C Programming Guide

3rd Edition

Jack Purdum

Que® Corporation
Carmel, Indiana

C Programming Guide, 3rd Edition

Library of Congress Catalog No.: 88-61496

ISBN 0-88022-356-1

91 90 89   8 7 6 5 4 3 2

Interpretation of the printing code: The rightmost double-digit number is the year of the book's printing; the rightmost single-digit number, the number of the book's printing. For example, a printing code of 88-4 shows that the fourth printing of the book occurred in 1988.

Dedication

To my family:
Karol, Katie, and John Paul

Publishing Director

Allen L. Wyatt, Sr.

Product Line Director

Bill Nolan

Editing

reVisions Plus

Technical Editor

Alan C. Plantz

Index

Sherry Massey

Illustrations and Figures

Stacy Kagiwada

Design and Production

Dan Armstrong
Brad Chinn
Cheryl English
Lori A. Lyons
Cindy L. Phipps
Joe Ramon
Dennis Sheehan
Peter Tocco

About the Author

Jack Purdum

Dr. Purdum received his B.A. degree from Muskingum College and M.A. and Ph.D. degrees from Ohio State University. He was a university professor for 18 years before becoming president of Ecosoft, a software house that specializes in microcomputer software. Dr. Purdum has received many teaching and research awards including a National Science Foundation grant to study microcomputers in education. He has published a number of professional articles; a BASIC programming text; and magazine articles in *Byte*, *Personal Computing*, *Interface Age*, and *Computer Language*. He has also authored several other C programming books, all published by Que Corporation.

Table of Contents

3   Operators and Selection Statements 81

4   Loops 115

9   Structures, Unions, and Other Data Types

Preface to the Third Edition

Much has happened since the first and second editions of this book were written. Perhaps the most important change is that the American National Standards Institute (ANSI) has completed its work on the standard for the C language. That document is out for public review as this is being written, and it appears that the standard is pretty well set now. New features have been added to the language, and those that seem certain are covered in this edition.

The next important change is that the price of quality C compilers has dropped dramatically. The $100 (or less) C compiler of today has more features than the $500 compilers of only two years ago. Even the least expensive C compiler now supports all data types and operators—most even have the ANSI enhancements to the C language. If you read the earlier editions of *C Programming Guide*, you will notice that this edition no longer assumes the reader is forced to use a "stripped down" C compiler. As a result, more interesting program examples are used. Appendix C has been expanded to present some of the many C products that are now available at a reasonable cost.

If you're familiar with earlier editions, you'll notice that the organization of this edition is different than before. This edition is a total rewrite and a total rethinking of previous editions. Most of the changes result from my experience in teaching seminars on C programming and from noticing the problems many programmers encounter when they learn the language. Each chapter now begins with a summary of the topics covered in that chapter and concludes with questions designed to test your understanding of the concepts discussed.

I find that over the years I have changed my own coding style. I think the change is for the better. Although there is nothing etched in stone about C programming style, the style used in this edition has been used in my own company and has worked well on team projects. The reader may find it worthwhile to use the style presented in this book.

I would be remiss in not mentioning a few of the many people that have contributed to this book. First, my friends and colleagues, Tim Leslie and Chris DeVoney, have made numerous comments and corrections that have protected the reader from silly errors that may have crept into the book otherwise. Both have contributed substantially in ways that have helped to make this a better book. Dave Cooper, Don Dudine, Chuck Lieske, Craig Miller, and Jim Rheude also have helped keep me on the straight and narrow while this book was being written. Alan Plantz, technical editor for this new edition, provided many helpful suggestions. Finally, I acknowledge the contributions of Bill Nolan, Allen Wyatt, and all the other people at Que who have worked tirelessly to transform gravel into diamonds. To all of them, my sincere thanks.

Jack Purdum
Indianapolis, 1988

Trademark Acknowledgments

Que Corporation has made every attempt to supply trademark information about company names, products, and services mentioned in this book. Trademarks indicated below were derived from various sources. Que Corporation cannot attest to the accuracy of this information.

ANSI is a registered trademark of American National Standards Institute.

CP/M is a registered trademark of Digital Research, Inc.

IBM is a registered trademark and PS/2 is a trademark of International Business Machines Corporation.

Macintosh is a registered trademark of Apple Computer, Inc.

MS-DOS is a registered trademark of Microsoft Corporation.

UNIX is a trademark of AT&T.

Introduction

In the five years that have elapsed since the first edition of this text was written, C has become one of the most popular languages of the day. Actually, C has been around since the early 1970s when Dennis Ritchie developed C as an extension of earlier work done by Ken Thompson. The stability that C has exhibited over the years is testament to the genius of Ritchie and Thompson.

C and the ANSI Standard

From its publication in 1978, the *de facto* C programming language standard of the time was *The C Programming Language*, by Brian Kernighan and Dennis Ritchie. So pervasive was this book as the standard by which C compilers were judged that vendors often advertised that they sold a "K&R" compiler.

Over the years, however, C went through a number of "unofficial" changes not present in the K&R standard. These changes, for the most part, were the result of features wanted by C programmers to overcome what were perceived to be shortcomings in the language. As these changes were implemented, however, code written for one compiler would not compile under a different compiler that lacked these new changes.

There was a genuine fear that C might suffer from this dialect problem the way that other languages, like BASIC, had suffered. The capability of moving programs among C compilers without having to change the program is often referred to as the "portability" of a program. Clearly, if different compilers follow different rules for C, portability would be lost.

In response to this pending problem, a group of compiler vendors, software developers, and other interested individuals petitioned the American National Standards Institute (ANSI®) to form a committee whose charge would be to develop a standard for the C language. The result was the creation of the ANSI Technical Committee X3J11 on the C Programming Language. The first meeting of X3J11 took place in the summer of 1983.

After almost five years of work, the committee has released the proposed standard for the C language: the *Draft Proposed American National Standard for Information Systems—Programming Language C*. The result of X3J11's work is a formal definition of the C language that builds upon the original work done by Kernighan and Ritchie. The new standard enhances the earlier standard, but attempts to do so in a way that "does not break" existing C programs. In other words, those programs written according to the K&R C standard should compile under a compiler that meets the ANSI standard for C.

The new ANSI standard is an incredible contribution to the C community. Not only does it clarify some past fuzzy points of C, it sets minimal criteria for previously unspecified areas of C (for example, something called the *standard library*, which we will talk about in a later chapter.)

All of these factors combine to make C's future even brighter than before. But why were programmers so enthusiastic about C in the first place? Why did C grow when many other languages withered on the vine?

Why C?

Although C's growth has been remarkable in the past 15 years, its growth in the last two years has been nothing short of explosive. C is the language chosen by most commercial programming companies. In addition, C has passed Pascal in popularity for those who program just for pleasure. Why has C enjoyed such phenomenal growth in the past several years?

There are many reasons why C has become the language of choice for so many people. First, C is a robust language whose large variety of operators and data types makes it suitable for writing everything from operating systems to accounting packages. You'd be hard pressed to find any program-

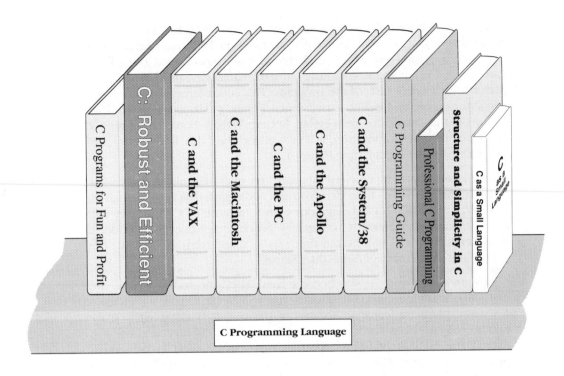

C Programming Language

ming task that couldn't be handled in C. In fact, many commercial C compilers were written in C.

C is also a portable language. If you write C programs with portability in mind (and the tips in this book will help you do that), you can have a C program working on any other computer with a minimum of change. The idea of writing a program just once takes on real meaning with C.

A related advantage is that the work by X3J11 has helped ensure that C won't be plagued by "dialects" common to other programming languages such as BASIC and, to a lesser extent, Pascal. This will reinforce C's portability into the future.

C lends itself beautifully to structured programming techniques. The language forces you to think about program design and encourages block-structure programs, in which each block has a specialized purpose or function. A C program involves little more than arranging these functions to perform the overall task of the program. This block-structure makes program debugging and maintenance much easier. (One aside here: While we're on the subject of debugging, Robert Ward's book *Debugging C*, published by Que Corporation, is an excellent book that is a worthy addition to anyone's programming library.)

C also is an extremely efficient language. Its operators allow you to "get down to the hardware" if needed. You can fiddle with data bits in much the same way that assembly language does. And because of C's intimacy with the computer's hardware, C compilers generate fast-executing code. In many applications, C will be ten times faster than interpreted BASIC programs, and almost always faster than Pascal.

C can grow with you. As you become more sophisticated in your C programming knowledge and techniques, you will begin to take advantage of C's many advanced features. Because of the way C is designed, you can bundle your previous work into something called a "library" and use it to extend the number of library routines that can be used in subsequent programming tasks. This "reusability" feature of C makes future programming tasks that much easier.

Although C has a rich set of operators, it is still a fairly small language. While there are relatively few C keywords to learn, they offer a means to solve virtually every programming problem in a concise, yet structured, manner.

Finally, C is an enjoyable language—not necessarily because it's the easiest language to learn, but because it's flexible and extensible. Having the freedom to create your own functions means that you can make C do just about anything you want. You can even create your own programming language in C!

Goals of This Book

The primary goal of this text is to help you learn C as quickly as possible. The basic strategy is to present a concept, and then show you how the concept is used in a simple program. There are two reasons for using simple programs. First, simple examples help you learn the concepts at hand without a lot of extraneous C code getting in the way. Second, you are more likely to type in and experiment with a short program than a long program. You will learn to program in C faster and retain the information longer if you experiment with the programs presented in this book.

Another thread that is woven throughout the book is to point out common problems that most beginning C programmers make while learning C. Knowing about these problem areas beforehand can save a lot of frustration later.

If you do experiment with the sample programs and work the problems at the end of each chapter, you will be surprised how quickly you will learn C. You will find C an extremely powerful language and one that is enjoyable to use.

Changes in This Edition

The most important change in this edition is coverage of the proposed draft for the ANSI standard for the C language. (The draft for the proposed standard is out for public review as this text is being written. Although additional changes may be made to the draft, it seems unlikely that any new or major changes will be made.) To reinforce your understanding of the new standard, all programming examples in this edition are written to conform to the new standard.

Another change in this edition is the addition of Programming Tips. At various points throughout the text, you will see a Programming Tip section that is relevant to the material being discussed. The topics covered in the Programming Tips range from things you should do or know about to stupid mistakes we all make. In some cases, the tip may show a coding shortcut or technique that might prove useful later on. In other cases, the tip might simply point out an error that programmers often make. Still other tips may provide an alternate way of viewing the material under discussion. In all cases, you should find the new Programming Tips feature a useful addition to the book.

This edition also includes a section at the beginning of the chapter that presents highlights of the material covered in the chapter. At the end of the chapter, review questions and exercises have been added. Answers are given to most of these questions, but not all of them. Hopefully, you will find it worthwhile to answer these questions (without looking at the answers!). This will help you learn the material presented in the chapter.

The teaching style used in this book presents the general view of a topic first and then develops the details around that topic. This allows you to

---

Programming Tip

Programming Tips Give Useful Advice

Important practical information is presented in boxes like this one. Each Programming Tip is designed to give you additional information related to the current discussion; information that could help you save time, avoid errors, discover shortcuts, and explore new programming techniques.

---

build your knowledge around a basic framework and fill in the details as the topic is developed further.

Finally, this edition is virtually a complete rewrite of the earlier editions. All of the chapters have been either rewritten or extensively modified. Several new chapters and appendixes have been added and some material has been deleted. In all cases, the changes are an attempt to make learning C easier and more enjoyable than before.

Assumptions about You

For you to get the most from this book, you should have access to a computer, a text editor (for entering the programs into the computer and saving them on disk), and a C compiler or interpreter. The exact compiler or interpreter doesn't matter. In fact, considerable effort was made to make this text as compiler-*nonspecific* as possible. If you do not have a C compiler, you may want to consult Appendix C after reading this chapter. Appendix C lists vendors of several inexpensive C compilers, along with numerous "add-on" products that you may find useful.

The programs in this book can be used on any compiler that supports the new ANSI standard for the C language. (Most of the programs will run on a K&R compiler with a few minor changes.) The important thing is that you experiment with the sample programs as they are presented in the text. You cannot learn a language by reading about it. You need to plunge right in.

I also have assumed that you are somewhat familiar with some elements of programming. This should not be viewed as a restrictive assumption. Many readers of the first and second editions of the *Guide* have learned C as a first language. However, the majority of readers have experience with some other programming language before learning C. Because BASIC and Pascal are a common base for those people, a few program examples with those languages are included as a bridge to learning C concepts in early chapters. If you don't know either of these languages, don't worry about it. Each concept can stand alone without support from other languages.

A third assumption is that you are under no pressure to master C by tomorrow evening. Some chapters may seem to dwell on a subject longer than you think is necessary. However, my experience in teaching C suggests that C is like a pyramid that must rest on a solid foundation. Take the time to master each concept before moving on to the next concept. Working each program example and the problems at the end of each chapter is a step in the right direction.

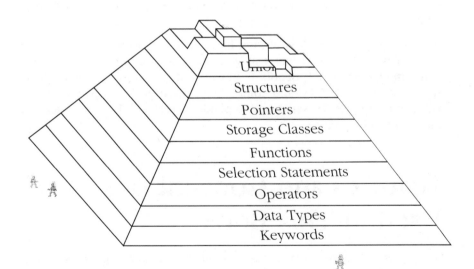

Finally, be sure to experiment and enjoy yourself while you're learning. Keep in mind that understanding what is written in this text is not the same as writing your own programs. At every opportunity, try to write programs of your own. You'll be amazed how well this approach to learning C pays off.

What Will You Find in This Book?

Chapter 1 provides an overview of a simple C program, and the rest of this book fills in the details. Chapter 2 discusses data types and their definition plus the important concepts of lvalues and rvalues. Chapter 3 covers C operators and control statements, and Chapter 4 examines loop structures. Chapter 5 explores the important new ANSI enhancement of function prototyping. Chapter 6 shows you how to use storage classes effectively. Because of their importance in C programming, pointers are explored in two chapters: Chapters 7 and 8. Chapter 9 discusses structures and unions and how they are used to organize your data. Chapter 10 investigates how disk data files are used, and Chapter 11 explains how the preprocessor is used.

In all chapters, the book is written in a "generic" fashion. That is, I have tried to write programs that will work on any computer with an ANSI-conforming compiler. Appendix B, however, does have information that is specific to the IBM® PC and compatibles. Additionally, Appendix A provides you with an ASCII chart, and Appendix C lists additional products you may want to investigate.

Features and Conventions Used in This Book

Starting with Chapter 1, each chapter begins with a list of the major topics covered in the chapter. If you need to review a topic, this list should help you isolate the areas for review.

When a program is discussed, all elements of the C language will appear in the same typeface used for program listings. This makes it easier to distinguish between the word hat and a variable named hat. As a further aid to clarification, function names will by followed by parentheses. Therefore, the word charge is visually different than the function named charge(). Finally, when a data array is discussed in the text, brackets will appear after the function name (for example, name versus name[]). These conventions should make it fairly easy to keep regular words distinct from program contructs even though they may appear the same (else versus else).

Because of a peculiarity in the type font used for listings, the plus sign (+) occupies more space than it should. This usually won't cause a problem, except in one case: the increment operator (++), introduced in Chapter 4. Listings may look like they have a space between the two plus signs that make up the increment operator, but you must not type a space between the plus signs; an extra space there will probably cause a syntax error.

Now that all of that's finished, we can turn to the task at hand: learning to program in C.

1

An Introduction to C

Concepts in This Chapter

- ☐ C keywords
- ☐ The parts of a C program
- ☐ How to use braces with functions
- ☐ What the C standard library is
- ☐ Differences between a compiler and interpreter
- ☐ Recommended C programming style

In this chapter, you learn the basic elements that are used to build a C program. You then see how the basic elements can be combined to form an infinite variety of building blocks that eventually become a C program. Additionally, you learn about the many pre-written building blocks that are available to you in something called the *C standard library*.

C Keywords

Each programming language contains words that have special meanings in that language. Such words are called *keywords*, and table 1.1 presents all the keywords available in C.

Table 1.1. *C Keywords*

auto	break	case	char	const
continue	default	do	double	else
enum	extern	float	for	goto
if	int	long	register	return
short	signed	sizeof	static	struct
switch	typedef	union	unsigned	void
volatile	while			

A few things become apparent when you review table 1.1. First, all keywords in C are written as lowercase letters. As you gain experience with C, you will find that (except for certain special constants in C) virtually everything in a C program is written in lowercase letters. Although the use of lowercase letters may seem strange to you at first (especially if you are used to programming in BASIC or Pascal), you should develop the habit of writing your programs in lowercase letters.

If you haven't guessed it, C is a case-sensitive language. That is, AUTO is not a C keyword but auto is. This means that you must use C keywords in lowercase letters. You can have a variable named AUTO, but not one named auto. Because the C compiler recognizes that keywords have special meanings in a program, keywords must not be used as variable names.

A second thing you might notice, after reviewing table 1.1, is that C does not contain many keywords. If you compare the list of keywords in table 1.1 to that of other languages (Ada for example), C's list of keywords seems pretty skimpy. Don't be fooled. The secret of C's success is not its long list of keywords, but rather how you can use those keywords to perform complex tasks.

Before you tackle the details of what each keyword means, you first must understand the broader scope of how a program is written in C. Only then will you be able to arrange the pieces to form a program.

Elements of a C Program

Despite all of C's powerful features and the virtually limitless ways you can combine keywords to form a program, C boils down to four basic elements:

- ❑ Expressions
- ❑ Statements
- ❑ Statement blocks
- ❑ Function blocks

The following sections present a brief discussion of these four parts, and then explain how they are used in an actual program.

Expressions

The first element of a C program is an *expression*. An expression may be created from operators and operands. If you think of programs as molecules, expressions are the protons and neutrons from which you create atoms. The following examples are all expressions:

```
b + c
a = b + c
32000
c < a
```

In the first example, variables b and c are called *operands*, while the plus sign is an *operator*. As you probably know, the plus operator causes b and c to be added together to form the sum of the two operands. This expression simply adds two variables together. Because there are two operands, the addition operator (+) is called a *binary* operator.

In the second example, variable a is assigned the sum of b plus c. b + c is a *subexpression* that must be evaluated before we can resolve the complete expression. After we know the sum of the subexpression b + c, we have an expression involving two operands (variable a and the sum of b + c) and the assignment operator.

The third example is simply a constant expression, but an expression nonetheless.

The last example is an expression that uses two operands (c and a) and a relational operator ($<$) to see whether c is less than a.

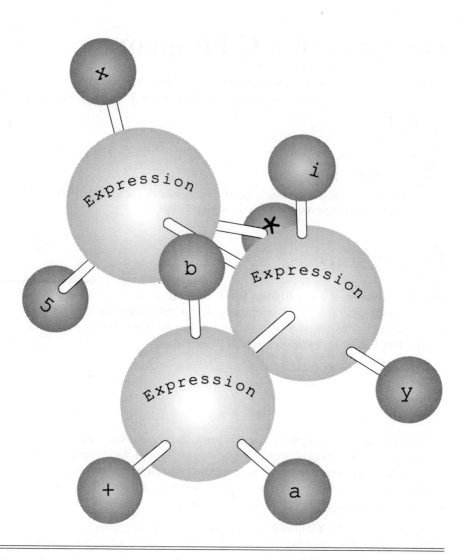

Remember that all expressions are resolved to a value. All of the preceding examples will yield a value after they are evaluated by the compiler. (Later chapters will explain why this is important.)

Statements

A *statement* is a complete C instruction. All C statements end with a semicolon. Usually, a statement in C is little more than an expression with a semicolon at the end. Some examples might include

```
i = 1Ø;
a = b + c;
```

The first statement is simply an expression that assigns the constant 10 into variable i. It is a statement because it contains an expression followed by a semicolon. The second statement is actually two subexpressions (an add subexpression followed by an assignment subexpression) followed by a semicolon to form a single C statement.

All statements in C must end in a semicolon. You can conclude then that the semicolon is also called a *statement terminator* in C. Carrying the chemistry analogy one step further, statements are the atoms from which elements are made.

Statement Blocks

A *statement block* consists of one or more statements grouped together so that they are viewed by the compiler as a single statement. The following is an example of a statement block:

```
if (...) {
    a = b + c;
    c = c + 1;
}
```

An opening brace ({) is used to indicate the start of a statement block. A closing brace (}) is used to indicate the end of a statement block.

In the example, the if keyword in C is followed by a set of parentheses (the three dots represent missing details that will be discussed in a later chapter) followed by an opening brace. The opening brace tells the compiler that all of the statements between the opening and closing braces are controlled by the if keyword.

Why is a statement block necessary? The answer is that most C keywords are designed to control a single C statement. In actual practice, however, you will often need two or more C statements controlled by a single keyword. The statement block allows you to do this. Statement blocks, therefore, allow you to combine elements to form elaborate and complex molecules.

Function Blocks

A *function block* is one or more C statement blocks or statements combined to accomplish a specific task. Each function, therefore, uses statements and statement blocks to create a single, cohesive module that is used to solve a particular aspect of a programming problem. For example, a function that solves the volume of a cube might look like

```
cube _volume()
{
    length = 10;
    height = 20;
    width = 5;
    volume = length * height * width;
    print _volume(volume);
}
```

In this example, cube _volume() is the name of a function block. It includes all statements beginning with the opening brace ({) right under the function block name, and ends with its matching closing brace (}). The statements between the opening and closing braces are called the *function body*.

Function blocks mold molecules and form them into materials that are used to build a program. All C programs are based upon the four elements presented in this section.

Writing, Compiling, and Linking a C Program

If you can learn the four basic concepts discussed in the previous section, you can write programs in C. Before you can write a C program, however, you must examine the steps necessary to write, compile, and link the source code to create an executable program.

If your previous programming experience is with an interpreted language such as BASIC, you will find that creating a program with a compiler is somewhat different. (If you are familiar with the use of compilers, you can skip to the next section.)

Writing a C program in a compiler environment requires the sequence of steps shown in figure 1.1.

The steps may seem like a lot of work, but actually they aren't. First, you write your C program with a text editor or word processor. Then you save the program to a disk file. This file contains what is called the *source code* for your program. Source code is written in a "human-readable" form that uses the English-like syntax of C and conforms to its rules. Usually, source code can be read and created by means of a standard text editor. The output from the editor is usually an ASCII (American Standard Code for Information Interchange) text file.

In the second step, you compile the ASCII source code file by using whatever command is required to run your compiler. For example, if the C program is called TEST.C, you might use the command

```
cc TEST
```

Once the compiler is invoked, your C program source code is passed through the *preprocessor*, which "processes" the code into a form usable by the compiler itself. The preprocessor is covered in detail in Chapter 11. For now, just think of the preprocessor as a separate process that is performed before the compiler actually sees your source code—it "pre-processes" some things in your program.

When the preprocessor is finished, the compiler takes the output produced by the preprocessor, checks it to make sure the program obeys the rules of C, converts it into an intermediate code form, and then writes it to a disk file. Because certain pieces of code needed to make the program run probably are not found in your program source code or in the compiler itself, the compiler must use an intermediate code form. The compiler, knowing that the program is not yet complete, leaves little "messages" in the intermediate code for the next step (the linker) in the compilation process.

Each message that the compiler leaves gives the linker the same type of information: (1) the name of the missing code, (2) where to find the code, and (3) where to place the code in the program. Therefore, the job of the linker is to find all of these messages, look for the missing code referenced

Fig. 1.1. *The procedure for writing a C program.*

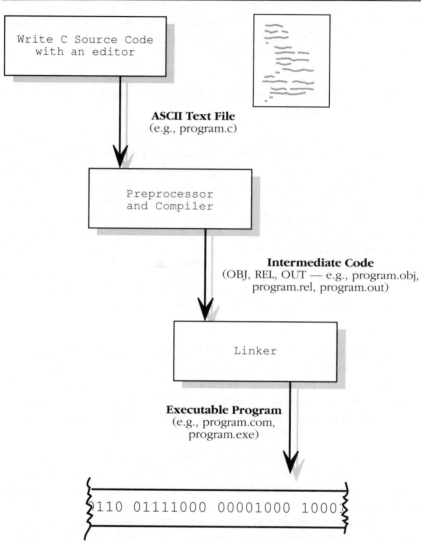

in the messages in the library, extract the missing code, and shove (link) it into the program at precisely the right spot. When the linker fills in all of the missing pieces, you have an executable program.

How long does all of this take? For the longest program in this book, the preprocessor-compiler pass took less than 10 seconds. Most of the programs require less than 5 seconds. The link step usually requires about twice as much time as the compiler. Still, most short programs can be compiled and linked in less than 30 seconds, if you use a personal computer.

Compiler versus Interpreter

If you have used an interpreter in the past, the steps needed to compile a program may seem time-consuming. True, the compiler does require more steps to develop the program, but once it is finished, it will run faster than the interpreted program—as much as ten times faster.

C interpreters do exist and they have some nice debugging features built into them. Compilers also have debuggers, but they normally are not an integral part of the compiler and, hence, are less handy to use.

The examples in this book are written with a C compiler and it is assumed that you also use a C compiler. This does not mean that you *must* use a compiler. For the simple programs that are used in this text, you can use either a C compiler or interpreter.

Writing Your First C Program

With the preliminary stuff out of the way, you can now write your first C program and analyze it in light of what you already know. Listing 1.1 is the source code for your first complete C program.

Listing 1.1. Your First C Program

```
/* This program prints a message on the screen */

#include  <stdio.h>

main()
{
    printf("This is my first C program.\n");
}
```

Although this is a short C program, several aspects need to be explained.

Comments in C

The first thing that you notice in listing 1.1 is that the first line begins with a slash-asterisk combination (that is, /*) and ends with the same two characters, but in reverse order (that is, */). Comments in C are similar to REM statements in BASIC or braces in Pascal. Everything between the opening comment mark (/*) and closing comment mark (*/) is ignored by the C compiler. Therefore, if the following three lines appeared in a C program, they would be ignored by the compiler:

```
/* You can write whatever you want between C comment marks */
/* and everything in between them is ignored by the C        */
/* compiler.                                                  */
```

Unlike comments in BASIC, comments in C do not increase the size of the executable program, nor do they affect the execution speed. (In fact, comments normally are stripped out by the preprocessor before the compiler sees the program!) Therefore, use comments in C programs to help document what the program or a specific section of code does. Such comments may come in handy three months from now when you try to debug the program!

Notice that most C compilers allow you to cross more than one line before the comment is closed. Consequently, you can also write

```
/*
    You can write whatever you want between C comment marks
    and everything between them is ignored by the C
    compiler.
*/
```

Because it requires fewer keystrokes, the second form is used more often than the first.

The ANSI standard does not allow comments within comments (that is, nested comments) even though some compilers do. Those "permissive" compilers would permit comments like this:

```
/* This is the 1st open
/* This is the 2nd open and close */
   and now the final close */
```

To conform to the ANSI rules, however, the comment would be written

```
/* This is the 1st open   */
/* This is the 2nd open and close */
/* and now the final close */
```

If you write code that might be moved to another system, avoid nested comments even if your compiler allows them.

Programming Tip

Use Comments To Simplify Debugging

Because the compiler ignores everything between /* and */, these comment characters (sometimes called comment *delimiters*) are a useful debugging tool. If you want to remove one or more C statements from the program to perform a test, enclose the lines in comment characters. This has the same effect as if you erased the lines. You can in effect remove one or more C statements from the program and not have to retype them later when you want to restore them. When the comment characters are removed, the previously "commented out" lines are restored.

The *#include* Directive and Header Files

The next thing you see in listing 1.1 is the line:

```
#include  <stdio.h>
```

All program lines that begin with a pound sign (#, sometimes called a "sharp") are flagged as special to the preprocessor. This particular preprocessor directive says "Go search for a disk file named stdio.h and place whatever you find in that file at this point in the program." A complete discussion of the C preprocessor is given in Chapter 11.

Because the #include directives to the preprocessor almost always appear at the head of a program, the files used with the #include are often called *header* files. Further, it is common practice to have header files end with ".h". The ".h" file extension makes it easy to recognize header files when you look at a directory of files.

Header Files, Quotes, and Angle Brackets

Notice that angle brackets surround the name of the stdio.h header file. Some compilers, however, may require quotation marks instead of angle brackets. In this case, the proper way to include the header file is

```
#include "stdio.h"
```

So what's the difference between angle brackets and quotation marks? Although we will postpone details on the preprocessor until Chapter 11, we can give a short explanation here.

Angle brackets that surround a header file tell the preprocessor to look in a file directory other than the current one for the requested header file. *Quotation marks*, on the other hand, tell the preprocessor to look in the current working directory for the header file before it looks elsewhere. The two forms of #include allow you to have two versions of the same header file in different places on the disk, yet you can select one version over the other. This can be handy, as you shall see in later chapters. For now, though, use the form that works.

What Is *stdio.h?*

The stdio.h file is a special file that comes with all C compilers, and it stands for standard input-output header file. You should use the #include directive to include stdio.h in any program that is expected to use input routines (such as getting a character from the keyboard) or output routines (such as displaying something on the screen or printer). Because almost all programs involve some form of input or output (hereafter called I/O), all programs should #include the stdio.h file.

The *main( )* Function

The next element in the program is called main(). main() is special to C programs for a number of reasons.

❑ Program execution begins with main( ). Regardless of any C statements you may see prior to the function named main( ), program execution begins with the main( ) function. You can think of any code prior to main( ) as a "setup" code that prepares things for main( ) so that the program can begin.

❑ Every C program *must* have a main( ) function. Obviously, since the compiler begins execution with the function named main( ), each program must have a main( ) function in it. It also follows that there can be only one main( ) per program. If you try to write a program with more than one main( ), the compiler issues a main( ) multiply-defined error message, and you have to remove one of the main( )s from the program.

❑ Program execution ends with main( ). When the statements contained within the main( ) function have been executed, the program ends. In listing 1.1, the main( ) function only has one statement. After that statement is executed, the program ends and control returns to the operating system.

One more point concerning main( ) must be noted. Because C does make a distinction between upper- and lowercase letters, Main( ), MAIN( ), and main( ) are all different functions. To execute your program, the required function is main( ), and it must be written in lowercase letters.

As a matter of style, most C programmers until recently did not use uppercase letters in function or variable names, nor did they mix upper- and lowercase letters in a single function or variable name. (This topic is covered later in this chapter.)

The Function Call to *printf( )*

You have learned that a function block is a set of statements combined to perform a specific task. You also know that main( ) is a special function in C. In this section, you will examine in greater detail the function call to printf( ) in listing 1.1:

```
printf("This is my first program.\n");
```

As you might guess, the C function call to printf( ) displays the message between the quotation marks. In more formal terms, the character string between the quotation marks is the *argument* to the printf( ) function call. Function arguments also are discussed later in this chapter.

The following sections explain some new things in the argument of the printf() function call.

The Newline Character

The first thing that might look a bit odd is the '\n' sequence at the end of the quotation. The '\n' is called a *newline* character in C. The newline character causes words printed after the message to print on the next (new) line. Hence the clever name "newline character." If you change the printf() to be

```
printf("This is my\nfirst program.\n");
```

The output looks like

```
This is my
first program.
```

and the cursor sits under the letter f in the word *first*. The newline character after the word *my* causes the different output.

Even though the newline character looks like two characters (a backslash and the letter n), and causes the computer to generate a carriage-return and a line-feed sequence, C compilers treat the newline character as though it were a single character. (This becomes clear when strings are explained in Chapter 7.) For now, simply remember that the newline character is treated as a single character.

A Closer Look at Functions

In the first discussion of listing 1.1, many details concerning the function call to printf() were ignored. Because functions are the building blocks of C, this section gives you an opportunity to study functions more closely.

Anatomy of a Function

You already know what a function block is. Now let's review that information in light of listing 1.1. Listing 1.1 is repeated without some of the details so that you can concentrate on the major components of a function. In its simplest form, a function consists of four parts, as shown in figure 1.2. Each of these four parts is discussed in the following paragraphs.

Fig. 1.2. The major parts of a function.

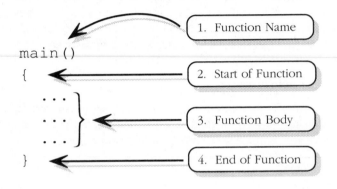

Valid Characters in a Function Name

The function name is exactly what you think it is: The name that is used to reference the function. A function name can use upper- or lowercase letters and the underscore (_) character. You can also use digit characters in the name, if it is not the first character in the name. Therefore, valid function names are

```
loan_interest      hat_size      weekday
printer2           _day4         Friday
```

On the other hand, the following are illegal function names:

```
1st_day            *fire         shoe-size
nat'l              .jim          +interest
```

1st_day is illegal because it begins with a digit, and *fire, .jim, and +interest are illegal because they begin with characters that are not part of the valid character set for variable and function names. The function name shoe-size is illegal because it contains a minus sign, and nat'l is illegal because it uses an apostrophe.

Programming Tip

Maintaining Uniqueness of Identifiers

The ANSI standard states that compilers shall treat the first 31 characters of an identifier (for example, names for variables and functions) as significant. As long as the name of two identifiers is different within the first 31 characters, the compiler should know that the two variables are different data items.

There is a catch, however.

If the identifier is a data item with external linkage (for example, a function name passed through to the linker), only the first six characters are significant. That is, the function names

```
johns_car()
{
...
}

johns_bike()
{
...
}
```

may confuse some compilers because the two function names are not unique within the first six characters. (This is a real restriction on early CP/M® compilers.) Another problem is that the linker may not recognize as many characters in a variable or function name as the compiler. That is, the compiler may send 31-character names to the linker, but the linker may be limited to as few as six characters. Check your documentation to see what limits apply to your compiler.

Notice that the function name is followed by an opening and closing parenthesis even though there is nothing between the parentheses. All function names are followed by parentheses that may or may not have something between them. (Look at the printf() function in listing 1.1 to see an example of a function that includes something between the parentheses.) The two parentheses make it easy to tell the difference between function and variable names. (What goes between the parentheses is discussed later in this chapter, in the section "Arguments to Functions.")

Start of a Function Block

As shown earlier, braces are used to mark the start and end of a block of statements. If the opening brace immediately follows a function name (and its parentheses), the brace marks the beginning of a function block.

Note how the opening brace is aligned with the first character of the function name. In figure 1.1, the opening brace is lined up immediately under the letter m in main(). This is a common C programming style convention, and a convention that you should adopt.

Function Body

The function body consists of the C program statement(s) between the opening and closing braces of the function block. These statements accomplish the task that the function was designed to do. A function body may have one statement or several hundred.

As a matter of style, statements found within a function block are indented so that it is easy to tell which statements are part of the function block. Indent statements by three or four spaces to mark the statements as belonging to a function. If you indent statements too much you limit the amount of information that can be written on a single line.

Programming Tip

One Task, One Function

When you design your own C functions, do not write functions that attempt to do too much. Such busy functions are difficult to write and even harder to debug. Limit each function to one task.

End of Function

The closing brace (}) marks the end of the function block. As with the opening function brace, the closing function brace is lined up with the first character in the function name (that is, the m in main()). This style convention makes it easy to see where the function block starts and ends.

Figure 1.3 shows how program control flows when you execute the main() function and a function named func1() within main().

Fig. 1.3. Program control during execution of the main() *function.*

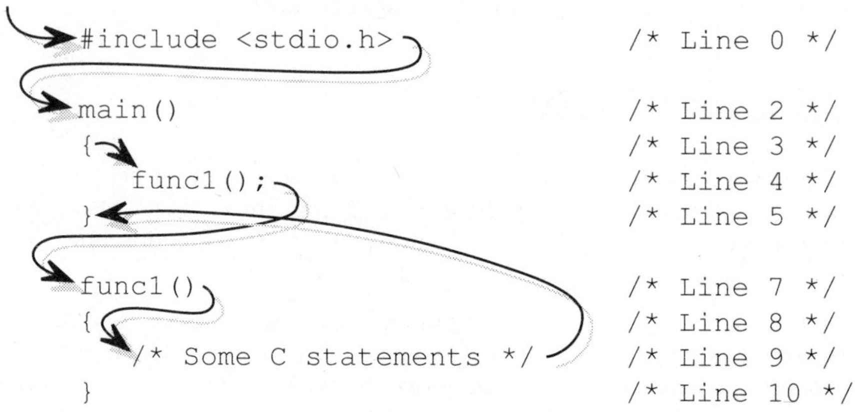

```
    #include <stdio.h>              /* Line 0  */

    main()                          /* Line 2  */
    {                               /* Line 3  */
        func1();                    /* Line 4  */
    }                               /* Line 5  */

    func1()                         /* Line 7  */
    {                               /* Line 8  */
        /* Some C statements */     /* Line 9  */
    }                               /* Line 10 */
```

When the program that is shown in figure 1.3 is run, the execution sequence is

    2, 3, 4, 7, 8, 9, 10, 5

After line 5 is executed, the program ends because line 5 marks the end of the main() function. Obviously, this also means that program control is returned to whatever caused the program to execute (normally the operating system). C functions behave similarly to subroutines in assembler and BASIC, or to procedures in Pascal. That is, program control is sent to the function to perform the task of the function and then control is returned to the statement that follows the function call.

With respect to figure 1.2, the closing brace (line 10) of func1() marks the end of the function block named func1(), but also causes program control to return to the point at which func1() was called. In the example, program control resumes after the call to func1() in line 4. Because there is nothing else on line 4, control resumes with line 5 (which is the closing brace for main()) and the program ends.

The example shown in figure 1.2 also shows that the main() function is different from other functions. When the closing brace of main() is reached, the program ends. When the closing brace of any other function is reached, program control returns to the expression or statement that follows the one that called the function.

Arguments to Functions

A function often cannot perform its task unless it is first given some information to work with. This information is called the *argument* of the function. Function arguments are listed between the parentheses that follow the function name.

In listing 1.1, the argument of printf() is "This is my first program.\n". This argument is simply a sequence of characters (normally called a *string*) that is displayed on the screen. The printf() function treats characters between quotation marks as a *string constant* for display on the screen.

Because each function is designed for a specific task and each task is different, expect each function to have different information requirements for performing its task. Therefore, any number of arguments can be passed to a function. If a function uses more than one argument, the function is said to have an *argument list*. Arguments in the list must be separated by commas.

Earlier in this chapter, for example, a function was shown that calculates the volume of a cube. In cube_volume(), we simply set the length, height, and width of the cube to values that are fixed in the function. This is not a very good cube function, however, because the function body must be changed when you want to use a different cube size.

A more versatile cube function is shown in listing 1.2. In this code, the dots represent missing details for the function. These details are discussed later.

Listing 1.2 (Fragment). *Volume of a Cube*

```
volume(length, height, width)
   ...
{
      ...
      ...
      ...
}
```

Listing 1.2 reflects the "old" (that is, K&R) way to define a function. The new ANSI standard has changed things just a bit, and a discussion of the new (and better) way to define a function is in a later chapter. (In fact, the "better way" is so important that we have devoted Chapter 5 to this topic alone.)

Figure 1.4 summarizes what has been discussed about functions thus far.

Fig. 1.4. *The parts of a function.*

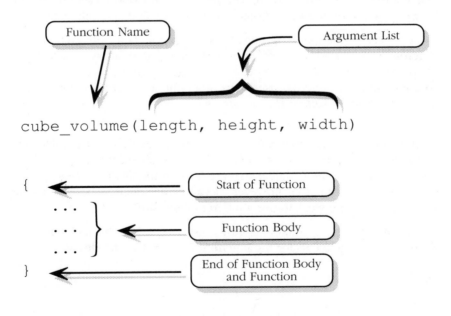

Note that a function might not have any arguments passed to it. In listing 1.1, main( ) was used with no arguments. You must still include the parentheses, however, so that the compiler knows that you are using a function instead of a variable.

The concept of function arguments may appear strange at first glance, but if you have programmed in other languages, you have probably used function arguments. The PRINT statement in BASIC or writeln in Pascal treats function arguments in a manner much the same as C. Function arguments are discussed in detail in later chapters. For now, simply think of function arguments as information needed by the function to complete its task.

Function Calls and Libraries

Looking at listing 1.1, the obvious question is "Where is the code for printf( )? I don't see it in the program." You know the code for printf( ) is executed by main( ), but it appears nowhere in the program. That question is answered in the pages that follow.

The Standard C Library

All C compilers have something called a *standard library*, which is a collection of commonly used C functions, such as printf( ), that have already been written for you.

If you write a program that uses a function call, the compiler first searches all the source code you wrote for the missing function. If the compiler cannot find the code for the function in your program, it marks the function as missing from the program and relies on the *linker* to fill in the missing code.

After the compiler performs its job, it passes control to the linker, more or less saying "Here's a list of functions I can't find—it's up to you to find them and place them at the proper places in the program." The linker proceeds to look through the standard C library for the missing functions (some compilers may require you to specify a list of library files to be searched by the linker). When the linker finds printf( ), it copies the printf( ) code from the standard library into the appropriate spot in your program. When the linker is finished, you have an executable program.

Clearly, the more functions you have in your standard C library, the fewer functions you have to write yourself. You can add whatever new functions you like. As your personal library of functions grows, programming in C becomes easier because you don't have to rewrite functions. Eventually, even highly complex programs become little more than a series of C library function calls.

Programming Tip

Writing Reusable C Functions

The trick to writing "reusable" C functions is to design them so they are generic. It sounds easy, but writing generalized functions takes a bit of practice. A function that attempts to do too many tasks is most likely not going to be reusable. If you constantly ask yourself "Can I simplify this function even further?" as you design a function, you have a better chance of writing functions that can be used in other applications.

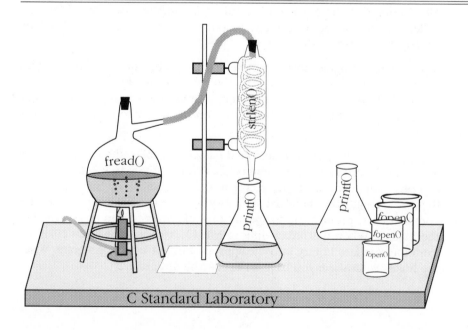

C Standard Laboratory

Depth of the Standard C Library

How many functions are in the standard C library? There is no fixed number. Some compilers have a few dozen library functions while others have over 300. There were no K&R rules about the content of the standard library. Fortunately, the ANSI standard defines over 150 standard C library functions and most compilers include them in their standard library. (Not all functions can be supported because of hardware and operating system differences.)

One benefit of the ANSI standard is that you can rely on the library functions in the standard library to use the same names and behave in the same manner regardless of the compiler vendor. In the "old days," one vendor had a function named putfmt() that behaved exactly the same as printf(). The different name was used out of fear of copyright infringement. Although this makes perfect legal sense, it's a nightmare when you are trying to write a program that is compiled with one compiler that uses putfmt() and another compiler that uses printf(). Such naming inconsistencies made "porting" (that is, moving a program from one computer system to a different one) very difficult.

The ANSI standard has placed naming inconsistencies behind us, and this should no longer be a problem.

It would be worth your time to scan the documentation that came with your standard C library. Don't be concerned if you don't fully understand everything that you read. That understanding will come soon enough. All you want to do now is get some idea of the extent of your standard library. Try to categorize the functions you find in the library (for example, those that work with string data, those that work with numbers, and so forth). The Quick-Reference Card included with this book should help you categorize the functions. All of the program examples in this text either use standard library functions or include the source code for functions that are not in the standard library.

(From now on, we will use the term *library* to refer to the standard C library. We will also assume that nonstandard names for those library functions are not a problem. With the ANSI standard upon us, this seems to be a safe assumption.)

Interpreting Linker Errors

If you have not had much experience with compiled languages, the linker and how it operates may be somewhat new to you. Further, it can issue error messages that are a bit terse at best. For example, if the linker cannot find the missing code for a particular function in the standard library, it will issue an error message. While the exact message varies among linkers, it will probably be something like Unresolved external followed by the name of what it couldn't find. Quite often such link errors are caused by misspelling the name of a function that is in the standard library. If you correct the name of the misspelled function in the source code and relink the program, the linker error should disappear.

You might want to misspell printf() in listing 1.1 on purpose to see what kind of message is produced by your linker under such circumstances. Seeing the types of error messages you get under controlled circumstances may make it easier for you to figure out what went wrong when you see the error "for real."

A Review of Functions

Now that you know something about C functions, let's review listing 1.1, labeling all of its parts (see fig. 1.5).

Figure 1.5 summarizes the major elements of a C program. If you feel uncomfortable with anything presented in figure 1.5, you should review that element before reading further.

Fig. 1.5. *A review of the functions in listing 1.1.*

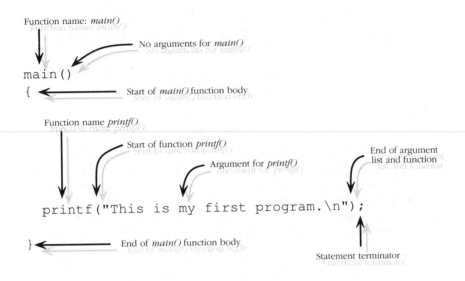

Some More Ideas about Programming Style

C is a "context free," or free-form, language. This means you are free to use whatever spacing, indentation, or other style considerations that you want. Indeed, we could have written listing 1.1 as

```
main(){printf("This is my first program.\n");}
```

and it would compile and execute without error. However, some programming styles are a little harder to read than others, especially on large programs.

You are free to select whichever style you like, but keep in mind that you want to write with a style that is easy to read. This will help make debugging easier. Select those style conventions you like, and then use them consistently in all of your C programming. If you are working in a programming shop where several of you will be sharing code, you should collectively select a style and all use it. It makes team projects easier to write and maintain.

What follows is a list of style conventions that are fairly popular among C programmers.

Lowercase versus Uppercase Letters

Each language develops its own style for variable names. For example,

```
HATSIZE
HatSize
hat_size
```

shows different style conventions typical to BASIC, Pascal, and C. Until recently, C programmers rarely used uppercase letters in variable names. That tradition is changing, but the programs in this book use lowercase for variable names. Uppercase letters are more often used for symbolic constants in C programs. (We will cover these in Chapter 3.) Many dialects of BASIC don't give you a choice; all variables must use uppercase letters.

Pascal programmers often use uppercase letters to start the name of a variable. If the variable is long or needs to be delineated for some other reason, uppercase letters are used to "break up" the name in an attempt to make it more readable.

C programmers break up long variable names or otherwise delineate a variable name with an underscore character, as in hat_size. Because so many C programmers follow the lowercase naming convention, you should get used to writing variable (and function) names in lowercase letters.

One more point. Because C does distinguish between upper- and lowercase letters, PRINTF(), Printf(), and printf() would all be viewed as different functions. Therefore, if you expect to use the printf() found in your compiler's standard library in a program, you have no choice but to use printf().

Placement of Braces and Indentation

Braces are used to group program statements together. As you have already seen, braces are used to mark the start and end of function and statement blocks. This section discusses how braces are often placed within function and statement blocks.

Braces and Functions

The opening brace for a function is placed below (and aligned with) the beginning of the function definition. (For now, the terms *function definition* and *function name* are used interchangeably.) The closing brace has the same alignment. Therefore, listing 1.1 was written

```
main()
{
    ...
}
```

using this style convention. Notice that the dots have been indented one tab position (to represent the missing printf( )). This is also a common C style convention. Indenting the statements that make up the function body makes it easier to see where the function definition starts and ends.

Some C programmers indent the opening and closing brace of a function by one tab position. This style would look like:

```
main()
    {
    ...
    }
```

I've asked programmers who use this style why they like it. They feel this style makes the function name stand out better. Relatively few C programmers use this style, but it is an alternative.

Braces and Statement Blocks

Braces can also group one or more program statements within a function. Suppose you want to add 1 to the variables x and y as part of a for loop. Listing 1.3 suggests one style that might be used. (Again, dots represent missing details we will cover later.)

Notice that the opening brace is at the end of the same line as the for keyword. The closing brace is aligned with the letter f in for. The braces serve to define the statement block controlled by the for loop. Also note that the statements controlled by the for are indented one tab position. The reason for indenting them is the same as for the function body state-

Programming Tip

Identifying Debugging Code

If you develop the habit of indenting statements within a function body by one (or more) tab positions, it can make debugging a little easier. For example, if you are working on a function and want to display a value for debugging purposes, you might use

```
complex_function()
{
        /* Many function body statements to do the task */

printf(/* missing details about debug stuff here */);

        /* More function body statements */
}
```

Because the printf() statement is *not* indented, you can tell at a glance that it is not part of the actual code for the function body but has been added for debugging purposes. This makes it easier to identify and remove such debugging code after the bug has been squashed.

Listing 1.3 (Fragment). Indentation within Function Body

```
main()
{
    ...

    ...
    for (...) {         /* start of loop */
        ...
        x = x + 1;
        y = y + 1;
    }                   /* end of loop  */
}
```

---

ments; it makes it easier to see that they are controlled by the for loop. An alternative form is shown in listing 1.4.

Listing 1.4 (Fragment). *Alternative Indentation within Function Body*

```
main()
{
    ...
    ...
    for (...)          /* start of loop */
    {
        ...
      x = x + 1;
      y = y + 1;
    }                  /* end of loop   */
}
```

This style uses the same alignment that was used with the braces that mark the start and end of a function. This indentation style is fairly common, but slightly less popular than the style shown in listing 1.3. The style shown in listing 1.3 is the one used throughout this book.

There are other style considerations that will be confronted in later chapters. However, they are best discussed at the time those C language constructs are explained. For now, consider the alternative styles presented thus far, select the ones you like, and then use them consistently in your own programming.

Review Questions and Exercises

1. What are the elements from which a C program is built?

2. Name the major parts of a C function.

3. What is an argument list?

4. What does the output of the following program look like?

```
#include <stdio.h>

Main()
{
    print("This program has\na few problems with it\n)
}
```

▼Answers

1. Expressions, statements, statement blocks, and function blocks.

2. Function name
   Function argument list (if any)
   Opening brace of function body
   Statement(s) that form the function body
   Closing brace of function body

3. An argument list is a list of variables that are given to a function so the function can perform its task. Each argument in the list must be separated from the others by a comma.

4. The program will not compile as it is written. First, Main() must be changed to main() for the program to execute. Second, the programmer probably meant to use printf() from the standard C library, rather than print(). Third, the string constant which is the argument to printf() needs a closing double quote before the closing parenthesis. Finally, because a call to a function is a C statement, a semicolon is needed at the end of the printf() statement. The correct program is

   ```
   #include  <stdio.h>

   main()
   {
        printf("This program has\na few problems with it\n");
   }
   ```

   and the output would be

   ```
   This program has
   a few problems with it
   ```

2

C Data Types

Concepts in This Chapter

- ❑ Keywords for several data types in C
- ❑ How to define variables
- ❑ lvalues and rvalues
- ❑ Modifiers to data types

In this chapter, you begin defining variables for several fundamental data types. You also learn an important distinction between defining and declaring a variable. This chapter shows how variables are stored in memory and how the terms lvalue and rvalue are used. (These terms will be important to understanding pointers in Chapters 7 and 8.) Finally, this chapter discusses special C keywords that can be used to modify several fundamental C data types.

Data Types

C offers a variety of data types. Table 2.1 presents the keywords for the basic data types that we will discuss in this chapter.

Table 2.1. *Keywords for Data Types (Partial Listing)*

char	int	float	double

Table 2.1 does not include all of the data types available to you; we will cover the rest of them in later chapters. You will find, however, that you can write a lot of useful programs using just those data types presented in table 2.1.

char Data Type

A char data type is usually a single-byte quantity (8 bits) and is used to represent a single character of the host machine's character set. Many computers use ASCII (American Standard Code for Information Interchange) for character representation, but alternative character sets exist. The ASCII character set only uses seven of the eight bits, yielding 128 (that is, 2^7) characters. (Some systems, such as the IBM PC, use the eighth bit for graphics and other special characters.)

> The word char can be pronounced two different ways. One form is like the first part of *charcoal*, as in *char* a steak. The second form rhymes with the word *care*, as in *tender loving care*. Because I prefer TLC to something that is burned, my personal preference is the second form, but the choice is yours.

Later in this chapter, you will be able to experiment with a program that uses character variables.

int Data Type

An int is an integer data type in C. int is a signed quantity so that it can represent both positive and negative integer numbers. The exact range of an int varies because the number of bits used to represent an int varies among systems. On the IBM PC, for example, an integer is normally a 16-bit quantity, while it is a 32-bit quantity on a Macintosh® and most UNIX® systems.

The high bit of an integer is used as a sign bit, leaving either 15 or 31 bits for the value. For a 16-bit integer the remaining 15 bits can represent 32,768 (that is, 2^{15}) unique values. Because zero is a valid integer value, the largest positive number would be +32,767. The largest negative number is –32,768.

A 32-bit integer, of course, has a significantly larger range of values (that is, 2^{31} or –2,147,483,648 to +2,147,483,647). The ANSI standard states that an int shall never be less than 16 bits, but the final choice is left to the vendor of the compiler. Often the decision on the size of an int is dictated by the sizes of the registers and the instruction set of the host Central Processing Unit (CPU).

float Data Type

A float data type is used to represent floating-point numbers, or numbers that may have fractional values (for example, 3.14). The ANSI standard does not state the memory requirements for a float data type. Rather, ANSI states that the range shall be at least plus or minus 1.0e37. It is fairly common for the float data type to use 32 bits to represent a floating-point number, yielding at least six digits of precision.

double Data Type

A double data type is also used to represent floating-point numbers but a double will normally use twice as many bits as a float. The ANSI standard does not *require* the range of the double floating-point number to increase. However, because a double typically uses more bits for storage, the ANSI specifications guarantee at least 10 digits of precision. (See your documentation for the number of significant digits for your compiler.)

Many compiler vendors have adopted the IEEE standard for binary floating-point arithmetic. For a 64-bit value, the range of a double is approximately ± 1.0e308. This range is fairly common on many personal computers (for example, the IBM PC). On other machines machines, however, it is not unusual to find 80 bits used for the double data type (mini and mainframe computers). You should consult your compiler's documentation for the specifics that pertain to you.

Using the *sizeof* Operator To Find the Size of a Data Type

As you might have guessed from the discussion above, the C standard permits some latitude in the size that various data types can have. This means that the range of values for the data types can also vary. These variations are permitted so that the vendor writing the C compiler can select the optimal data size for the CPU being used. Some CPUs are most efficient when working with 8 bits (for example, the Z80 and 6502) while others are best with 16 bits (such as the 80286), and still others with 32 bits (such as the 68020 and 80386). By not restricting a given data type to a fixed number of bits, the compiler writer can select whatever size is best for the machine being used.

Because the C standard allows variable data sizes, C also needs to provide a means by which the programmer can determine how large a data item is. This can be done by using the sizeof operator. sizeof is a compile-time operator that tells us the number of bytes required to store a given data item. The general form for the sizeof operator is

```
sizeof expression
```

If you have an integer variable named months, the following statement would assign into variable i the number of bytes required to store the variable named months:

```
i = sizeof months;
```

On the other hand, if you want to know the size of a data type using a C keyword, you *must* use parentheses around the data type in question, such as

```
i = sizeof(int);
```

Notice that this example does not use a variable name; it uses the C keyword int.

> Parentheses are required when the expression for the sizeof operator is a C keyword for a data type.

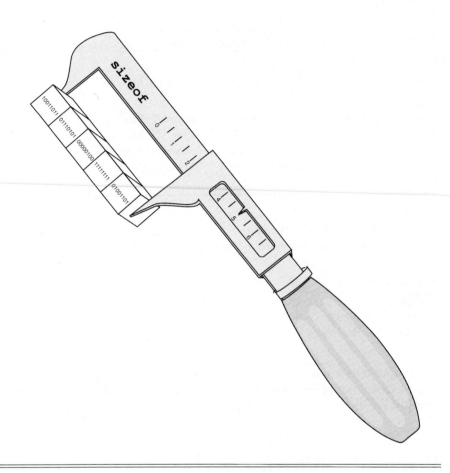

You can, however, use parentheses with variable names, such as

```
i = sizeof(months);
```

In typical C programs, you will find that the parentheses are always used because you can use either C keywords or variable names.

Listing 2.1 shows an example of how the sizeof operator can be used.

Listing 2.1. *Using the* sizeof *Operator*

```
#include  <stdio.h>

main()
{
    printf("size of a char   = %d\n", sizeof(char) );
    printf("size of an int   = %d\n", sizeof(int) );
    printf("size of a float  = %d\n", sizeof(float) );
    printf("size of a double = %d\n", sizeof(double) );
}
```

If you run listing 2.1 on your system, you can tell quickly the sizes of the basic C data types. For my system, the output of listing 2.1 is

```
size of a char   = 1
size of an int   = 2
size of a float  = 4
size of a double = 8
```

This output tells you that a char requires one byte for storage, an int two bytes, a float four bytes, and double eight bytes. Other uses for the sizeof operator are illustrated in later chapters.

Variable Names in C

Now that you know about a few C data types, you need to know what constitutes a valid name for a data item in C. The rules are simple. You can use

- ❑ Characters *a* through *z* and *A* through *Z*
- ❑ The underscore character (_)
- ❑ Digit characters 0 through 9, in any position but the first

Using these rules, the following are valid variable names:

fred	kilowatts	June	dollars
pay _period	i	birthday45	_interrupt

By the same rules, the following are not valid variable names:

```
?response      45th_birthday      -loss        @discount
2percent       not-good           nat'l_bank   $past_due
```

To help you learn C's naming conventions, consider why each of the preceding variables are not valid names in light of C's rules for variable names.

C Variable-Naming Conventions

When it comes to naming variables, certain conventions exist in almost every programming language, and C is no exception. First, it is common in most languages to use the variable names i, j, and k for variables that control program loops. It is also common practice to use x, y, and z for floating-point variable names.

Another convention is that special variable names used by the manufacturer of the compiler begin with an underscore character. Because the vendor may use special variable names with a leading underscore character, most C programmers avoid using the underscore character as the first character in a variable's name. This practice minimizes the chance of picking a variable name that would "collide" with a hidden variable name used by your vendor.

Finally, you should *never* use the name of a function that appears in your standard library as a variable name. Attempting to use a variable named printf, for example, will produce an error message if you later try to use the function named printf().

Defining Data Types

Now that you know something about data types and valid names for variables, you need to learn how to create a variable so that you can use it in a C program.

All variables must be defined before they can be used in a C program. This is different from some other languages, such as BASIC, in which definitions are not necessary because all variables default to a certain data type. C gives you much more control in that you define exactly the type of variable you want to use.

Listing 2.2 shows a short program that defines three integer variables, assigns values to two of them, and adds them together and displays the result, using printf().

Listing 2.2. *Adding Two Integer Numbers*

```
#include <stdio.h>
#include <stdlib.h>

main()
{
    char buff[20];
    int a, b, c;            /* Definition of integers */

    printf("Enter a value for a: ");
    a = atoi(gets(buff));
    printf("Enter a value for b: ");
    b = atoi(gets(buff));
    c = a + b;
    printf("The sum of %d and %d is %d\n", a, b, c);
}
```

The preprocessor directive #include <stdio.h> is needed because of the function call to printf(). Next appears the only function defined in the program: our old friend main(). The opening brace marks the start of the statements that form the function body of main().

Defining Variables

The first statement within the main() function body is the definition of a character array named buff[]. (The details about array variables are explained in Chapter 7. For now, you just need to know that buff[] is a character array capable of holding up to 20 characters.)

Our program now comes to the statement that defines the variables a, b, and c in the program. When the compiler reads this line, several things happen.

First, the compiler reads the word int. In more formal terms, the word int is called a *type specifier*. The purpose of a type specifier is to tell the compiler the type of data that you want defined. Next, the compiler reads the

```
a, b, c;
```

and now knows that you want to define three integer variables named a, b, and c.

We could have also written the first line in main() as three separate lines:

```
int a;
int b;
int c;
```

It is much more common, however, to define multiple variables of the same data type as shown in listing 2.2. In that listing, a single type specifier is followed by a list of variable names separated by the comma operator. Either form will work just fine.

The first line within main()'s function body, therefore, contains two important pieces of information for the compiler:

1. The type specifier for the data item(s) being defined

2. The name(s) of the data item(s) being defined

Note that once the type specifier is read in a data definition, the compiler knows how big each data item is. That is, the compiler knows how much storage must be allocated in memory for each data item. For this example (assuming a PC-type computer), we will assume that each integer variable needs 16 bits of storage.

When the compiler reads the semicolon at the end of the line, it knows that the statement is complete. The compiler must now allocate enough space for each data item in the list. Basically, the compiler sets aside three chunks of memory, each of which is 16 bits wide. The purpose of the type specifier, therefore, is to tell the compiler how big each chunk must be. The compiler then labels each chunk with the appropriate name; a, b, and c. (The compiler keeps track of the location of each of these named memory chunks in something called a *symbol table*. You don't need to worry about these details, however; the compiler does it for you.)

Data definition is a fundamental concept in C and one that is a common cause of confusion. We will return to the concept many times in this book. The importance of the concept will become clear as you gain a greater understanding of how C is used properly.

The defining of variables is a basic, yet important function per-formed by the compiler. The important thing to remember is this:

The *definition* of a data item in C causes the compiler to allo-cate storage for the data item.

Defining Multiple Variables

When defining a list of variables with the same type specifier, you are free to use a single type specifier followed by a list of variable names, each separated by a comma, such as

```
int a, b, c;
```

Or you can use one type specifier for each variable, as in

```
int a;
int b;
int c;
```

Either form works just fine and should cause the compiler to generate identical code.

As program complexity grows, however, it becomes more impor-tant to identify clearly the task of each variable. Often, the name is not enough to jog your memory months later when you are work-ing on the code. A common technique is something like the following:

```
int units,      /* Units of widgets produced/month */
    shipped,     /* Widgets shipped each month */
    returned;    /* Widgets returned each month */
```

This is actually the same form of definition shown in listing 2.2, except that each variable is followed by a comment on its own line to help make clear what each variable does in the program.

You might want to consider this convention, especially for long or complicated programs. (You may want to do it on every program!)

Simple Data Input

The next thing you see in listing 2.2 is

```
printf("Enter a value for a: ");
a = atoi(gets(buff));
```

followed by a similar pair of statements for variable b. The printf() call is nothing more than a prompt so that the user knows what is to be entered. The second statement is built up from two function calls. Although you are not ready to understand fully the details of the two function calls, a brief explanation is needed.

The function gets() ("get string") is found in the standard library. The function simply accepts characters from the keyboard and places them in the character array named buff[]. The input from the keyboard ends when the user presses the Return key.

atoi() is another standard C library function, whose purpose is to convert ASCII digit characters to an integer value. In this example, atoi() takes the contents of the characters in buff[] and forms an integer value from them. In listing 2.2, if the user enters a 5, it will be stored in buff[] as the character digit 5. The function atoi() then processes the contents of buff[] to form an integer (binary) value of 5. The same sequence is repeated for variable b.

The atoi() function is verbalized as "a to i" and stands for *ASCII to i*nteger. Many C standard library function names follow similar naming conventions. The function ftoa() converts a floating-point number to ASCII (that is, "f to a"). You will catch on to these "memory joggers" as you gain experience with the C standard library.

Binary Operators

Listing 2.2 uses two C operators; the addition (+) and assignment (=) operators. Although these operators were used in listing 2.2, they haven't been explained yet. All binary operators have the general form

```
expression_1 binary_operator expression_2
```

As you can see, any binary operator requires two expressions to perform properly (hence the clever name *binary* operator). C offers many operators, two of which we will discuss in this section.

Don't Confuse ASCII with Binary Values

The digit characters '0' through '9' are not the same as integer values 0 through 9. For example, the digit character for '0' has a binary representation in memory of

```
00110000            /* ASCII character digit 0 */
```

but the number zero is

```
00000000            /* Numeric value of 0 */
```

Characters entered from the keyboard are ASCII character digits that must be converted to integer values before arithmetic operations are perform on the data. The conversion process may also be written as

```
gets(buff);         /* Get the character digit(s) */
a = atoi(buff);     /* Convert to binary values */
```

but the form shown in listing 2.2 is more commonly used.

Assignment Operator

The *assignment operator* in C is a single equal sign (=). Because the assignment operator is a binary operator, it requires two expressions, or *operands*, to function properly. As you probably have guessed, the general form for an assignment operator is

```
expression_1 = expression_2
```

(For this example, we will assume that expression_2 is always resolved before expression_1, although C does not require this ordering.) In listing 2.2, the two lines

```
a = atoi(gets(buff));
b = atoi(gets(buff));
```

each use the assignment operator. If you are familiar with programming languages you know that in an assignment operation, the expression on the right side of the equal sign is resolved first and the result of the right expression is then assigned into whatever is on the left side of the equal sign. In the two C program statements above, variables a and b are both equivalent to expression_1 and 5 and atoi() and gets() function calls are both equivalent to expression_2. In this example, expression_2 in both statements resolves to an integer, the value of which is determined by what was entered by the user from the keyboard. The result is that integer values are assigned into variables a and b.

Addition Operator

The addition binary operator appears in listing 2.2 as

```
c = a + b;
```

and involves two binary operators: assignment and addition. The expression on the right side of the equal sign is resolved *before* the assignment into the expression on the left side of the equal sign takes place. This means that we must do the addition of a and b before we can assign the result into c.

If you use your thumb to cover up c =, you will see

```
a + b
```

which is the same as the general form for any binary operator. Variable a is expression_1 and b is expression_2 and the binary operator is the addition operator (+). If the values of a and b are 5 and 10 respectively, the problem is

```
5 + 1Ø
```

or 15. The integer value 15, therefore, is the resolved value for the addition operation. Note that this resolved value becomes expression_2 for the next binary operation. That is, the integer value 15 is used to create the final binary form

```
c = 15
```

which is the required form for an assignment operation. After the compiler performs the assignment, variable c holds the integer value 15.

This is the standard way to view such binary operations. However, it also helps to see things from a different point of view (see fig. 2.1).

Fig. 2.1. Evaluation of subexpressions.

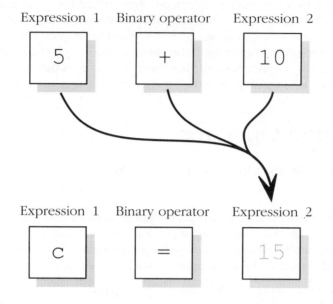

Operator Precedence

Some binary operators are executed before others. For example, the multiplication operator (*) has higher precedence than does addition. Therefore, 4 + 5 * 2 resolves to a value of 40, not 18, because the multiplication is performed before addition. If we truly wanted the value of 18, we would have to change the expression to (4 + 5) * 2. Chapter 3 discusses the precedence of all C operators.

Variable Definitions and Binary Operators from the Compiler's Point of View

Now let's look at addition and assignment from the compiler's point of view. An in-depth discussion of this now will be extremely helpful in later chapters.

You already know that when the compiler reads the line

```
int a, b, c;
```

the compiler defines storage for three integer variables. We have assumed that each integer variable requires 16 bits (2 bytes) of storage. After reading the definition for the variables a, b, and c, the compiler attempts to find an "unused" place in memory for each variable. Upon finding enough free memory to store the variables, the compiler creates an entry for each variable and assigns each variable a memory address. The information kept is the name of the variable and its location in memory (that is, its memory address). More formally, this information is kept in the compiler's symbol table. Assume that each variable is given the memory locations shown in figure 2.2.

Fig. 2.2. *Memory image for variables* a, b, *and* c.

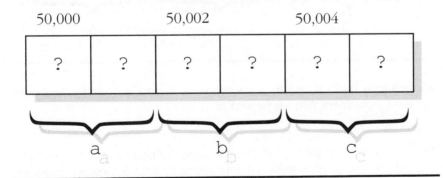

Because each integer variable requires two bytes (16 bits) for storage, variable a was given memory locations 50,000-50,001, variable b occupies 50,002-50,003, and variable c occupies 50,004-50,005.

Important note: A definition of a variable in C similar to those shown in listing 2.2 does *not* mean those memory addresses are cleared to zero as is done in some other languages (BASIC, for example). The contents of memory locations 50,000-50,006 are whatever (junk?) happened to be there when the program started.

Let's suppose that the user enters the character digit '5' from the keyboard. After the gets() and atoi() functions have been called, we can view the statement as though it were

    a = 5;

The compiler is now ready to perform the assignment of 5 into variable a. The compiler now looks in its symbol table for variable a and finds that it is located in memory at addresses 50,000-50,001. The compiler then takes the integer constant 5 and stores it in those two memory locations. The memory image now looks like the one shown in figure 2.3.

Fig. 2.3. The memory image after a is assigned a value.

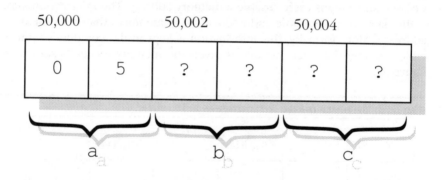

Assuming the user enters the character digits '1' and '0' from the keyboard, the next assignment may be viewed as

    b = 1Ø;

Once again the compiler performs the same "table lookup" for variable b and assigns the integer value 10 into the appropriate memory locations. Figure 2.4 shows what the memory image now becomes.

Fig. 2.4. *The memory image after variable b is assigned a value.*

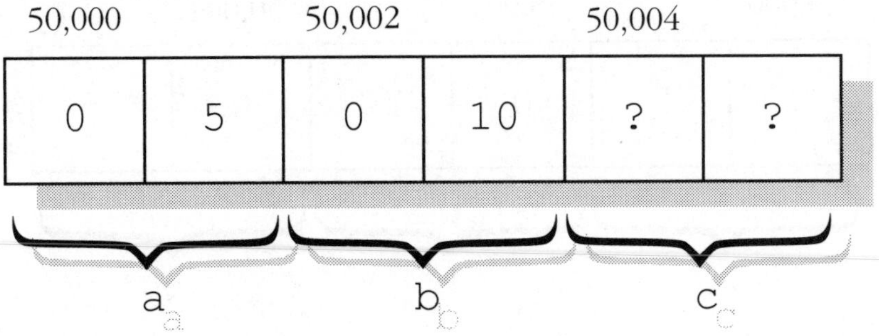

50,000   50,002   50,004

| 0 | 5 | 0 | 10 | ? | ? |

a   b   c

The next line

```
c = a + b;
```

requires the compiler to first resolve the right expression (or subexpression a + b) of the assignment operation. To resolve the subexpression, the compiler must

1. Find where variable a is stored (50,000-50,001) and get its value (5).

2. Find where variable b is stored (50,002-50,003) and get its value (10).

3. Add the two values together to get 15.

The compiler has now resolved the right side of the assignment operation to the integer value 15. The compiler is now ready to perform the assignment operation.

To perform the assignment into variable c, the compiler must once again look in the symbol table to find where c is stored. The symbol table will divulge the address of c as memory locations 50,004-50,005. The compiler will then place the integer value 15 into those memory locations. Figure 2.5 shows what the memory image now becomes.

The compiler has completed most of the difficult parts of listing 2.2.

Fig. 2.5. The result of evaluating the assignment expression.

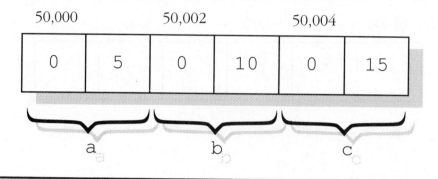

lvalues and *rvalues*

Another useful way to illustrate a memory image has a slightly different, but very important, approach. This approach is illustrated by using variable a, as shown in figure 2.6.

Fig. 2.6. Alternative memory image for variable a.

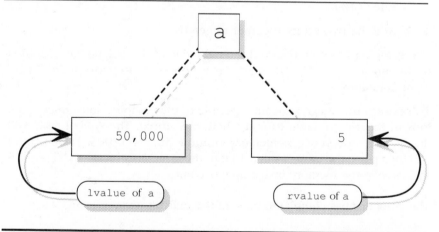

In figure 2.6, variable a is shown with two "legs." The left leg is called the lvalue for variable a. An *lvalue* is the memory address for a data item. From figure 2.2, you can see that the lvalue for variable a is memory address

50,000. This is exactly the same as the memory image explained earlier, only viewed in a different way.

The right leg for variable a in figure 2.6 is called the rvalue for variable a. The *rvalue* of a data item refers to what is stored in the data item. More formally, the rvalue of a variable is what is stored at that variable's lvalue. Think about it.

If you think of lvalues as "left values" and rvalues as "right values," the left value is the address of a data item and the right value is what is stored there. Every data item in a program *must* have an lvalue and an rvalue.

One more thing for you to think about: The compiler must know the lvalue of every variable. If it cannot find the lvalue, the compiler will issue a variable undefined error message. Once the compiler has an lvalue, getting what is stored there (that is, its rvalue) is easy.

Remember the following points:

- ☑ lvalue is a memory address of a data item
- ☑ rvalue is a value stored at an lvalue
- ☑ compilers need lvalues to get rvalues

Take a moment to explain the following lines in terms of lvalues and rvalues:

```
int a, b, c;

a = 5;
b = 1Ø;
c = a + b;
```

You may find it worthwhile to use a diagram similar to the one in figure 2.5. Understanding the concepts of lvalues and rvalues is an important step to understanding C. Having this understanding will make the material presented in later chapters *much* easier.

Using *printf( )*

The final statement in listing 2.2

```
printf("The sum of %d and %d is %d\n", a, b, c);
```

uses some features of printf() that have not been discussed. This time, printf() has a double-quoted string followed by a list of three variable names. This section explains what printf() does with such an argument list.

Programming Tip

Problems with *scanf( )*

Ever since the first edition of this book was published, I've been asked why I don't use the scanf() function for data input. That is, listing 2.2 could have replaced the statement

```
a = atoi(gets(buff));
```

with the scanf() equivalent of

```
scanf("%d", &a);
```

There are several reasons why scanf() is not used. First, it uses aspects of C that we will not cover until much later in the book. Second, it is used differently with simple and aggregate data types—its use is not consistent across all data types. Third, it makes it difficult to enter things that might have blank spaces in them, such as first and last names and street address. All of these considerations make scanf() prone to error. Last, but not least, it is a huge and complex function that represents an H-bomb-to-kill-an-ant approach to data input. With one compiler, using scanf() increased the code size by more than 20 percent.

scanf() is discussed in some detail in a later chapter. For now, however, I suggest that you defer using the scanf() function.

---

printf( ) and Output Conversions

Notice the percent signs (%) in the double-quoted string. A percent sign within double quotes in a printf() function call is called a *conversion character* and has a special meaning. The letter immediately following the conversion character tells what type of data will be converted. In the example, the "%d" stands for decimal conversion.

Computers store data in binary form, and the actual memory image for variable a is shown in figure 2.7. (For simplicity, always assume that the high byte is stored before the low byte for an integer.) The binary image is a little difficult for most people to read. The %d conversion character, therefore, tells printf() to convert the integer data stored in binary form to a decimal form that humans can more easily understand. (The binary values for decimal values 0 through 255 can be found in Appendix A.)

Fig. 2.7. *The memory image of an integer variable.*

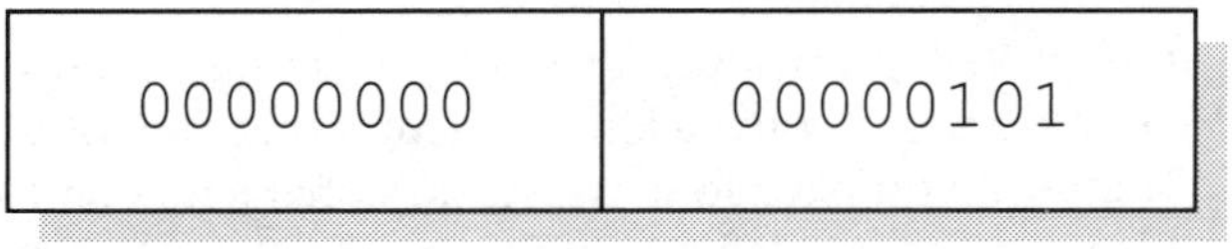

00000000	00000101

So how does printf() know which variable to convert? It knows which variable to use by the order in which they appear within the argument list used for the printf() function call. This is illustrated in figure 2.8.

Fig. 2.8. *Matching conversion characters and variables in* printf( ).

```
printf("The sum of %d and %d is %d\n", a, b, c);
```

Figure 2.8 shows that the conversion characters within the double quotes are matched up with the variable names appearing in the list which begins after the closing quotation mark and comma. Notice that variable names are separated by the comma operator. Because our printf() statement has three conversion characters within the double quotes, there must be a list of three variable names, each separated by a comma. The output produced by printf() statement is

```
The sum of 5 and 1Ø is 15
```

Having displayed the results of the addition of two numbers, the program encounters the closing brace for main() and listing 2.2 ends.

Programming Tip

Be Careful with *printf( )* Arguments

Although it is probably obvious, all kinds of strange things can happen if you have more conversion characters that variables in a printf(). That is, if you have four conversion characters and only three variables, be prepared for trouble. In some cases, nothing strange will happen and you may even get reasonable values for the missing variable. In other cases, the program will "go west" (that is, lock up the system). If you are getting strange values in a program, never dismiss this type of error—we all have made it at least once!

Other Conversion Characters for *printf( )*

The printf() function would not be useful if it were limited to simply displaying integer values. Table 2.2 shows some other possible conversion characters for printf().

All but the last two entries in table 2.2 are used to convert from a numeric binary format (as stored in memory) to a human-readable format for display by a program.

Table 2.2. printf( ) *Conversion Characters*

Conversion Character	Interpretation
%d	Convert integer to decimal (base 10)
%ld	Convert long integer to decimal
%x	Convert integer to hexadecimal (base 16)
%lx	Convert long integer to hexadecimal
%o	Convert integer to octal (base 8)
%lo	Convert long integer to octal
%u	Convert unsigned integer to decimal
%lu	Convert long unsigned integer to decimal
%e	Convert floating-point to scientific notation (for example, 1.23e10)
%f	Convert floating-point to decimal (for example, 2.14)
%g	Convert floating-point to the shortest of %e or %f
%p	Convert pointer value
%c	Convert byte to character
%s	Convert bytes to string

The %c conversion character is used to convert a single binary byte into its printable equivalent character. Usually, this means converting from binary to an ASCII character for display. (Appendix A presents a list for the ASCII character set.)

The %s conversion character behaves much the same way, only it operates on a series of characters stored in memory to print out a "string" of characters on the screen. Therefore,

```
printf("%s", name);
```

would print out all of the characters stored at the lvalue of name until a termination character is read. (The details of how this works are explained in a later chapter.)

Escape Sequences and *printf( )*

Now you know that the control string for printf() can contain special conversion characters as well as normal ASCII characters. In addition, the control string may also contain special control characters, or *escape sequences*, as shown in table 2.3.

Table 2.3. *Escape Sequences*

Escape Sequence	Meaning
\n	Newline (corresponds to a line feed)
\b	Backspace
\t	Tab
\r	Carriage return
\f	Form feed
\'	Single quote
\"	Double quote
\\	Backslash
\ddd	Octal integer
\xddd	Hexadecimal integer
\a	Alert (bell)
\v	Vertical tab
\?	Question mark

Note: d represents a digit.

You have already seen the newline escape sequence in several programs. The other are new. To give you an idea of how some of these sequences work, consider the statement

```
printf("12345\b\b\b");
```

When this statement is executed, the cursor would be sitting on top of the character '3' because the cursor was backspaced on the screen three positions.

As another example, the ANSI device driver code sequence for clearing the screen and homing the cursor is the character sequence

```
ESC   [   2   J
```

That is, when we send an Escape character, a right bracket, the character '2', and the character 'J' the screen will be cleared and the cursor will be in the upper left (home) position. However, because the Escape character is a nonprinting character, we must use an escape sequence to represent the Escape character. Therefore, the proper string to use could be written as

```
"\Ø33[2J"
```

in octal format, or as

```
"\x1b[2J"
```

if you prefer hexadecimal. If we simply used "27[2J", that's exactly what you would see on the screen. The backslash is necessary for nonprinting characters.

We have only touched on a few of the many things that printf() can do. You should read your standard library documentation to see some of the other features offered by printf().

Additional Program Examples with Different Data Types

By now, you have a pretty good idea of some of the data types that are available to you, how they are defined and stored in memory, and how you can use printf() to display their values in a program. This section presents several program examples, using some of the data types you have studied.

If you look for the ASCII representation for the letter 'A' in Appendix A at the back of this book, you will find that it is the 65th character in the ASCII character set. Listing 2.3 shows you four ways to print the letter 'A' on the screen.

The output of the program is

```
A   A   A   A
```

Notice that single quotes are used to denote a single character constant in C. (As you will recall from Listing 1.1 in Chapter 1, double quotes are used for a string of characters.) Therefore, the first call to printf() uses the %c conversion character of printf() to display the character constant A.

Listing 2.3. Display the Letter 'A'

```
#include <stdio.h>

main()
{
    printf("%c   ", 'A');
    printf("%c   ", 65);
    printf("%c   ", 0x41);
    printf("%c\n", 0101);
}
```

The second call to printf() also displays the character 'A' on the screen, but reflects our knowledge that the decimal number 65 represents the ASCII equivalent for the letter A (see Appendix A). If the %d conversion character had been used, you would have seen "65" displayed on the screen. Because the %c conversion character was used, printf() knows you want the character (for example, ASCII) representation of the number 65, so A is displayed on the screen.

The last two calls to printf() also rely on the use of the numeric ASCII value for the letter A, but use the hexadecimal and octal numbering systems. That is, decimal 65 is 41 in hexadecimal (base 16) and 101 is decimal 65 in octal (base 8). Note that all hexadecimal numbers are preceded by 0x and octal numbers have a leading 0 as the first digit. (Can you explain why removing the 0x in the third printf() would display a closing parenthesis? Why would deleting the leading 0 in the fourth printf() display a lower-case letter e?)

Some machines (the IBM PC, for example) use the remaining 128 characters for graphics characters. Your compiler's documentation will tell you whether the remaining 128 characters are available for use.

Character Variables

Thus far, we have shown only examples that used character constants (for example, 'A' or 0x41) that are "hard-coded" in the program. Listing 2.4 shows how to get a single character from the keyboard.

Programming Tip

Choosing between Numeric and Character Representations

Given that you can display a letter by using its character representation in single quotes ('A') or in numeric form (65), which is better? Although either form will work, clearly the character representation in single quotes ('A') is easier to read. Therefore, in most circumstances the single-quoted character representation is the better choice. A possible exception is when you need to use a nonprinting ASCII character. In those cases, most C programmers use a hexadecimal representation of the number (for example, Escape = 0x1b).

Listing 2.4. Using Character Variables

```
#include <stdio.h>

main( )
{
    char response;

    response = getchar( );

    printf("\nThe character just entered was %c\n", response);
}
```

Notice the call to the function getchar( ). The purpose of the getchar( ) call is to read a character from the keyboard. After getting the keystroke, getchar( ) returns that value from the function call. In listing 2.4, we then take the value returned from getchar( ) and assign it into response. The printf( ) call then displays the character on the screen.

Even though getchar( ) is an ANSI standard C library function, it may behave differently for various compilers. In some cases, you will have to press the Enter (or Return) key after typing in the letter. Other implementations return the keystroke immediately without waiting for you to press the Enter key.

One more thing about the getchar( ) function: getchar( ) is defined to return an integer value, but we are assigning it into a char data type. Some compilers may issue a warning because of the mismatched data type assignment. (Usually, the program will work fine, and you will see how to deal with the warning in Chapter 9, in the section about the cast operator.) You may wish to type in listing 2.4 just to see how your version of getchar( ) works.

Using *float* and *double* Data Types

Thus far, most of the examples have used either char or int data types. In this section, you will see how the floating-point data types float and double are used.

A *floating-point number* is any number that can assume a fractional value. The constant pi (3.14. . .) is a common example of a floating-point number. If you tried to assign pi into an integer (and if the compiler lets you do it), the integer variable would be assigned the value 3; the fractional part would be "lost in translation." Therefore, you must define a variable of the floating-point data type if the number can assume a fractional value.

Using Floating-Point Numbers

Listing 2.5 uses both float and double data types in calculating the present value of $100 a year from now. As you might recall, the present value of money in the future is a function of the amount of money invested today and the interest rate. For example, if you invested about $90.91 cents in the bank today at 10 percent interest, a year from now it would be worth $100.00. Alternatively, if you promise to give someone $100.00 a year from now and the interest rate is 10 percent, anyone buying the promissory note from you today should not pay more than $90.91 for your note.

Listing 2.5. *Present Value Program with Floating-Point Numbers*

```
#include  <stdio.h>

main( )
{
    float rate1, dollar1, discount_factor1;
    double rate2, dollar2, discount_factor2;

    dollar1 = 100.0;
    discount_factor1 = 1.1;

    dollar2 = 100.0;
    discount_factor2 = 1.05;

    rate1 = (discount_factor1 - 1.0) * 100.0;
    rate2 = (discount_factor2 - 1.0) * 100.0;

    printf("The present value of $100 at %g%% ",  rate1);
    printf("in a year is %g\n\n", dollar1 / discount_factor1);

    printf("The present value of $100");
    printf(" at %g%% in a year is %g\n\n",
            rate2, dollar2 / discount_factor2);

}
```

The present value of any asset for one year is simply the value of the asset divided by 1.0 plus the interest rate. We have defined variables `rate1`, `dollar1` and `discount_factor1` to be `float` data types and `rate2`, `dollar2`, and `discount_factor2` to be `double` data types. This example was chosen because it illustrates several quirks about floating-point numbers and their use in C.

Floating-Point Constants

You will notice that in each of the assignment statements, all floating-point constants have the decimal point present even when the value does not have a fractional part (for example, 100.0 and 1.0). Although all C compilers should interpret the constant properly, some C compilers get confused. Why might it have been confused? Perhaps the reason was because the default data type for a numeric constant in a C program is an integer. Therefore, when you wrote

```
y = 100;
```

the compiler tried to assign an integer (2 bytes) into a double (8 bytes). By using the decimal point

```
y = 100.0;
```

you let the compiler know that a floating-point constant is being used. This defensive coding practice should not be necessary with most commercial C compilers.

> Always use the decimal point with any floating-point constant, even if there is no fractional value. The decimal points helps to jog your memory that a floating-point number is being used and no compiler should confuse the floating-point constant with an integer value.

What Is %g%%?

In the printf() function call

```
printf("The present value of $100 at %g%% ",  rate1);
```

you can see that rate1 is printed out, using a %g%% character sequence. What does this do? As you can see from table 2.2, the %g is used to print out a floating-point number. The %g causes the value of rate1 to be displayed on the screen.

The two consecutive percent signs (%%) after the %g are used to print a single percent sign in C. Because the percent sign is the conversion character and has special meaning to printf(), if you want to print a percent sign on the screen, you must use the conversion character (the first %) followed by a second percent sign (the one we wish to show on the screen). This tells printf() that there really is no variable value to convert, rather you just want to display a percent sign.

Formatting Floating-Point Numbers

When listing 2.5 is run, the output is

```
The present value of $100 at 10.000003% in a year is 90.909089
The present value of $100 at 5% in a year is  95.238095
```

While the program works, the output is a bit messy. Dollar amounts are usually not viewed to six decimal places. The same is true for interest rates. Fortunately, the printf() function provides a way to solve the problem. If you change the printf() statements to

```
printf("The present value of $100 at %2.0f%% ", rate1);
printf("in a year is %5.2f\n\n", dollar1 / discount_factor1);

printf("The present value of $100");
printf(" at %2.0f%% in a year is %5.2f\n\n",
    rate2, dollar2 / discount_factor2);
```

the output becomes

```
The present value of $100 at 10% in a year is  90.91
The present value of $100 at 5% in a year is 95.24
```

which looks a little better. To make these changes, you use the %f conversion character with a format field. The general form is

Conversion Character	Total Field Width	Decimal Point	Decimal Field Width	Floating Point
%	field_width	.	decimal_width	f

Therefore

```
%2.0f
```

has a field width of two and no decimal places. The %5.2f specification says that you want to print the number in a field of five places (total) with two places (for cents) after the decimal point. If the width of the number exceeds the field width, the number is not truncated (you will see the entire number). The field width, therefore, is the minimum field width used by the number but it may be larger if needed. As you can see, the change has little impact (other than rounding) on the result.

In a field specification such as %5.2f, the first number (5 in this example) specifies the total width of the field used to display the number—not the number of places to the left of the decimal point.

float or *double*: Which Is Best?

As an experiment, change listing 2.5 so that the float and double variables use the same values and see whether there is any difference in the two results. (Instead of using a %5.2f conversion, just use %f.) If your results are similar to mine, the float values become incorrect after the fourth decimal place (for example, 95.238100 instead of the correct value of 95.238095).

One disadvantage of the float data type is that it does not have very much precision—typically only six digits. But, you say, "True, but since it is only half the size of a double, it's probably twice as fast in computations."

float and Automatic Conversions

Not necessarily true. Normally, all C floating-point computations are done in double precision arithmetic. This is true for float and double data types. As a result, a float computation may actually be slower. How come? Because the compiler is required to do computations in double precision, the compiler must first convert the float variable to a double, perform the computation, and then de-convert the double back to a float so the result can be assigned into the float variable. All of these conversions take time. A double, on the other hand, simply performs the computation—no conversions are necessary.

If a float has relatively poor precision and might even be (computationally) slower, why even have a float data type? One primary reason: storage space. If you have limited memory or disk storage and need to store a large array of floating-point numbers, you may have no other choice than to use the float data type.

ANSI C and Floating-Point Arithmetic

Note that pre-ANSI C required all floating-point operations be done in double precision arithmetic. The ANSI standard, however, does permit float arithmetic and leaves the decision up to the compiler manufacturer. While this change in the floating-point arithmetic rules may muddy the waters a bit, it does make sense. There are a lot of applications where 14 digits of precision are not needed but speed is (for example, 3-D graphics). The new rules gives users greater freedom to select a compiler that best suits their needs.

You may want to see whether your compiler supports float arithmetic.

Data Type Modifiers

To enable you to have greater control over the data, several additional keywords can be used to modify some of the basic C data types. These keywords are

unsigned   signed   short   long

These modifiers can be used only with certain C data types, as explained below.

unsigned Modifier

The keyword unsigned is used to tell the compiler that the data type being defined will not use a sign bit. The use of unsigned is limited to int and char data types only (including both long int and short int). For example, if you define variable i as

    unsigned int i;

you are defining i to be an integer value that can only assume positive values (including zero). In the case of a 16-bit unsigned integer, there are 65,536 (that is, 2^{16}) unique values available. Therefore, the range for a 16-bit unsigned integer is 0 through 65,535. (Zero is, after all, one of those unique values.) For machines that use 32-bit unsigned integers, the range is extended to 0 through 4,294,967,295.

The unsigned modifier also resolves certain problems incurred when converting from a character to integer data type. Without the unsigned modifier, result of a conversion from a char to an int is implementation-specific. That is, is the char sign expanded or not when converted to an integer? In other words, is the value of the high bit of the char copied into all bit positions for the high byte? By using the unsigned modifier with the char data type, you have an unambiguous conversion from a char to an int without sign expansion.

signed Modifier

The signed modifier is a new keyword that has been added by the ANSI committee. The int data type is a signed quantity by default. In a practical sense, therefore, the signed modifier only has meaning when used as a modifier for the char data type. Therefore, the definition

```
signed char c;
```

says that we want to define a character variable c that can assume a value from –127 to +127. Typically, a char may or may not be a signed quantity—it is implementation specific. By using the signed modifier, the programmer can define a signed char variable that is not dependent upon the compiler's char details of implementation.

Fig. 2.9. *Memory image of a* float.

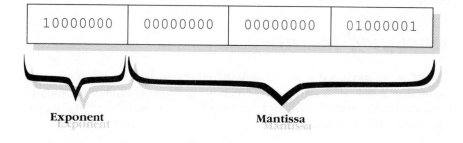

short Modifier

The short modifier allows you to define a data type that may use less storage than its unmodified counterpart. For example,

```
short int i;
```

on a machine that uses a 32-bit integer may use 16 bits for a short int. This is especially useful when you are defining loop counters. Because few bits must be manipulated, a short int can process loops faster than a default (32-bit) int.

Beware of Data-Type Mismatches

C is different than some languages (BASIC, for example) because each data item must be defined before it can be used. This can cause some confusion at the start if you're not used to it. The following code fragment illustrates a common mistake:

```
float b;

b = 65.Ø;

printf("The value of b is %d\n", b);
```

Notice the mistake. Suppose that b is stored with an lvalue of 50,000 and an rvalue of 65.0. Let's simplify things further and assume that 65.0 (in binary) is stored in memory as shown in figure 2.9.

Even though we should print b as a floating-point number, a %d conversion character was used by mistake. This will cause printf() to grab only an integer-sized chunk of memory (that is, two bytes). Because the first two bytes at b's lvalue (memory locations 50,000 and 50,001) are all zeros, printf() does exactly as asked and displays an integer value of zero. Therefore, the output is

```
The value of b is Ø
```

which is incorrect. Now you can see why the type specifier is important in both defining the variable and using the variable in a function. If the data type and conversion character don't match, all kinds of weird things can happen.

Make sure your data types match throughout a program.

long Modifier

The `long` modifier allows you to define an integer value that is capable of holding a range of values from –2,147,483,648 to +2,147,483,647. For most systems, a `long` will use 32 bits for storage with the high bit used for the sign. Therefore, the data definition

```
long int big_num;
```

defines `big_num` to be a `long` integer data type. By default, a `long int` data type is a signed number.

Because of differences in machines, you will find some compilers where an `int` and a `long int` have the same size and range.

Modifiers and Implied Data Types

When using the `unsigned` and `long` modifiers, you can omit the keyword `int`. Therefore, you could write

```
unsigned i;
long big_num;
```

which is the same as defining

```
unsigned int i;
long int big_num;
```

The compiler will use either pair of definitions in the same manner. Most C programmers tend to omit the `int` keyword when using a `long` or `unsigned` modifier with integer data types. A summary of the basic data types and their extensions is presented in table 2.4.

Table 2.4. *Basic Data Types and Modified Data Types*

Basic Data Types			
char	int	float	double

Modified Data Types

Long:	`long int, long double`
Short:	`short int`
Signed:	`signed char, signed short int,` `signed short, signed long int,` `signed long`
Unsigned:	`unsigned char, unsigned int,` `unsigned short int, unsigned long` `int, unsigned long`

▼ Review Questions and Exercises

1. Write a program that constructs a table of the data types discussed in this chapter for your compiler. Use the `sizeof` operator.

2. What is a type specifier and why it is important?

3. What does the following program display?

```
#include  <stdio.h>

main()
{
    printf("%c  %x  %d  %o", 'Y', 'Y', 'Y',    'Y');
}
```

(Hint: You might want to look at Appendix A.)

4. Write a program of your choice that tests the accuracy of `float` and `double` data types. Don't forget that you can use a format field as big as you need (for example, `%2Ø.18f`).

5. What does it mean to define a variable?

6. Explain the statement

   ```
   a = b;
   ```

   in terms of lvalues and rvalues. Is it true that this type of assignment results in one rvalue replacing another?

7. Write a program that, on purpose, uses the wrong conversion characters with variables of different data types, such as

   ```
   char letter;
   int val;
   unsigned int num;

   letter = 'A';
   val = -1;
   num = -1;

   printf("%d %u %f", letter, val, num);
   ```

   and see how your compiler handles such things. Experiment with all data conversion types.

▼ Answers

1. Because the signed and unsigned type modifiers for a data type will always use the same amount of storage, we need only consider the basic data types. The following program is one possible solution:

   ```
   #include <stdio.h>

   main()
   {
      printf("     char: %d     int: %d\n",
              sizeof(char), sizeof(int));
      printf("short int: %d    long: %d\n",
              sizeof(short int), sizeof(long));
      printf("    float: %d  double: %d\n",
              sizeof(float), sizeof(double));
   }
   ```

   The specific output will vary depending upon the host system.

2. A type specifier sets the attributes, or properties, that a variable will assume in a program. The type specifier is important because the attribute of the variable determines how the variable can be used in a program.

The attribute of a variable is also important when arrays are used because the type specifier sets the scaling value for array arithmetic. For those readers familiar with arrays, the memory location of element 5 of an integer array

```
num[5]
```

is found in a manner not unlike

```
num[Ø] + sizeof(int) * 5;
```

Notice why the type specifier int is important in determining how many bytes in memory to "skip over" to find element 5 of the array.

3. The output of the program is:

```
Y    59    89    131
```

which represents the character, hexadecimal, decimal, and octal value of the character 'Y'. The conversion characters for printf() give you a variety of ways to view the same data.

4. Reader's option.

5. Some writers intermix the terms "declare" and "define" in C, but the terms are *not* interchangeable. When you define an object in C, you cause storage to be allocated for that object. That is, the compiler will request enough storage from the operating system to hold the data item being defined.

When you declare a variable, you are simply telling the compiler what the attribute list of the variable is in the program—*no storage is allocated for the data item*. (This distinction will become clearer in the chapter that discusses storage classes for data objects.)

6. Every variable in C has an lvalue and an rvalue. To process the statement

```
a = b;
```

the compiler performs the following sequence of steps:

a. Look in the symbol table for variable b. If not found, issue a `variable undefined` error message. If found, get the address in memory (the `lvalue`) of where b is located.

b. Go to the `lvalue` of b and get what is stored at that memory address. This is its `rvalue`. The number of bytes that must be used to form the `rvalue` were set by the type specifier of variable b (for example, if the type specifier was an `int`, look at `sizeof(int)` bytes of memory).

c. Look in the symbol table for variable a. If not found, issue a `variable undefined` error message. If found, get the address in memory (the `lvalue`) of where a is located.

d. Go to the `lvalue` of a and place the `rvalue` of b into that memory address (that is, the `lvalue` of a). Variable a now has an `rvalue` that is the same as the `rvalue` of b.

As you can see, the `rvalue` of b does in fact replace whatever `rvalue` may have existed in a prior to the assignment taking place.

7. Reader's option.

3

Operators and
Selection Statements

Concepts in This Chapter

- Arithmetic operators
- Relational operators
- Bitwise operators
- "Shorthand" versions of operators
- if statements
- Logical operators
- Switch statements

In this chapter, you will learn about the arithmetic, relational, bitwise, and logical operators. These operators allow you to manipulate data in your programs and to perform tests on the data. You will also learn about the first of several C statements that enable you to determine the flow of control through a program. In summary, this chapter lays the foundations for writing programs that make decisions.

81

More Arithmetic Operators

In Chapter 1, the addition operator was used to add two integer values. Obviously, other arithmetic operators exist. In this section, the other available arithmetic operators are discussed. These are presented in table 3.1.

Table 3.1. *Arithmetic Operators*

Operator Symbol	Interpretation
+	Addition
–	Subtraction
*	Multiplication
/	Division
–	Unary minus
+	Unary plus
%	Modulus (remainder after division)

Most of these operators are identical to those used in ordinary mathematics and provided in other programming languages. Perhaps the only strangers are the last two in the list: the unary minus and the modulus operator.

Unary Minus Operator

The only nonbinary arithmetic operator, the unary minus is used to alternate the sign of the data item. For example, in the code fragment

```
int i, j;
i = 5;
j = -i;
```

variable j will have the value –5. The unary minus operator can be used with any data type.

Modulus Operator

The modulus operator is a little different in two ways. The first difference is what it does, and the second is that certain data-type restrictions apply to the use of the modulus operator.

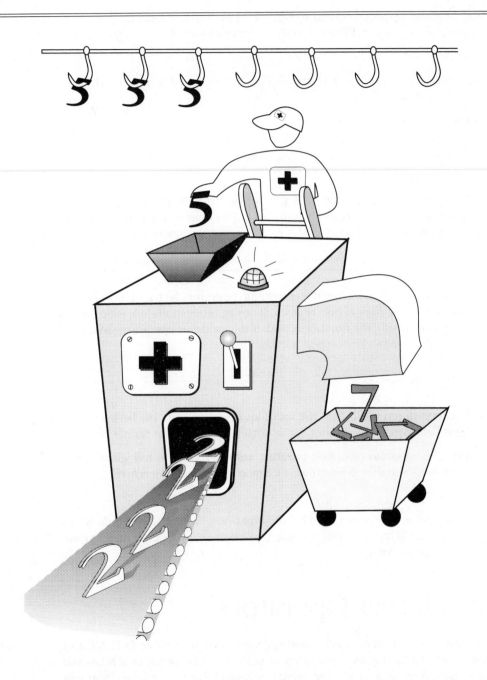

The modulus operator is used to find the remainder of a divide operation. As you know, integer division ignores any remainder. For example,

```
17 / 4 = 4
```

when integer division is performed. The remainder of 1 is ignored. In C, you could write

```
int a, b, c;

a = 17;
b = 4;
c = a / b;
```

and c would hold the value 4. If you replace the divide operator with a modulus operator, the answer would be 1. The reason is that *the modulus operator yields the remainder of a division*, not the quotient.

> One common use for the modulus operator is to determine whether a number is odd or even. If any number modulo 2 yields a non-zero result, the number is odd. If the modulus operation yields a value of zero, the number is even.

The second difference is that the modulus operator can only be used with integral data types. You cannot use it with a floating-point number.

Finally, the modulus operator is rarely verbalized in its full glory. Most programmers simply refer to it as the "mod" operator. Therefore

```
c = a % b;
```

is verbalized as "c equals a mod b," or sometimes "c equals a modulo b." (I thought I would mention this because you never know when it might come up at a cocktail party.)

Relational Operators

The usual complement of relational operators is also available in C. A list of the relational operators is provided in table 3.2. The result of a relational operation is either logical False (zero) or logical True (non-zero). You will see an example of how these logical values are used later in this chapter.

Table 3.2. *Relational Operators*

Relational Operator	Interpretation
>	Greater than
>=	Greater than or equal to
<	Less than
<=	Less than or equal to
==	Equal to
!=	Not equal to

If you're familiar with other programming languages, only the last two operators in table 3.2 will be unfamiliar to you. The double equal sign is used in C to differentiate it from the assignment operator. While this makes it easy to tell whether a relational test or an assignment is being performed in the program, beginning C programmers should expect to forget this at first. This can cause problems, however, as you shall soon see.

The test for inequality is also different in other languages. The simplest way to remember it is that the exclamation mark in C is the *not* operator. Combining the *not* operator with the equal sign yields the "not equal to" operator.

Bitwise Operators

One of the early driving forces behind C was the goal to create an operating system (UNIX) that could be easily moved from one hardware system to another. Operating systems must be on "intimate terms" with the computer hardware; sometimes a single bit conveys an important message such as "1 for error, 0 for OK." Obviously, the C language had to be able to perform bit manipulations to realize that goal. The result is that C offers a number of bitwise operators not found in other languages. These operators are listed in table 3.3.

With one exception, all bitwise operators require two operands. The exception is the bitwise NOT (or "one's complement") operator, which requires only one operand.

As the term implies, *bitwise* operators perform operations on data at the bit level. The arithmetic operators, by contrast, perform operations on bytes

Table 3.3. *Bitwise Operators*

Bitwise Operator	Interpretation
&	AND
|	OR (inclusive)
^	XOR (exclusive OR)
>>	Right shift
<<	Left shift
~	NOT

and larger data items as a whole. Each bit in the result of a bitwise operation is determined by corresponding bit(s) in the operand(s).

Bitwise AND (&)

With a bitwise AND, the result bit is 1 if corresponding bits are 1 in both operands. Any other combination produces a 0 for the bit position. Thus

```
5 & 9 = 00000101 & 00001001 = 00000001
```

Figure 3.1 shows how the operands are evaluated bit by bit to produce the result.

Bitwise OR (|)

If either bit position is 1, the result of a bitwise OR is a 1. Only when both positions are 0 is the result 0. Therefore

```
13 | 2 = 00001101 | 00000010 = 00001111
```

Bitwise Exclusive OR (^)

If one or the other bit is 1, the result is 1. The exception is when both bits are 1, which produces a zero result.

```
13 ^ 3 = 00001101 & 00000011 = 00001110
```

Fig. 3.1. *Bitwise evaluation of 5 AND 9.*

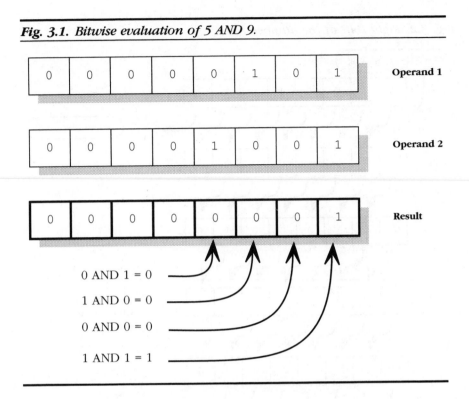

Bitwise Right Shift (>>)

The bitwise right shift operator shifts the bits of the left operand to the right by a number of bits equal to the right operator. Therefore

```
139 >> 1 = 10001011 >> 1 = 01000101
```

causes all bit positions to move to the right by one position. Note that a zero replaces the high bit.

Figure 3.2 shows what happens when the value 139 is shifted right 8 times.

Bitwise Left Shift (<<)

The bitwise left shift operator shifts the bits of the left operand to the left by a number of bits equal to the right operator. Therefore

```
2 << 2 = 00000010 << 2 = 00001000
```

Fig. 3.2. Right shift of the number 139.

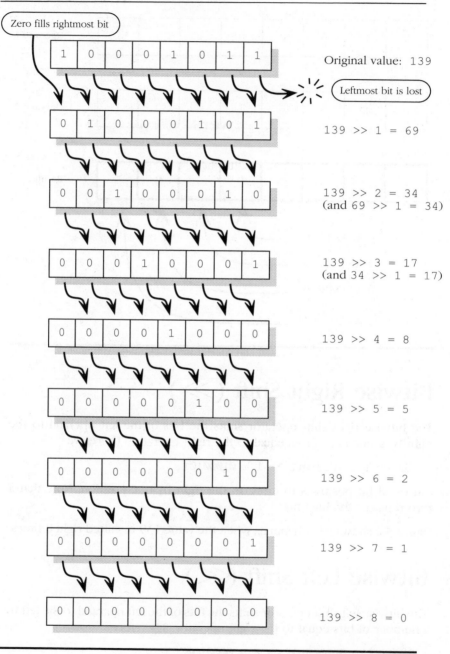

Zero fills rightmost bit

| 1 | 0 | 0 | 0 | 1 | 0 | 1 | 1 |

Original value: 139

Leftmost bit is lost

| 0 | 1 | 0 | 0 | 0 | 1 | 0 | 1 |

139 >> 1 = 69

| 0 | 0 | 1 | 0 | 0 | 0 | 1 | 0 |

139 >> 2 = 34
(and 69 >> 1 = 34)

| 0 | 0 | 0 | 1 | 0 | 0 | 0 | 1 |

139 >> 3 = 17
(and 34 >> 1 = 17)

| 0 | 0 | 0 | 0 | 1 | 0 | 0 | 0 |

139 >> 4 = 8

| 0 | 0 | 0 | 0 | 0 | 1 | 0 | 0 |

139 >> 5 = 5

| 0 | 0 | 0 | 0 | 0 | 0 | 1 | 0 |

139 >> 6 = 2

| 0 | 0 | 0 | 0 | 0 | 0 | 0 | 1 |

139 >> 7 = 1

| 0 | 0 | 0 | 0 | 0 | 0 | 0 | 0 |

139 >> 8 = 0

You can also treat bits within an integer as fields, too. The discussion of this feature is postponed until Chapter 9.

Programming Tip

Fast Multiplication and Division by Powers of Two

As you can see from the discussion of the shift operators, shifting a number by one bit position to the left has the effect of multiplying the number by 2, provided that bits don't flow out of the top position and that an unsigned integer is used.

Shifting right one position has the effect of dividing the number by two. If you need a fast multiply or divide operation and the data can be expected to meet the limitations, the shift operators could be just the solution.

Bitwise NOT (~)

The bitwise NOT operator—the only unary bitwise operator—performs a logical complement of the operand: if the operand bit is a 0, the result bit is a 1; if the operand bit is a 1, the result bit is a 0. Therefore,

```
~ 170 = ~ 10101010 = 01010101
```

Shorthand Form for Operators

If you have done much programming, you already know that certain operator sequences, such as

```
a = a + b;
```

are used often. In fact, they are so common in programming that C provides special operators to abbreviate such sequences. For example, you can use

```
a += b;
```

instead of

```
a = a + b;
```

The result is the same in either case: The value of b is added to the contents of a. Table 3.4 shows the operators for which a shorthand form is available.

Table 3.4. *Shorthand-Form Operators*

Operator	Example of Long-Form Equivalent
+=	x = x + a;
—=	x = x – a;
*=	x = x * a;
/=	x = x / a;
%=	x = x % a;
&=	x = x & a;
^=	x = x ^ a;
|=	x = x | a;
< <=	x = x < < a;
>>=	x = x >> a;

In all cases, you will notice that the leading operator of the shorthand form is the binary operator for the long-form equivalent of the operator.

Although the compiler will generate identical code with either the long or short versions of the operators, the short-form versions of the operators can save you considerable typing.

if Statements

A fundamental task in any program is to decide what to do next. Like other languages, C has statements that "select" the next thing to do by examining the value of one or more variables. These *selection statements* allow you to determine (or control) the flow of execution through the program. The simplest if these selection statements is the if statement.

Perhaps the most common use of the relational operators is in an if statement. The general form of the if statement is

```
if (test_criterion)
    statement;          /* do this statement if test is logic True */
```

If test_criterion is logical True (that is, non-zero), the statement following the if is executed. If test_criterion is logical False (that is, zero), the statement is skipped. The term *test criterion* is used instead of the more formal *conditional expression* to reinforce the idea that a relational test is performed by an if statement to decide what the program will do next.

> Unlike some other languages, C requires that conditional expressions be enclosed in parentheses. Therefore,
>
> ```
> int i;
> i = 5
> if i == 5
>     printf("i is five\n");
> ```
>
> will produce an error message. The correct syntax is if (i == 5).

Listing 3.1 shows a simple use of the if statement.

Listing 3.1. Use of the if *Statement*

```
#include <stdio.h>
#include <stdlib.h>

main()
{
    char buff[2Ø];
    int b;

    printf("Enter a value for b: ");
    b = atoi(gets(buff));

    printf("The variable b does ");

    if (b != 5)
      printf("not ");

    printf("equal 5.\n");
}
```

The first line within main( ) defines a character buffer (buff[ ]) used to hold the user's input for b. The second line defines an integer variable b. The next two lines prompt the user for a value and convert it to an integer value for use in the program. (How these statements work is explained in Chapter 2, in the section "Simple Data Input.") The calls to printf( ) display a short message on the screen. The if statement tests the value of b, determining whether the word *not* is displayed as part of the message.

Values Associated with Logical True and Logical False

This is the point where we must tie in the workings of the if statement with the way relational tests are evaluated. Any relational test can only have one of two possible states: logic True or logic False. If a test is logic False, the result of the test is 0. If the relational test is logic True, the result is non-zero. (Notice we said non-zero, not just one.) Now let's see how this applies to listing 3.1.

Assume that the value of b is 3, but the if statement is asking "Is it True or False that b is not equal to 5?" In the example, the test is logic True—it is True that b does not equal 5. In this case, the test b != 5 yields a non-zero value (that is, the value 1). As you can see from the general form of an if statement shown earlier, if the test criterion is logical True, the statement controlled by the if is executed. The output from the program becomes

```
The variable b does not equal 5.
```

You can also create a variation of listing 3.1 that illustrates the non-zero status of a logical True condition. This is shown in listing 3.2.

The only important difference between listings 3.1 and 3.2 is the if test:

```
if (b)
```

Let's continue to assume that the user entered the value 3 for b. Because any non-zero value is a logical True value and b is non-zero, the test criterion is logical True and the printf( ) call will display the word *not* as a result of the test. It should be clear that the test criterion for an if statement does not have to be 1; any non-zero value equates to logical True.

You should also convince yourself that, if the user had entered a 0 for b, the word *not* is omitted from the display screen.

Listing 3.2. *Use of the* if *Statement and Non-zero Logical True*

```
#include <stdio.h>

main()
{
    char buff[20];
    int b;

    printf("Enter a value for b: ");
    b = atoi(gets(buff));

    printf("The variable b does ");

    if (b)
        printf("not ");

    printf("equal 0.\n");
}
```

Expressions and Values in C

Every expression in C yields a value of some kind. In this way, the language differs from others such as Pascal, and the difference can lead to problems if you're not careful. (See the Programming Tip entitled "Don't Confuse Assignment with Comparison.")

Obviously, the expression

```
3 + 2
```

yields a value, namely 5. But it may not be so obvious that the expression

```
b = 5
```

also yields the value 5. In C, an assignment expression—that is, an expression using the (=) assignment operator—yields the result of the assignment.

Programming Tip

Don't Confuse Assignment
with Comparison

The following is a common mistake made by all C programmers (even the experienced ones!):

```
if (b = 5)
    printf("Variable a equals 5.\n");
```

Notice that we performed an *assignment* operation (b = 5) as part of the if statement, rather than performing a relational test (b == 5). Because the expression within the parentheses is non-zero (after all, b now equals 5 because of the assignment operator), the if statement takes the test criterion as logic True *in all cases*—this if statement can never assume a logic False state and the call to printf() would always be executed.

Now consider the opposite case:

```
if (b = Ø)
    printf("Variable a equals 5.\n");
```

What is the result of this code? Because b is 0, the if statement views this as a logic False condition and will never execute the printf() associated with the if.

One way to prevent this type of error is to code the test so that the constant is on the right side of the expression, such as

```
if (Ø == b)
```

If you write

```
if (Ø = b)
```

by mistake, the compiler will issue an error message because you cannot assign a variable into a constant.

If your code seems always to skip a section of code no matter what test data you feed to it, check all of your relational tests for possible assignment operators.

The *if* Statement and Programming Style

Notice how we indented the statement controlled by the if. The programming style used in listing 3.1 is very common, but not the only style used. An alternative style is

```
if (b != 5) printf("not ");
```

The style shown in listing 3.1 seems to be the most popular, but either form will work. Throughout this text, the style shown in listing 3.1 will be used. You should select one style and stick with it.

if and Multiple Statements

You will notice in listing 3.1 that the if statement only controls one program statement. In that program, the if statement determined whether the printf("not ") function call was made or not.

You won't often want to control several statements by using a single if statement, however. Consider the following code fragment:

```
if (b == Ø)
    printf("zero detected");

if (b == Ø)
    zero_counter += 1;
```

Obviously, the code fragment wants to display a zero-detection message and to increment a counter each time the program detects a zero value for b. (Notice the use of our shorthand operator to add 1 to zero_counter.)

The preceding code fragment will work, but the duplicate if statement is inefficient. The better way to write the code fragment is

```
if (b == Ø) {                      /* statement block start */
    printf("zero detected");
    zero_counter += 1;
}                                  /* statement block end  */
```

Just as braces were used in Chapter 1 to mark the start and end of a function body (or function block), they also are used to mark the start and end of any type of statement block. The opening brace is usually placed one space after the `if` test criterion (enclosed in parentheses). The closing brace for the statement block is aligned with the letter i of the `if` statement that controls the statement block. (Note: The term *statement block* as used here can also be called a *compound statement*.)

The use of a statement block with the `if` statement is more efficient because the program must execute only one test on variable b while the first code fragment had to execute two tests on b. (By the way, the code shown above is not the best way to increment a variable in C. Some alternatives will be discussed in later chapters.)

> When you want a single `if` statement to control multiple statements, use braces before and after the statements to be controlled.

Again, the placement of braces is a matter of style. Some programmers prefer

```
if (b == 0)
{                                    /* statement block start */
    printf("zero detected");
    zero_counter = zero_counter + 1;
}                                    /* statement block end */
```

where the opening brace of the statement block is also aligned under the letter i in the `if` keyword. Still others will also indent the braces (aligning the { with the *p* of `printf()` and the } with the *z* of `zero_counter`) so the `if` stands out more clearly. Although we will use the form that places the opening brace on the same line as the `if` statement, either form may be used.

Brace alignment may seem to be a trivial issue, but it can make debugging much easier. This is especially true when `if` statements are "nested" within one another. For example, consider the code fragment in listing 3.3.

Some programmers will place comments near the closing braces of `if` statements and other program structures (for example, loops). This also helps to identify what the closing braces belongs to.

Listing 3.3 (Fragment). *Aligning Braces for Clarity*

```
#define ON      1
#define OFF     Ø
#define DONE    9Ø

    .

    .

if (valve1 == ON) {
    if (valve2 == ON) {
        if (heat == ON) {
            open_vats();
            add_mixture();
            close_valves();
            if (time == DONE) {
                heat_off();
                cool_down();
            }                           /* Close if (time    */
            printf("Mixture cool");
        }                               /* Close if (heat    */
    }                                   /* Close if (valve2  */
}                                       /* Close if (valve1  */
```

---

if . . . else Statement

The if . . . else statement is an expansion of the simple if statement. The general form is

```
if (test criterion)
    statement;      /* do this statement if test is logical True */
else
    statement;      /* do this statement if test is logical False */
```

The following code fragment shows a simple example of the if . . . else statement.

```
/* Assume x = Ø if male, otherwise female */

if (x == Ø)
    printf("Male\n");
else
    printf("Female\n");
```

Avoid Trouble Later—
Use "Extra" Braces Now

Throughout this book, we have cultivated the habit of *always* using braces with any if statement, even when only one statement is controlled by the if. (The braces were left out of program 3.1 just to make a point.) There are two reasons why braces are purposely used. First, more often than not it seems that as we develop a program, we sooner or later add one or more statements that must be controlled by the if. Having the braces there from the start makes it easy to add the new line(s).

Second, you often need to put debug statements after the if to see the value of some variable. For example,

```
if (b == Ø)
printf("b is zero");
```

and perhaps you also want to inspect a second variable c (defined elsewhere in the program) if b is zero. To do this, you would add

```
    if (b == Ø) {
        printf("b is zero");
printf("\nwith b == Ø, c = %d\n", c);
    }
```

Because you must have the braces to add the second print() statement anyway, you might as well place them in the program in the first place. Also notice that debug codes are always placed on the extreme left of the screen. This makes debug statements easy to find and remove once the bug is fixed. (See the Programming Tip entitled "Identifying Debugging Code" in Chapter 1.)

Therefore, I suggest that you use

```
if (b == Ø) {
    printf("b is zero");
}
```

even though the braces are not required.

The if . . . else statement is what we might call *precise-default*. That is, the only way to display the word *Male* is if (and only if) x equals 0. On the other hand, any other value of x will cause the word *Female* to be displayed. Therefore, the relational test for the statement controlled by the if part of the if . . . else statement is a precise test. If that test fails, the else is executed as though it were a "catch-all," or default, condition.

Of course, as the next code fragment indicates, you can also use braces to group more than one statement with an if...else:

```c
/* Assume x = 0 if male, otherwise female */

if (x == 0) {
    printf("Male\n");
    male += 1;
} else {
    printf("Female\n");
    female += 1;
}
```

Note how the braces are placed for the if and the else. While other styles can be used, the style shown here (with its use of indentation and placement of the braces) makes it easy to see what controls which statements and which else is associated with which if. Listing 3.4 shows another use of if . . . else.

Listing 3.4. if . . . else *with Modulus Operator*

```c
#include <stdio.h>

main()
{
    char buff[20];
    int b;

    printf("Enter a value for b: ");
    b = atoi(gets(buff));

    printf("b is ");

    if (b % 2) {
        printf("odd\n");
    } else {
        printf("even\n");
    }
}
```

So how does the program work? The if statement is controlled by the evaluation of b % 2. Because the modulus operator yields the remainder of division, b % 2 yields a remainder of 1. Because the expression controlling the if statement (b % 2) is non-zero (that is, b % 2 is equal to 1), it is evaluated as logic True, and the message

```
b is odd
```

is displayed on the screen. The if and if ... else control statements are a basic part of the C language, and you will use them often

Logical Operators

C provides for three logical operators, as shown in table 3.5.

Table 3.5. *Logical Operators*

Operator	Interpretation
&&	logical AND
||	logical OR
!	logical negation

Notice the similarities between the logical AND and OR operators and their bitwise counterparts: bitwise AND is a single ampersand (&), and bitwise OR is a single vertical bar (|). The resemblance is more than skin-deep: the bitwise logical operators perform logical operations on their operands at the bit level, and the (non-bitwise) logical operators perform the same operations at the level of expressions as a whole (not the bits that represent them).

Logical AND Operator (&&)

A common use of the logical AND operator (&&) is within an if test. For example,

```
int month, day;

month = 1;
day = 1;

printf("Today ");

if (month == 1 && day == 1) {
   printf("is");
} else {
   printf("isn't");
}

printf(" New Year's Day.\n");
```

In this code fragment, the logical AND operator is used to expand the test criterion for the if statement to test two variables before deciding which course of action to follow. The line

```
if (month == 1 && day == 1) {
```

might be verbalized as "If it is True that month equals 1 *and* if it is also True that day equals 1, then execute the next statement; otherwise, execute the statement following the else." With a logical AND operator, two logical tests may be performed and the result is logical True if, and only if, both tests are True. (If the first test on month is logical False, the second test on day would not even be evaluated.)

The output from the preceding example is

```
Today is New Year's Day.
```

because it is True that month and day are both equal to 1. Table 3.6 is a truth table for the AND operator.

As you can see from table 3.6, only when the Month and Day logical tests are both True is the result logical True. If, for example, month equals 2, the month == 1 test criterion would be logical False, or 0. If day equals 2, the day == 1 would also be logical False. If both test criteria are logical False, table 3.6 shows that their combined tests result in a logical False condition for the if test.

Table 3.6. *Logical AND Truth Table*

Month	Day	Logical Result
0	0	False
0	1	False
1	0	False
1	1	True

Logical OR Operator (||)

A typical use for the logical OR operator (||) is to test whether one of two or more possible conditions is True and respond accordingly. A common use for the logical OR operator is to test whether the user entered an upper- or lowercase letter, as in entering a *y* or *Y* to answer "Yes" to a program question. For example,

```
c = getchar();
printf("The answer is ");
if (c == 'y' || c == 'Y')
    printf("yes");
else
    printf("no");
```

As you will recall from the previous chapter, getchar() reads a character from the keyboard and then assigns it into variable c. A truth table for the logical OR for this code fragment is shown in table 3.7

Table 3.7. *Logical OR Truth Table*

'y'	'Y'	Logical Result
0	0	False
0	1	True
1	0	True
1	1	True

The first two columns of table 3.6 represent the possible results of the two test criteria in the if statement. If the user entered either a *y* or a *Y* for variable c, the result is a logical True condition. Only when the input is something other than a 'y' or a 'Y' (that is, the first row in table 3.6) does the logical result become False.

Notice again that if the first test is logical True, there is no need to evaluate the second test; the if is logical True. Therefore, we might verbalize the line

```
if (c == 'y' || c == 'Y')
```

as "If it is True that c equals a lowercase letter y *or* if it is True that c equals an uppercase letter Y, then the answer is Yes and the test result is logical True."

Programming Tip

Test Likely Conditions First
with Logical OR

Because logical OR tests are True if either test condition is True, you might consider placing the statement most likely to be True first in the OR sequence. This will cause program execution to skip the second test of the OR.

The reverse test placement would be used with a logical AND test. Because both test criteria must be logical True for an AND to be logical True, you might consider placing the test most like to be logical False as the first test executed. If the first test is logical False, the code for the second test can be skipped by the program.

The time saved by these two tactics is small, but it could be significant if the tests are performed within a highly repetitive loop structure.

Logical Negation

The result of a logical negation is either a 1 or a 0. Sometimes use of a logical negation can simplify an if test. Consider a code fragment we discussed earlier in this chapter:

Bitwise and Logical: Which is Which?

Notice that the logical AND (&&) and OR (||) operators are only slightly different from their bitwise AND (&) and bitwise OR (|) counterparts. If you're not an expert typist, it's easy to miss the second ampersand or vertical bar when doing a logical test. Even if you're a keyboard whiz, you can simply confuse the logical and bitwise counterparts. Because both bitwise and logical operators are binary operators, there is no way for the compiler to sense this type of error—it can be a difficult one to detect.

If you use a bitwise operator when you intended to use a logical operator, usually your program will compile and run. The result will not be what you expect, however.

Here's an aid to memory:

The bitwise operators work on the smaller objects (bits), so the bitwise operators themselves are "smaller" (a single character).

```
/* Assume x = Ø if male, otherwise female */

if (x == Ø) {
    printf("Male\n");
} else {
    printf("Female\n");
}
```

You could also write

```
if (!x) {
    printf("Female\n");
} else {
    printf("Male\n");
}
```

In this example, if x does equal 0, its logical negation would be 1. Because a non-zero value is associated with females, a !x when x is male (that is, 0) is the same as saying x is female.

The logical negation operator is less often used than the other logical operators. As shown in the preceding example, however, it does provide an alternative logic structure that may prove useful in certain situations.

The *switch* Statement

Suppose that you want to print one of the first three days of the week based upon the value of an integer variable named day. Your first attempt might be

```
if (day == 1) {
   printf("Monday");
}
if (day == 2) {
   printf("Tuesday");
}
if (day == 3) {
   printf("Wednesday");
}
```

While this form will work, it is not very efficient. The reason is that, even after a successful match is found, the program continues to execute the remaining if tests. Each if test requires a new comparison between day and an integer constant. For example, if day equals 1, the program prints Monday on the display and then proceeds to execute two more if tests even though they can't possibly be logical True.

Because this form is not good enough, you might try nested if statements, such as

```
if (day == 1) {
   printf("Monday");
} else {
   if (day == 2) {
     printf("Tuesday");
   } else {
     if (day == 3) {
        printf("Wednesday");
     } else {
        printf("No day");
     }
   }
}
```

This form will also work and has the saving grace that once the correct value is found, no further if statements are executed. On the other hand, the levels of if statements are a little confusing to read quickly.

Because programming problems similar to this are fairly common, C provides the switch statement. The general form for the switch statement is

```
switch (expression) {
   case integer_constant:
      statement;
}
```

Notice that a case keyword is followed by an integer_constant value and then a colon. For those who are familiar with BASIC, the switch has features similar to the ON . . . GOTO statement.

The following code fragment implements a switch in light of the problem discussed above, and the paragraphs that follow the code explain how the code behaves.

```
switch (day) {                    /* opening brace of switch */
   case 1:
      printf("Monday");
   case 2:
      printf("Tuesday");
   case 3:
      printf("Wednesday");
   default:
      printf("No day");
}                                 /* Closing brace of switch */
```

If you ran a program using this form, and day equals 1, the output would be

```
MondayTuesdayWednesdayNo day
```

So what happens with a switch statement? The parenthetical expression (for example, switch (day)) is used to determine which of the case conditions is to be executed. Each case (and default too) actually serves as nothing other than a label for a jump: program control jumps to the matching case label. The switch on day determines which of the case labels is the "target" of the jump. That is, the switch test on day causes a jump to the given case label. Figure 3.3 shows the behavior of a switch when the variable day equals 3.

If there is no match on any of the integer_constant values associated with a case label, program control is sent to the default label. The default label, therefore, is a catch-all if there is no match between day and any of the case values. If there's no default and the test variable doesn't match any given case, nothing happens. The switch has no effect.

In our example, because day equals 1, we jump to case 1: and execute its printf(). However, because a case label is NOT the equivalent of an if

---

Fig. 3.3. *Execution of a* switch *statement.*

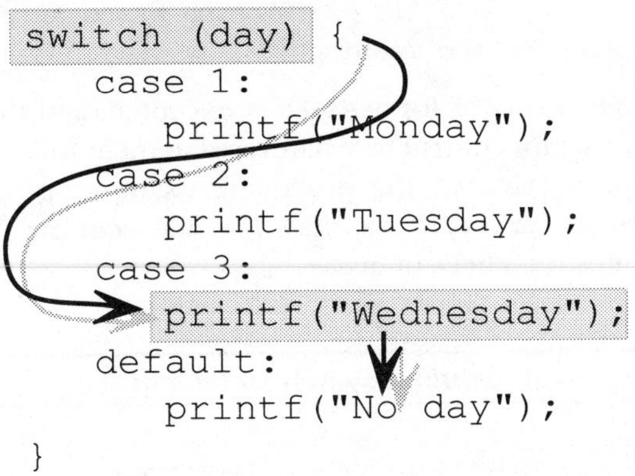

```
switch (day) {
    case 1:
        printf("Monday");
    case 2:
        printf("Tuesday");
    case 3:
        printf("Wednesday");
    default:
        printf("No day");
    }
```

---

statement, the program falls through each case, executing every statement contained within the switch. Clearly, this isn't exactly what we want.

break Keyword

We can solve this problem by introducing the break keyword. When a break is executed, program control is sent to the next statement outside the statement block controlled by the switch. To correct the problem, you would write

```
switch (day) {                    /* opening brace of switch */
    case 1:
        printf("Monday");
        break;
    case 2:
        printf("Tuesday");
        break;
    case 3:
        printf("Wednesday");
        break;
```

```
    default:
        printf("No day");
        break;
}                              /* Closing brace of switch */
    printf(" is okay for the meeting");
```

If day equals 1, the printf() for case 1: is executed, and then the break statement sends program control to whatever statement follows the closing parenthesis of the switch. In the preceding example, program control would be sent to the printf(" is okay for the meeting"); statement. Figure 3.4 illustrates the effect of break.

Fig. 3.4. Effect of break *within a* switch *statement.*

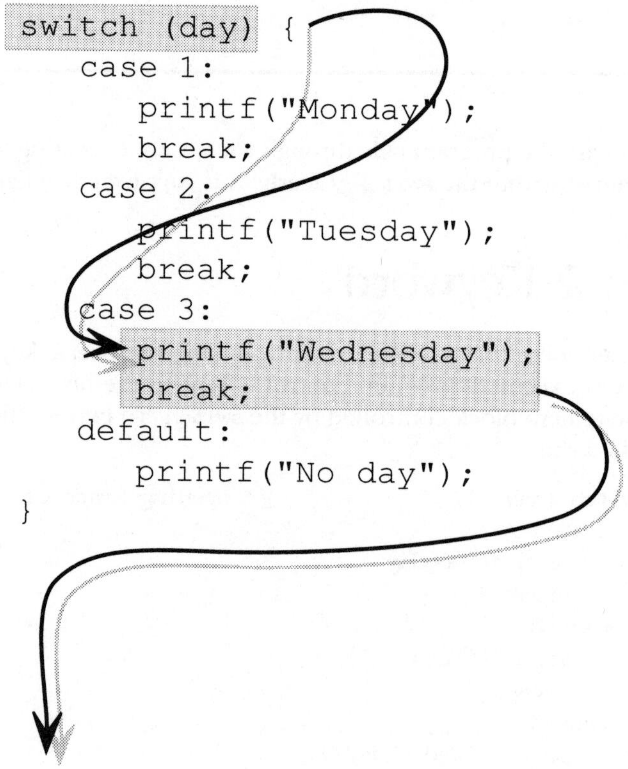

Programming Tip

Use *default* To Trap Unanticipated Values

Note that the default statement is shown as the last label in the switch. It does not have to be the last statement. Indeed, you do not need to have a default statement in a switch. However, it has been my experience that surprising values for the control variable (for example, day) do creep in every once in a while, and the use of the default label is a nice bit of defensive coding if strange values for the control variable suddenly appear.

Precedence of Operators

We have now discussed many of the operators that C has to offer. Table 3.8 presents the order of precedence of the operators. Don't be concerned that some of the operators have not been introduced yet; this table, listing all of the operators, will be useful for reference when you've learned about the rest of the operators.

Operators in table 3.8 are listed in order of precedence from the highest (level 1) to the lowest (level 14). The +, –, and * operators seen in level 2 are unary operators and represent the unary plus, unary minus, and indirection operators.

When you write complex expressions involving several operators at the same level of precedence, you need to take into account how the operators "associate," or are grouped, in an expression. All of the operators in table 3.8 associate left to right, except those operators at levels 2, 12, and 13, which associate from right to left.

Table 3.8. *Precedence of Operators*

Level	Operators
1	() [] -> .
2	! ~ ++ -- + *(unary)* – *(unary)*
	* *(indirection)* & *(address)* (cast) sizeof
3	* *(multiplication)* / %
3	+ *(binary)* – *(binary)*
4	<< >>
5	< <= > >=
6	== !=
7	& *(bitwise AND)*
8	^
9	|
10	&&
11	||
12	?:
13	= += –= *= /= %= &= ^= |= <<= >>=
14	, *(comma)*

Keep in mind that C does not guarantee any particular order of evaluation for function arguments. That is,

```
i = 5;
printf("i = %d  i = %d", i ++, i);
```

may print

```
i = 5  i = 6
```

or

```
i = 6  i = 5
```

If you need to be certain of the value of i, it should be incremented outside of the call to printf().

▼ Review Questions and Exercises

1. What is the value of j?

```
i = 5;
j = i == 5;
```

2. Why might the following cause a problem?

```
double x;

/* some more statements */

if (x != Ø) {
/* do these statements */
}
```

3. What is the output from the following code fragment?

```
i = 5;
j = Ø;

if (i && j) {
    printf("First");
} else {
    printf("Second");
}
```

4. Suppose that you are teaching a class and a variable named grade holds
the current test grade (1 equals an A, 4 equals a D) for each student in a
class. Another variable named student_id holds the student's identifica-
tion number. You now want print out the student's id number and grade
on the screen. Write a code fragment to print the report.

5. What is the output from the following code fragment and why?

```
i = 5;
j = Ø;

if (i & j) {
    printf("First");
} else {
    printf("Second");
}
```

▼ Answers

1. First, we must resolve the subexpression i == 5;. Because i does equal 5, the relational test is logical True. This means the result of the relational test is 1 (logical True). The value 1 is then assigned into variable j. Hence, j now equals 1, not 5.

2. There are two potential problems. First, the if test is done against the integer constant 0 instead of the floating-point constant 0.0. By using 0.0, you let the compiler know without a doubt that the test is against a floating-point number. If the compiler functions properly, this should not be a problem.

    The second problem is more difficult. Because floating-point numbers normally are stored in binary format (binary coded decimal could be used, but usually is not), some numbers cannot be represented exactly. In testing against 0.0, it is possible for x to be non-zero, but extremely close to zero. This type of problem arises because of something known as the *epsilon error*. More formally, the epsilon error is the largest number that can be added to 1.0 and NOT change the number. The ANSI standard suggests that for a double, the epsilon error should be approximately 1.0e–9 and 1.0e–05 for a float. The epsilon error is even smaller on compilers that use the IEEE standard for floating-point numbers. The float.h header file will give you the applicable epsilon values.

    In the problem posed here, if x has a value just above the epsilon threshold, it would be viewed as 1.0 when in fact it should be 0.0. As a result, you should normally rewrite the test of x using the < = or > = operators if possible. Another alternative is to test against 0.0 plus the epsilon error. (The float.h header file for compilers that support the ANSI specifications will define the epsilon errors for a float and a double.)

3. The output will be "Second". The reason is that the if test uses a logical AND on i and j. However, because j is 0, it is viewed as logical False. This would be viewed as the same as the third row in table 3.5 and, hence is a logical False result on the if test.

4. One solution might be the following fragment.

```
printf("Student ID number: %d  Grade: ", student_id);
switch (grade) {
    case 1:
        printf("A");
        break;
    case 2:
        printf("B");
        break;
    case 3:
        printf("C");
        break;
    case 4:
        printf("D");
        break;
    default:
        printf("F");
        break;
}
```

This problem could, of course, be written with `if . . . else` statements, too.

5. You probably thought this is a repeat of question 3. The output is still "Second", just as in question 3. However, we used a bitwise AND instead of a logical AND in the `if` statement. Because we did a bitwise AND with j equal to zero, the resulting bit pattern will be all zeroes leading to a logical False condition for the `if` test.

Suppose that we actually meant to perform a logical test, but simply did not type the second ampersand sign? The fact that both the bitwise and logical AND produced identical results even though it was not the type of test we thought we were performing suggests that this kind of error could be extremely difficult to detect.

Perhaps a better way to write the logical form for the test would be the longer, albeit more explicit, form

```
if (i != 0 && j != 0)
```

4

Loops

Concepts in This Chapter

- ☐ goto statement
- ☐ while statement
- ☐ #define preprocessor directive
- ☐ do...while statement
- ☐ for statement
- ☐ Increment and decrement operators
- ☐ Infinite loops
- ☐ break and continue statements

Loops are used whenever one or more program statements are to be executed until some desired condition is reached. C makes a number of different loop statements available to you. In this chapter, you will learn about each of these loop statements and see how they are used in a program.

Regardless of the specific loop statement used, all loops have two things in common:

1. One or more variables are initialized to some starting value. The initial value may be set prior to entering the loop or may be part of the loop statement itself.

2. At least one variable is tested to see whether another pass through the loop is required.

If these two loop characteristics are ignored, the program likely will not behave in an expected manner. This might cause a loop that does not execute when it should, or perhaps an "infinite" loop that continues to execute forever.

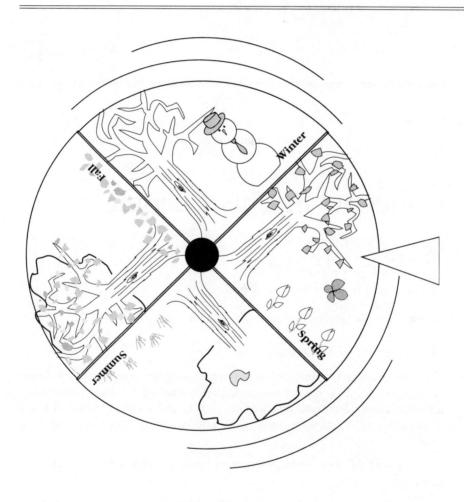

Simple Loops with the *goto* Statement

Many programming experts feel it's a crime to use a goto statement in a program. Perhaps a more tempered approach is needed. There are situations where use of a goto statement results in a program that is more natural and easier to understand than a convoluted structure without a goto. Although I do not advocate using goto statements in every program, they can be useful in some cases, and they can be used to form a simple program loop structure.

The goto statement actually has two required parts. The first part is the goto statement itself. The second part of the goto is a named point where program control is sent when the goto is executed. The place where program control is to be sent is called the *label* (or *target*) of the goto statement. The general form of a goto statement is

```
label _name:

    /* statements */

    goto label _name;
```

The label _name has the same syntax restrictions as a variable name (for example, it must start with a letter or underscore). Notice that the label name is followed by a colon (:) and *not* by a semicolon. One reason a semicolon is not used is because a label does not require processing by the compiler. The only purpose of a label is to establish a memory address (that is, an lvalue) to which the program control can be sent when necessary.

The label can appear either before or after the goto statement in a program, but the goto and its associated label must appear within the same function. You cannot use a goto to transfer control to a label outside of the function that contains the goto statement.

Now let's see how to build a simple loop structure with a goto statement. The program appears in listing 4.1.

Listing 4.1. *Creating a Loop with a* goto *Statement*

```
#include <stdio.h>

void main()
{
    int i;

    i = Ø;

  do_over:                          /* label  for goto */
    if (i < 1Ø) {
        printf("i = %d\n", i);
        i = i + 1;
        goto do_over;             /* goto  statement */
    }
}
```

Note that this program follows the rules for using the goto statement: (1) the label named do_over is in the same function block that contains the goto statement, and (2) the label obeys the rules for a valid label name.

Now let's see whether the rules for writing a well-behaved loop were followed. First, variable i is initialized to zero before program control enters the loop. Second, variable i is tested by the if statement to control the looping sequence (immediately after the do_over label). Thus we can expect the loop to behave in a predictable manner.

On the first test of i in the if statement, i equals 0. Because i is less than 10, the if test is logical True and the statement block controlled by the if statement is executed. That is, the program prints out the current value of i by means of a call to printf(), and then increments i. The goto statement then is executed and sends program control back to its associated label (do_over).

Note that this do_over is just a label that marks a point to which program control is sent. In terms of the actual machine instructions, do-over would correspond to the memory address (lvalue) of where the machine code for the if statement is located.

Because i is still less than 10, the loop repeats until i has been incremented to 10. At that time, i is no longer less than 10, the if statement becomes logical False, the statements within the if statement block are no longer executed, and the program ends.

Is the last value printed on the screen 9 or 10? Think about it.

Notice that the goto loop structure involves an explicit test on a variable (i in the preceding example) and a possible jump (or "branch") to the label, depending on the outcome of the if test. That is,

```
do_over:                        /* label for goto */
   if (i  < 1Ø) {               /* Explicit test  */
      printf("i = %d\n", i);  /* loop code */
      i = i + 1;
      goto do_over;             /* Branch if True */
   }
```

Most loops use this type of "test-and-branch" sequence, which is shown explicitly in the preceding code fragment and diagrammed in figure 4.1. However, most loop structures hide some of the details from the programmer. That is, you can't see the explicit test of the control variable or the transfer of program control. This test-and-branch sequence will be shown explicitly when we discuss the do...while loop.

Fig. 4.1. The test-and-branch sequence of a loop.

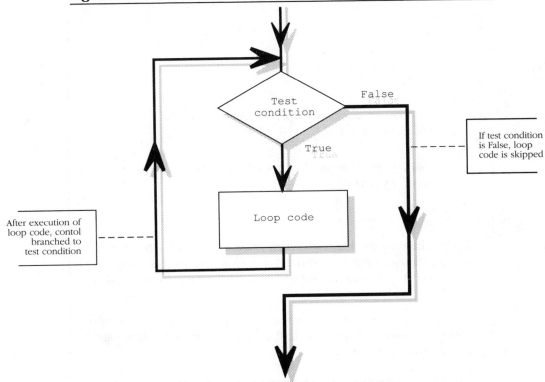

If test condition is False, loop code is skipped

After execution of loop code, contol branched to test condition

Programming Tip

Use *goto* as an "Emergency Exit"

Later in this chapter, you'll learn about use of the break statement to cause an early escape from a loop—an escape, that is, before the loop's test condition becomes logical False. A break statement can transfer program control only out of the current loop. If the current loop is nested within another loop, execution of the outer loop continues. That may not be desirable, because the condition requiring an escape from the inner loop could also require an escape from the outer loop. The goto statement is the best solution to a problem like this one.

For instance, you might have something like the following code fragment:

```
int i;
for (...) {
    for (...) {
        if (i == -1) {
            goto bail_out;
        }
    }
    /* Code we don't want to execute if an */
    /* error is sensed                     */
}
/* Additional code we don't want to execute if an */
/* error is sensed                                 */

bail_out:
    error = -1;
```

In this code fragment, a test is performed on i, and if i is equal to -1 (indicating an error condition), a goto is used to send program control past code that should not execute if an error condition is sensed.

In almost all cases, you can write a program without a goto statement. However, C does provide the goto as part of the language, and it can come in handy on occasion.

while Loops

A while loop executes one or more program statements as long as its test criterion is logical True. The general format for a while statement is ·

```
while (test_criterion) {
    statements;
}
```

Listing 4.2 illustrates how a while loop is used.

Listing 4.2. Printing ASCII Characters with a while Loop

```
#include <stdio.h>

void main()
{
    int i;

    i = 65;

    while (i <= 90) {
        printf("%c ", i);
        i = i + 1;
    }
}
```

As in all well-behaved loops, an initialized variable (i) is used to control the while loop. The while loop tests i to see whether it is less than 91. If i is less than 91, the call to printf() causes i to be printed *as a character* rather than an integer. The program then increments i, and program control goes back to the while statement again.

As long as i is less than 91, the test criterion used by the while statement is logical True and the statement block controlled by the while statement continues to be executed. When i is eventually incremented to a value of 91, the while test becomes logical False, the while statement block is skipped, and the program ends.

Depending on the result of the logical test performed by the while, the statements in the block controlled by the while may or may not be executed. If, for example, we had initialized i to a value of 91 rather than 65, none of the statements in the while statement block would have been executed. A while loop, therefore, will execute its statement block only if the test is logical True. It is quite possible that the statement block controlled by the while is never executed.

Also notice that the "test-and-branch" sequence exists in the while loop. The test on i determines whether another iteration of the loop is performed. The closing brace of the while loop has the effect of causing a jump back to the test on i at the top of the loop. This "test-and-branch" continues until the test on i becomes logical False. At that time, the while loop no longer executes the statements controlled by the while statement, and the loop ends. The while loop therefore uses the same test-and-branch sequence previously shown in figure 4.1.

#define Preprocessor Directive

You may have a hard time figuring out what program 4.2 does, if you just read the program. But when you execute the program, you can see that it prints out the alphabet in capital letters. The program produces this result because we used a %c conversion character in printf() to display the values of i. Had we used %d instead, the numbers 65 through 90 would have been displayed.

Another reason that the function of listing 4.2 is not obvious is that some of the constants (such as 65) don't seem to mean much by themselves. You have to study the program closely in order to understand the meaning of the numbers. Clearly, anything you can do to make the program more understandable is a step in the right direction. One such step is something called the #define *preprocessor directive*. (The preprocessor was introduced in Chapter 1, and it's discussed in more detail—along with #define and other preprocessor directives—in Chapter 11.)

One use of the #define preprocessor directive is to define a symbolic constant for use in a program. Program 4.2 has been modified to use #define directives for two numeric constants. The change is shown in listing 4.3.

Listing 4.3 uses the #define preprocessor directives to define two symbolic constants. LETTER _A is a symbolic constant for a numeric value of 65, and LETTER _Z is the symbolic constant for the letter Z. Although the program is still a little bit cryptic, it's less so than before.

Listing 4.3. Illustration of #defines

```
#include <stdio.h>

#define LETTER_A          65        /* 65 is  ASCII for A */
#define LETTER_Z          90        /* 90 is  ASCII for Z */

void main()
{
    int i;

    i = LETTER_A;

    while (i  <= LETTER_Z) {
       printf("%c  ", i);
       i = i  + 1;
    }
}
```

When you compile this program, the C preprocessor (that is, a precompile pass that looks at your program) will see the two #define directives and store the information for the two symbolic constants for later use. When the program finds either symbolic constant in the program, it will substitute the value associated with symbolic constant. Therefore, when the pre-processor pass finds LETTER_A in the program, it will substitute the value 65 in place of the symbolic constant. When the preprocessor finds LETTER_Z in the program, it substitutes 90 in its place.

> The use of symbolic constants improves the readability of a program. By replacing "magic numbers" with symbolic names, you give a better idea of the purpose that the numeric constants serve in the program. A #define can help document your program.

There is another reason for using #define to define numeric constants in a program. Suppose that you are writing a large program and a specific input/output port (for example, port number 2) is used 100 times in the program. Now suppose further that you take your program to a friend's machine, and his machine requires that the I/O port number be port 3 rather than port 2. Now, you must go through the source code for the program, editing 100 port 2 entries, and making them all port 3.

If you used a #define for the port number when you wrote the program in the first place, you would only have to change one #define and recompile the program. All 100 port 2 references would automatically be changed to port 3 by the preprocessor pass. By using the #define preprocessor directive

```
#define PORT_NUMBER 2
```

near the beginning of the program when you first wrote it, you might save a lot of editing at some later date if the port number ever needs to be changed.

Remember that all a #define does is cause the preprocessor to perform a *textual* substitution in the program. That is, if a program contains

```
#define THIS    1
```

the preprocessor replaces every occurrence of THIS with 1 in the program before the program is actually compiled. Indeed, some compilers allow you to inspect the program after the preprocessor pass to see all of the substitutions that were performed by the preprocessor. The only time a replacement does not occur is when the symbolic constant appears within a double-quoted string constant. That is,

```
printf("THIS is the answer\n");
```

is *not* replaced with

```
printf("1 is the answer\n");
```

because the symbolic constant THIS appears within a double-quoted string.

> Common practice is to use uppercase letters for symbolic constants in a program. This convention makes it relatively easy to find where the symbolic constants are used in a program.

You need to remember two rules about using #define directives. First, the #define directives must appear in the program before the symbolic constants are used. For example, if you tried to use PORT_NUMBER before its associated #define, the preprocessor wouldn't know what PORT_NUMBER was and would probably give you an "undefined variable" error. Second, unlike most C program statements, a #define preprocessor directive does *not* have a semicolon at the end of it. (This is one reason why we have called it a directive rather than a C statement.)

You should consider using the #define preprocessor directive for any number in a program that might change at some time in the future. Doing so now can save you a lot of editing time down the road.

do. . .while Loops

A do...while loop is similar to the simple while loop with one important distinction: the statements controlled by a do...while are always executed at least one time. The do...while is singular to the repeat...until construct in Pascal, except that the do...while executes as long as the test criterion is logical True. The repeat...until construct, however, executes *until* the test criterion is logical True.

The general form for a do...while loop is

```
do {
   statements;
} while (test criterion);
```

The do...while performs the loop test at the bottom of the loop, after the statements within the do...while statement block have been executed. This means that even if the test criterion is logical False, the statements already will have been executed at least once by the time the test is made. If the test criterion is logical True at that time, the statements within the braces are executed again. This test-and-branch sequence is shown in figure 4.2.

If the test criterion is logical True (the test), program control is sent to the first statement after the opening brace of the do...while (the branch). This continues until the test criterion becomes logical False.

Listing 4.4 shows an example of a do...while loop.

In listing 4.4, a do...while statement block simply contains a function call to getchar() and assigns the value returned from getchar() into variable i. (As you will recall, getchar() is designed to get a character from the keyboard. For most compilers, you will have to type a letter and then press the Enter or Return key for getchar() to work properly. If you don't understand why the value returned from getchar() is an int, see the section "Character Variables" in Chapter 2.)

After a letter is assigned to i, the test criterion is evaluated to see whether the letter entered was a pound sign (#). As long as it is True that the user

Fig. 4.2. Test-and-branch sequence for a do...while *loop.*

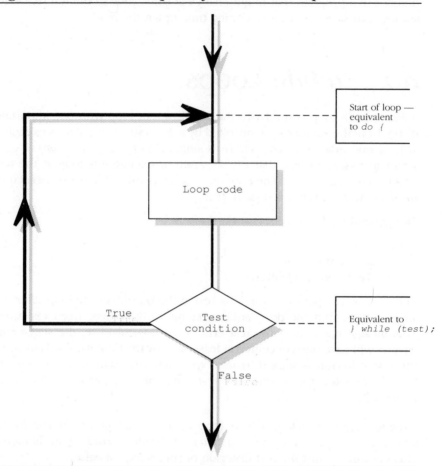

Listing 4.4. do...while Loop

```
#include <stdio.h>

void main()
{
    int i;

    do {
        i = getchar();
    } while (i != '#');
}
```

did not enter a pound sign, the do...while loop continues to execute. If the user does enter a pound sign, the test becomes logical False and the program ends.

Note that listing 4.4 still meets the requirements for a well-behaved loop: it initializes and tests a control variable. Also note that the control variable is initialized within the loop body, not before the loop begins. We can get away with initializing the control variable (i) within the loop itself in a do...while because the test criterion is performed at the bottom of the loop. Therefore, the control variable i is set to its initial value before the loop-control test is performed.

As is typical in C, the exact positioning of the braces in a do...while is a matter of style—within reason. The opening brace for the do...while statement block must be after the do and before the first statement in the block. The closing brace must be after the last statement in the statement block and before the while. Therefore,

```
do { i = getchar(); } while (i != '#');
```

will work just as well as the form shown in listing 4.4. However, the style in listing 4.4 is more common and perhaps a little easier to read.

for Loops

By contrast, the FOR loop in BASIC increments its control variable at the end of the loop, as in

```
100 FOR I = 0 TO 5
110 PRINT"I=";I
120 REM Possibly dozens of additional code lines
...
500 NEXT I:REM Variable I is incremented here
```

And in Pascal, the increment (or decrement) of the control variable is hidden away within the internals of the language implementation—plus, you're limited to an increment of 1 or –1! The for loop in C is easier to read and is much more flexible.

To this point, all of the loop constructs look similar to their counterparts in other languages. The for loop, on the other hand, looks a bit strange at first. However, C's for loop structure is actually more convenient than those found in other languages because it places all of the relevant information in one place.

The general form of a C for loop is

```
for (expression1; expression2; expression3) {
    statements;
}
```

The for statement uses three expressions, separated by semicolons. Usually, expression1 is used to initialize one (or more) variables that are used in the loop. The second expression (expression2) often performs a relational test on one of the loop variables. The final expression (expression3) normally increments the variable controlling the loop. In their most common form, we might summarize for loops as

```
for (initializers; test criterion; increments) {
    statements;
}
```

Listing 4.5 shows a simple program that displays the printable ASCII character set plus the special graphics characters found on many PC-type machines.

Listing 4.5. *Using a* for *Loop to Print ASCII and Graphics Characters*

```
#include <stdio.h>

#define ASCII _START   32
#define ASCII _END     255

void main()
{
    int i;

    for (i = ASCII _START; i <= ASCII _END; i = i + 1) {
        printf("%c ", i);
    }
}
```

The two #defines set the starting and ending characters to be printed. Because the printable characters start with 32 and end with 255 on my machine, those are the values used. If your machine uses just the normal ASCII character set (with no graphics characters), you would set ASCII _END to 127 for your program. The use of #defines makes it simple to change these constants, and the names (that is, symbolic constants) of the numbers give some idea of what the numbers are all about.

Now, let's look at the for loop:

```
for (i = ASCII_START; i <= ASCII_END; i = i + 1) {
```

Obviously, variable i is used to control the loop. The first expression assigns ASCII_START into i when the loop begins. Next, expression2 (i <= ASCII_END) is evaluated. Because i is less than ASCII_END on the first pass through the for loop, the statement(s) controlled by the for loop are executed. (The statements controlled by the for loop are called the *for statement block*.)

As a matter of style, I place the opening brace of the for statement block at the end of the line that begins the for loop. The closing brace of the for statement block is aligned under the f of the for keyword. You are free to use other forms if you wish, although the form shown in listing 4.5 is used throughout this book.

The only statement in the for statement block is the call to printf() to display the character on the screen. Because there is only one statement, the opening and closing braces are not required. (Without braces, the for statement controls a single statement.) However, the examples in this book always use braces with a for loop, and I urge you to adopt the same practice. Braces make it easier to add debugging code when necessary or to add "real" code when required.

Programming Tip

Use Braces with All *for* Loops

Although a for loop can control a single statement without the use of braces, you should always use an opening and closing brace with a for loop. The braces help delimit the control structure of the for loop, plus you can insert debugging code when necessary or add "real" code when required.

When the character has been printed on the screen, all of the statements in the for statement block have been executed. At this point, the third expression is executed. That is, in listing 4.5, i is incremented by 1. Then the second expression (i <= ASCII_END) is evaluated to see whether another pass through the loop is required.

This is the "test-and-branch" sequence again. Expression 2 is the test, and, if that expression is logical True, the for loop statement block is executed. Control then is sent to evaluate the third expression. After expression 3 is evaluated, control is sent to expression 2 again; this is the branch. Figure 4.3 shows the test-and-branch sequence for the for loop.

Fig. 4.3. *The test-and-branch sequence of a* for *loop.*

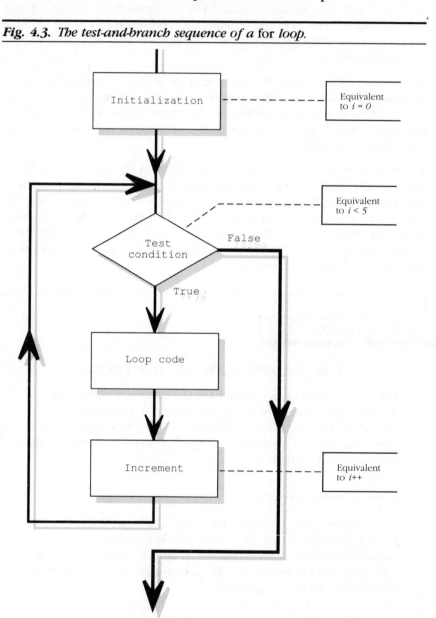

The sequencing of the expressions that make up a for loop is important. Using the for statement from listing 4.5 as a model, consider figure 4.4.

Fig. 4.4. *Typical use of expressions in a* for *loop.*

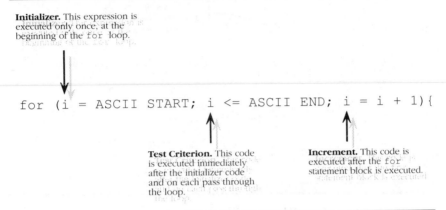

Initializer. This expression is executed only once, at the beginning of the for loop.

```
for (i = ASCII START; i <= ASCII END; i = i + 1){
```

Test Criterion. This code is executed immediately after the initializer code and on each pass through the loop.

Increment. This code is executed after the for statement block is executed.

The first expression is evaluated only once: when the for loop begins. The second expression then is evaluated immediately. If the second expression evaluates to logical False on the first pass through the loop, the statements in the for statement block are not executed. Therefore, it is possible that a for statement block is never executed.

Finally, after the for statement block is executed, the third expression is evaluated. In this example, this step is a simple increment of variable i. If you want to set things visually in your mind, the loops behaves as though it were written as in figure 4.5.

Therefore, expression1 is executed only once, expression2 is executed at the top of the loop, and expression3 is executed at the bottom of the loop. Indeed, the for loop above looks very much like a while loop.

Fig. 4.5. Diagram of the for *statement block.*

```
i = ASCII_START;

for (i = ASCII_START; i < ASCII_END; i = i + i;) {
      /* The for statement block */
      i = i + i
}
```

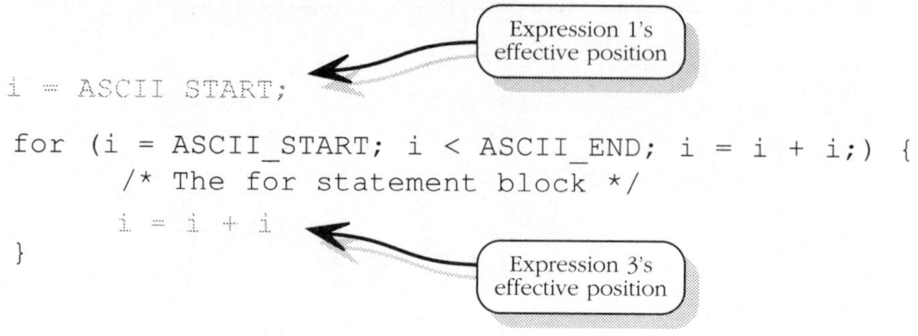

Multiple Initializers in a *for* Loop

Sometimes you may want to initialize more than one variable in a for loop. C provides nicely for this need. Consider the following code fragment:

```
int i, j;

for (i = Ø, j = 5Ø; i < 1ØØ; i = i + 1) {
     /* for statement block */
}
```

Notice that we have initialized i and j as part of expression1. The only requirement is that we separate initializers with a comma. Listing 4.6 shows the sequencing of the three expressions in a for loop.

In listing 4.6, multiple expressions are used for each of the three basic expressions found in a for loop. Each expression also includes a printf() that allows you to see which expression is being evaluated as the for loop executes.

If you run this program, the output is

```
Initializer
test i=Ø increment
test i=1 increment
test i=2 increment
```

Programming Tip

for Loops, Programming Style, and the *null* Statement

Like the if statement discussed earlier, the for statement does not require a semicolon at the end of it. However, I doubt whether any C programmer has not written

```
for (i = Ø; i < MAXIMUM; i = i + 1);
```

at least once. Using the common style for a for loop, the line becomes

```
for (i = Ø; i < MAXIMUM; i = i + 1)
    ;
```

The semicolon on the line by itself is called a null statement. A null program statement is simply a statement with no expression. In other words, it is just a lone semicolon. This is perfectly valid C syntax, but it can cause problems. Consider, for example, the following fragment:

```
for (i = Ø; i < MAXIMUM; i = i + 1);
    sum = sum + func(i);
```

The misplaced null statement is more apparent in the following lines:

```
for (i = Ø; i < MAXIMUM; i = i + 1)
    ;
sum = sum + func(i);
```

To guard against this error, *always* use braces with a for loop, even if only one statement is being controlled. Since I started writing both braces *before* writing the code controlled by the for loop, this kind of error has virtually disappeared for me.

```
test i=3 increment
test i=4 increment
test i=5 --out of the loop!
```

This shows that the first expression is executed only once: at the beginning of the for loop. Listing 4.6 also shows that a test and an increment are performed for each pass through the loop. The final test is not followed by an increment because the condition for terminating the loop (i < 5) has been reached, so the for loop ends.

Listing 4.6. Sequencing of a for *Loop*

```
#include <stdio.h>

void main()
{
   int i;

   for (printf("Initializer\n"), i = Ø;       /*   expression 1 */
        printf("test i=%d ",i), i < 5;         /*   expression 2 */
        printf("increment\n"), i = i + 1) {  /*   expression 3 */

      ; /* do-nothing statement block */
   }
   printf("--out of the loop!\n");
}
```

Increment and Decrement Operators

Incrementing and decrementing a variable is a common occurrence in any program, especially within program loops. Because these operations are so common, C provides special operators for incrementing and decrementing variables. Each increment and decrement operator has two varieties available: a prefix form and a postfix form. These are usually called *pre-increment* (or pre-decrement) and *post-increment* (or post-decrement) operators.

Pre-increment or pre-decrement causes the increment or decrement of the variable to occur *before* an assignment takes place. A post-increment or post-decrement causes the increment or decrement of the variable to occur *after* the assignment has taken place.

The increment and decrement operators are shown in table 4.1.

Table 4.1. *Increment and Decrement Operators*

Syntax	Meaning
++i	pre-increment
i++	post-increment
--i	pre-decrement
i--	post-decrement

Note: The variable i *is used to show the syntax of the operators.*

Programming Tip

Using Multiple Expressions

As you can see in listing 4.6, C allows you to use multiple expressions where the syntax requires a single expression. The only requirement is that expressions be separated by commas. Notice how the initialization of i and the printf() of expression 1 in listing 4.6 are separated by a comma.

One word of caution about using multiple expressions: There is no guarantee about the order of their evaluation in function calls. For example,

```
i = 5;
printf("i = %d i = %d", i = i + 1, i);
```

could print out

```
i = 6      i = 5
```

or

```
i = 6      i = 6
```

Keep this in mind when you use multiple expressions in function calls.

As you might guess, the increment operators add 1 to the current value of the variable, and the decrement operators subtract 1 from the value. Therefore,

```
++i;    is the same as    i = i + 1;
--i;    is the same as    i = i - 1;
```

With this in mind, what is the value of j in the following code fragment?

```
int i, j;

i = 5;
j = ++i;
```

Because we have used the pre-increment operator, we increment i *before* doing the assignment into j. This means that both i and j will equal 6 after those code lines are executed. Had we written the code fragment as

```
int i, j;

i = 5;
j = i++;
```

the value of j would be 5 and i would be 6, because we used the post-increment operator in this example. This means that we perform the assignment of i into j and then increment i (hence the term *post-increment*: the increment is performed *after* the assignment).

The decrement operators behave in similar fashion. In the following fragment,

```
int i, j;

i = 5;
j = --i;
```

i and j would both be equal to 4, and

```
int i, j;

i = 5;
j = i--;
```

would find i equal to 4 and j equal to 5.

Increment and Decrement Operators in *for* Loops

Now that you understand the increment operator, you can rewrite the for loop from listing 4.5 as

```
for (i = ASCII_START; i <= ASCII_END; ++i) {
    printf("%c ", i);
}
```

Notice the third expression in the for loop. Because we are not using variable i in an assignment, it does not matter whether we use the pre- or post-increment operator.

We can also use multiple increment operations in expression3 if needed. For example,

```
int i, j;
for (i = 0, j = 50; i < 100; ++i, j--) {
    /* for statement block */
}
```

would increment i but decrement j. The only requirement is that the subexpressions be separated by the comma operator.

Infinite Loops and the *break* Statement

A "true" infinite loop in a program is a loop from which there is no exit. Because this means there is no way to terminate the program, a true infinite loop is usually an error. On the other hand, if you have a means of exiting from an otherwise infinite loop, these loops can be a perfect solution to many types of programming problems.

Consider the following code fragment, which is designed to force a Yes or No response to a question.

```
#include <ctype.h> /* for tolower() */
#define TRUE 1

char answer;
```

---

lvalues and Increment Operators

The + + and — operators differ in some important ways from those we've discussed so far. Most of the other operators yield values based on their operands, but they do not *modify* their operands. (An obvious exception is the assignment operator.) But the increment and decrement operators do change their operands.

Also, most of the operators we've studied are binary operators, which require two operands. The increment and decrement operators are unary operators, which use only one operand.

Because the increment and decrement operators do modify a variable's value, some subtle points need to be made. First, because a value is being changed, there must be an lvalue that allows the value to be fetched from memory, incremented or decremented, and then stored back into the lvalue. The first point implies the second point. That is, intermediate expressions or constants cannot be used with the increment/decrement operators. For example,

```
--5;              /* constant has no lvalue */
++(a  + 5);       /* intermediate expr has no value */
```

are not valid statements because neither expression has an lvalue.

```
while (TRUE) {
   printf(" Enter a Y or an N:");
   answer = getchar();
   answer = tolower(answer);
   if (answer == 'y' || answer == 'n')
      break;
}
```

Recall that a while loop continues to execute its statement block as long as the test criterion evaluates to logical True. The while loop in the preceding code fragment sets up an infinite loop because the test criterion expression is defined as having a value of 1 (that is, TRUE). Because logical True is any nonzero value, the while loop in the code fragment will execute forever.

The statements within the while statement block simply ask for the user to enter a Y or N. The call to getchar( ) gets the user's response and assigns it into answer. Next, the program calls a library function called tolower( ), which converts answer to a lowercase letter. (If this wasn't done here, we would have to check for upper- and lowercase letters in the if statement.) If the user enters a Y or an N, the if test is logical True, and the break statement is executed.

In Chapter 3's discussion of the switch statement, you were introduced to the keyword break. The behavior of a break statement in the context of a loop is quite similar to its behavior in a switch. A break statement is used to exit from the current for, while, or do...while statement block. Program control is sent to the next program statement following the current for, while, or do...while statement block. In this example, control would be sent to whatever statement followed the closing brace of the while statement block.

As an alternative, we could have written the sample code fragment as

```
char answer;

for (;;) {
    printf(" Enter a Y or an N:");
    answer = tolower(getchar());
    if (answer == 'y' || answer == 'n')
        break;
}
/* Control transfers here on break */
```

Notice how an "empty" for statement was used to create the infinite loop. If the second expression (the test) of a for loop is omitted, it is assumed to be logical True. Because this empty for loop's test expression always is logical True, an infinite loop results. The for statement block continues to execute until a Y or N is entered by the user. When the user enters a Y or N, the break statement transfers program control out of the for statement block to whatever statement follows the program comment.

If the second expression (the test) of a for loop is omitted, it is assumed to be logical True.

Programming Tip

Use *#define* To Clarify "Unusual" Code

A good example of using a #define to document what a statement does can be illustrated with an infinite for loop. Consider the code fragment

```
#define EVER ;;
/* statements */

for (EVER) {
    /* other statements */
}
```

The textual substitution of the #define results in

```
for (;;)
```

in the for loop. The #define makes it quite clear what the content of the for loop is in the program.

The last example also shows a common convention in C; namely that of *nesting* function calls. Here is an example of nested function calls:

```
answer = tolower(getchar());
```

As you can see, nesting function calls simply means that one function call becomes the argument of a second function call. The sequencing—or the order in which the function call is executed—is the same as you would expect with any parenthesized expression: getchar() is called first and the letter entered by the user is returned. The return value from getchar() becomes the argument for the call to tolower(), which converts the letter (if necessary) to lowercase. The lowercase letter returned from tolower() is then assigned into answer. Both the "unnested" and "nested" versions behave the same, although the nested version is more common in practice.

As we discussed earlier, the break statement only breaks you out of the controlling statement block in which it appears. For example,

```
for (;;) {
   i = func1();
   for (;;) {
      if (i == 10) {
         break;
      }
      /* More statements here */
   }              /* End of inner for */
   printf("i = 10");
}                 /* End of outer for */
printf("Done with both for loops");
```

Suppose the call to func1() returns a value of 10, which is assigned into i. Program control enters the second, or inner, for loop and the if statement is executed. Because i does equal 10, program control is sent to the printf("i = 10") statement, not the last printf(). If we wanted to break out of the outer for loop, we would need another break statement after the printf("i = 10") statement.

A break statement transfers program control out of *only* the switch, for, while, or do...while statement block in which the break statement appears. If the switch, for, while, or do...while statement is itself part of an outer switch, for, while, or do...while statement block, the rest of the outer statement block is executed.

See the Programming Tip entitled "Use goto as an 'Emergency Exit,' " earlier in this chapter, for a solution to a programming problem nested loops can pose.

---

continue Statements and Loops

You have seen how the break statement transfers control out of a loop. There are times, however, when you will want to stay in a loop but skip over the rest of the statements within the loop's statement block and continue with the next iteration of the loop. The exact point where program control resumes depends upon which loop structure is being used.

continue with *while* and *do. . .while*

Program control in a while loop is illustrated in figure 4.6. Program control is sent to the while loop's test expression as long as i is greater than 50. This is also true for a do...while loop, as shown in figure 4.7.

Fig. 4.6. *Program control with* while *and* continue.

```
while (i < 100) {
    if (i > 50) {
        continue;
    }
    sum = sum + 1;
    i++;
}
```

Fig. 4.7. *Program control with* do...while *and* continue.

```
do {
    i++;
    if (i > 50) {
        continue;
    }
    sum = sum + i;
} while (i < 100)
```

As you can see in figures 4.6 and 4.7, the continue statement sends program control to the test expression that is used to control the while or do...while loop.

continue with *for*

Program control with a for statement is different. When the continue statement is executed in a for loop, program control is sent to the third expression. This is often an increment operation (not a test), as shown in figure 4.8.

Fig. 4.8. Program control with for *and* continue.

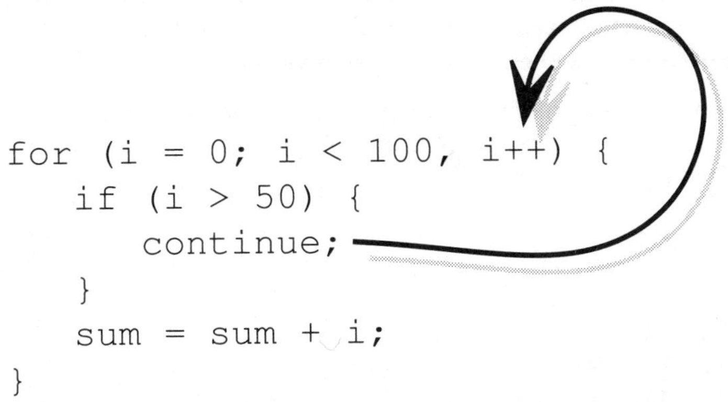

```
for (i = 0; i < 100, i++) {
    if (i > 50) {
        continue;
    }
    sum = sum + i;
}
```

With the for loop, control is sent to expression_3, i is incremented, and then we test i against 100. The behavior of a continue within a for loop, therefore, is as though program control is sent to the bottom of the loop to execute expression_3.

Now, consider the following code fragment:

```
#define OKAY    1

int i;

for (;;) {
    i = monitor();
    if (i == OKAY)
        continue;
    sound_alarm();
```

```
        turn_on_sprinklers();
        call_fire_department();
    }
```

In this example, we are in an infinite for loop that calls a function named monitor(). Assume that monitor() always returns 1 if everything is normal. As long as everything is normal, we don't want to do anything but call monitor() again. However, on any value other than 1 returned from monitor(), we assume there is a fire, and we want the program to sound an alarm, turn on the sprinkler system, and call the fire department.

Such a task is perfectly suited to the continue statement. The continue statement does nothing more than send program control to the top of the current loop for another iteration of the loop. Nothing happens there, because expression_3 (the increment) of the for loop is empty. The continue statement therefore sends program control back to the monitor() function call and skips the calls to sound_alarm(), turn_on_sprinklers(), and call_fire_department().

If the continue statement appears in a loop nested within an outer loop, control is sent to the top of the inner loop that holds the continue statement. That is,

```
#define OKAY    1

int i;

for (;;) {
    do_power_up();
    for (;;) {
        i = monitor();
        if (i == OKAY)
            continue;
        sound_alarm();
        turn_on_sprinklers();
        call_fire_department();
    }
}
```

The continue statement sends program control to the call to monitor(), not to do_power_up().

It should be clear that the break statement provides a way of breaking out of a loop, and a continue statement provides a means of doing another iteration of the same loop.

▼ Review Questions and Exercises

1. Write a program that increments a variable from 0 to 25,000 and sounds the computer's bell when it is done. You might want to think how this could be done with goto, for, while, and do...while loops.

2. Write a program similar to the one mentioned in Problem 1, but use a break statement for loop termination.

3. Write a program similar to the one mentioned in Problem 1, but use a continue statement.

4. Some time ago, I discovered (purely by accident) an unusual way to square a positive number. While I'm sure someone has a formal statement of the algorithm, it is basically this: The square of a positive number n is equal to the sum of n odd integers, starting with 1. Write a program to demonstrate this algorithm.

5. Explain the difference between a pre-increment and post-increment operation. When does it not make any difference which one is used?

6. What does the output of the following program look like?

```
#include  <stdio.h>

  main( )
  {
     int i, j, k;

     for (i = Ø; ;i ++) {
        for (j = Ø; ; j ++) {
           for (k = 1; ;k ++) {
              if (k % 1Ø)
                 printf("%d ");
              else
                 break;
           }
           break;
        }
        break;
     }
  }
```

▼**Answers**

1.
```
#include <stdio.h>

int main(void)
{
   int i;
   for (i=Ø, i<25ØØØ; i++){
       ;
   }
   putchar(ØxØ7);
}
```

About the only strange thing in this program is the call to putchar( ). The purpose of putchar( ) is to write a single character to the screen. Because we call putchar( ) with a value of seven, it sounds the bell.

2. The program is simple.

```
#include <stdio.h>

#define GOAL 25ØØØ

main()
{
   int i;

   for (i = Ø; ; i++) {
      if (i == GOAL)
         break;
   }
   printf("i = %d", i);
}
```

Notice that we have omitted the second expression from the for loop. This has the effect of turning it into an infinite loop. The if statement has the same purpose as the missing for expression; it terminates the loop when GOAL is reached and the break statement is executed.

3.
```
#include <stdio.h>
#define TRUE 1

int main(void)
{
   int i=Ø;
   while (TRUE) {
        if ( i < 25ØØØ ) {
```

```
            i++;
            continue;
        }
        break;
    }
    putchar(0x07);
}
```

4. This exercise is a test on how well you can implement an algorithm from a verbal statement of the algorithm. The algorithm states that the square of a number is the sum of that many odd integers starting with 1. If you want to square the number 3, the answer should be

```
9 = 1 + 3 + 5
```

The sum of the first 3 odd integers (starting with 1) does yield the correct answer. If you try this on the value 5, you get

```
25 = 1 + 3 + 5 + 7 + 9
```

Now let's write the program.

```
#include <stdio.h>
#include <stdlib.h>

main()
{
    char buff[20];
    int i, j, sum;

    printf("Enter a number to be squared: ");
    j = atoi(gets(buff));
    i = 1;
    sum = 0;

    printf("the square of %d", j);

    while (j--) {
        sum = sum + i;
        i = i + 2;
    }
    printf(" is %d", sum);
}
```

Although this could be implemented more directly with a for loop, I used a while just to be different. The only twist on things is the use of j to control the while loop. The nested calls to gets() and atoi() return an integer value, which is then assigned into j. Next i is set equal to the first odd integer (1), and sum is cleared to zero.

In the while loop, i is added to sum, and then 2 is added to i, so that i holds the next odd integer. Notice that j is decremented on each iteration of the loop. As long as j is nonzero (logical True), the while statement block continues to execute. When j becomes zero (the logical False value), the while loop terminates and the answer is displayed.

5. A pre-increment causes the rvalue to be changed before any use of the expression is made. Therefore,

```
int i, j;
i = 5
j = ++i;
```

causes j and i to equal 6. With a post-increment, the increment is performed after all other expressions are resolved. Therefore,

```
int i, j;
i = 5;
j = i++j;
```

will find j equals 5 and i equals 6. This is because the assignment expression into j is performed before i is incremented.

If the increment expression is not part of some other expression, it does not matter whether a pre- or post-increment is used, such as i in the following for statement:

```
for (j=0;j < MAX; i++) {
    /* statements */

}
```

6. Because none of the for loops use the second expression for exiting the loop, you must rely on the break statements to prevent an infinite loop. The innermost break statement, however, cannot be executed until the if test becomes logical False. Because modulus division can only return a value of zero when the number being divided is an even multiple of the divisor, the output must be

```
1 2 3 4 5 6 7 8 9
```

When k equals 10, the first break statement rather than the printf() is executed. The other break statements are needed to send control out of its for statement block.

5

Function Prototypes

Concepts in This Chapter

- ❑ The parts of a function
- ❑ Prototyping; differences between K&R and ANSI C
- ❑ Header files

In this chapter, you will take a close look at functions; in particular, you will see how functions are written and used. You will also examine new "safety" features that are now available when you use C functions.

This chapter also covers some of the major changes introduced by the ANSI standard committee. In this chapter, the acronym K&R (that is, Kernighan and Ritchie) is used to represent the standard for C as it existed prior to the work done by the ANSI standards committee.

K&R versus ANSI Functions

In Chapter 1, you read that a function has five major parts. The description given was for a function written under the old K&R standard for C. These function parts are repeated in figure 5.1.

Fig. 5.1. *Major parts of a K&R C function.*

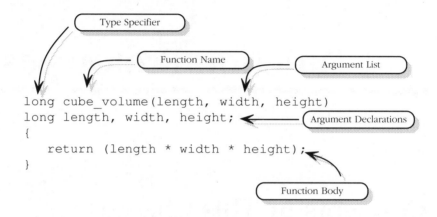

The form shown in figure 5.1 illustrates how functions were defined before the work was done by the ANSI committee. Note that the type specifier determines the type of data value that is returned from the function. In our example, cube _volume() returns a long integer value that is the product of length times width times height.

> If you omit the type specifier from a function definition or declaration, the default return value is int.

Figure 5.2 presents the same function, using the new ANSI form. You won't see too much difference between figures 5.1 and 5.2, except that the argument list and argument declarations in figure 5.1 have been combined into something called a *prototype* for the function in figure 5.2. A function prototype simply declares the names and data types of the function arguments.

Fig. 5.2. *Major parts of an ANSI C function definition.*

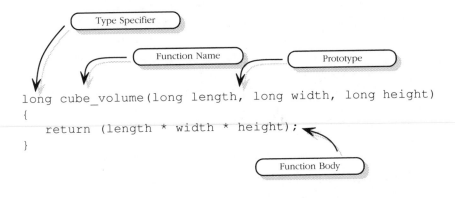

The Purpose of Prototyping
==========================

The major purpose of function prototyping is to allow the compiler to perform type checking on arguments that are sent to a function. *Type checking* refers to the checks that the compiler can perform to see whether the data type used in a function argument agrees with the type of data that the function expects for that argument. To see how this type checking is performed, consider listing 5.1.

Notice that this example uses the new ANSI form for defining the functions main() and cube_volume(). (The void argument for main() is explained later in this chapter.) When I compiled this program, one warning message was generated, but an executable program was produced. When I ran the program, the output was

```
The answer is -31872
```

which is not the correct answer. What went wrong? The warning message produced during compilation gives us a clue. The message was Assignment mismatch: int into long in line 7. This is where the return value from cube_volume() is assigned into answer. Obviously, the compiler thought that cube_volume() returned an int data type. There are other problems, too. Clearly, we need a way of telling main() the type of data being returned by cube_volume().

Listing 5.1. Partial Function Prototyping

```c
#include <stdio.h>

void main(void)
{
   long answer;

   answer = cube_volume(200, 50, 10);
   printf("The answer is %ld", answer);

}
/*****
                       cube_volume()

     Function determines the volume of a cube.

Argument list:      long length      length of cube
                    long width       width of cube
                    long height      height of cube

Return value:       long             volume of the cube
*****/

long cube_volume(long length, long width, long height)
{
   return (length * width * height);
}
```

Function Declarations and Prototyping in C

Now let's see how we can solve the compiler's confusion in listing 5.1 by using function declarations with the complete prototyping features permitted under the new ANSI standard. Listing 5.2 shows how this is done.

Notice that the first line of the function definition for cube_volume() was copied to a place just before main(). After the line was copied, a semicolon was added to the end of the line. Because the function *declaration* for cube_volume() appears *before* main(), main() now has information about the function that it did not have in listing 5.1. Specifically, the compiler now knows three things that it didn't know before:

Listing 5.2. Complete Function Prototyping

```
#include <stdio.h>

long cube_volume(long length, long width, long height);

void main(void)
{
   long answer;

   answer = cube_volume(200, 50, 10);
   printf("The answer is %ld", answer);

}
/*****
                    cube_volume()

      Function determines the volume of a cube.

Argument list:      long length      length of cube
                    long width       width of cube
                    long height      height of cube

Return value:       long             volume of the cube
*****/

long cube_volume(long length, long width, long height)
{
   return (length * width * height);
}
```

1. The type specifier for cube_volume() tells the compiler that this function returns a long data type. In listing 5.1, the compiler thought the return value was the default return type of int. Because my compiler uses 16-bit integers and 32-bit longs, the answer shown was incorrect.

2. The prototype portion of the function declaration tells the compiler that each argument must be a long data type.

3. The prototype enables the compiler to detect a difference between the number of arguments in the function *definition* and the number of arguments in a *call* to that function. (Note: The ANSI C standard supports an important exception to the third point; the exception and the problems it can cause are discussed later, in the section "Prototyping Functions with Variable Arguments.")

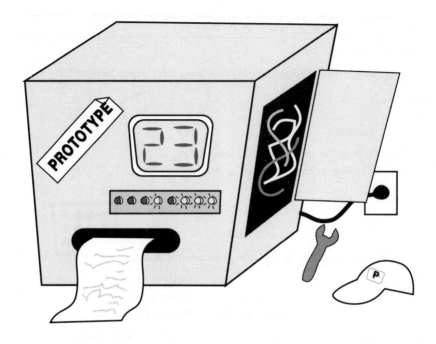

The following sections explain each of these three facts in detail so that you can understand the impact they have on the program.

The Return-Value Problem and Function Declarations

First, consider what happens when listing 5.1 (without the declaration) is compiled and executed.

Suppose that the compiler is ready to generate the code to process the return statement in cube _volume(). The type specifier indicates that cube _volume() returns a long data type, which typically requires four bytes of storage. The compiler calculates the answer and stores the answer where main() can find it. (Perhaps the answer is stored on the stack.) After this code is executed, program control returns to main().

Once program control returns to main(), we find that the answer produced by the function call to cube_volume() is to be assigned into answer. This is where the trouble starts. First, unless stated otherwise, all functions in C return an integer value; int is the default return type from a function call. That is, the default type specifier for all functions is int. Because main() hasn't been told differently, it thinks the answer produced by cube_volume() has the default function-return data type of int. And because an int is often a two-byte quantity, main() grabs only two bytes of a four-byte answer!

Listing 5.2 solves this problem by placing a full function declaration (including the prototype) just before the start of main(). Notice that all we did was take the first line of the function definition, copy it to the top of the program before main(), and add a semicolon to the end of the line. The type specifier in the function declaration tells the compiler that cube_volume() returns a long data type. The compiler will now generate code to grab the full four bytes for the return value from the function call to cube_volume().

That solves the first problem.

The Argument-Value Problem and Prototypes

The second problem with listing 5.1 is that cube_volume() expects each of the three arguments to be a long data type. We know this from the function definition of cube_volume() that appears near the end of the program. In listing 5.1, when the compiler sees the line

```
answer = cube_volume(200, 50, 10);
```

it assumes that the numeric constants (that is, 200, 50, and 10) are integer data types. After all, numeric constants default to an int unless the compiler is "told" otherwise. Now, consider how the compiler might process these three constants.

If we assume that an integer is two bytes, the compiler sets aside two bytes for each constant and places these six bytes where cube_volume() has access to them (perhaps on the stack again). Program control then is sent to cube_volume( ) for processing.

Once program control reaches cube_volume( ), the first thing the function does is get the three arguments passed to it from main( ). Here's where things get messed up. Because cube_volume( ) expects long data types from main( ), it grabs *12* bytes (that is, four bytes for each of the three long data types) for the arguments, but main( ) only supplied six bytes! The result is that cube_volume( ) is going to use six bytes of junk to form its answer to the problem.

If you compile listing 5.2 with the prototype for cube_volume( ), the compiler should tell you that the arguments in the line

```
answer = cube_volume(200, 50, 10);
```

don't match those given in the prototype of the function declaration for cube_volume( ).

The solution to the problem is to tell the compiler to form long data types instead of ints for the numeric constants. The changed line would look like

```
answer = cube_volume(200L, 50L, 10L);
```

Anytime a numeric constant is followed by the letter L or l (the last is an "el", not a "one"), the compiler converts each constant to a long data type. As a result, the proper values are now available to the function. Although you can use an upper- or lowercase el, we would suggest an uppercase 'L'. This makes it easier to see that the letter is an el, not the digit 1 (one).

The corrected version of the program is shown in listing 5.3.

Listing 5.3 produces the correct answer of 100,000.

Finally, because of the function prototype for cube_volume( ), the compiler can also check that the proper number of arguments are passed to the function. This is the third piece of information that function prototypes provide.

Advantages of Prototyping

A function declaration with prototyping allows the compiler to perform type checking on the data type of the function's return value (as determined by the type specifier) and on its arguments. This reduces the debugging burden on you by pushing it onto the compiler.

Listing 5.3. *Complete Function Prototyping with Corrected Numeric Constants*

```
#include  <stdio.h>

long cube_volume(long length, long width, long height);

void main(void)
{
    long answer;

    answer = cube_volume(200L, 50L, 10L);      /* Note long modifiers */

    printf("The answer is %ld", answer);

}
/*****
                              cube_volume()

        Function determines the volume of a cube.

Argument list:      long length     length of cube
                    long width      width of cube
                    long height     height of cube

Return value:       long            volume of the cube
*****/

long cube_volume(long length, long width, long height)
{
    return (length * width * height);
}
```

You should adopt the habit of using prototypes for all of your C programming. Prototyping will make you more productive by reducing the time required for debugging.

Always Specify Return Values

If you omit the type specifier from a function definition or declaration, the compiler assumes the type specifier is int. Therefore, the declarations

```
int func1(void);
```

and

```
func1(void);
```

both declare that func1 returns an int. The second form relies on the default type specifier (int).

I strongly urge you *never* to rely on the default type specifier. Always write it out explicitly. It has been my experience that once you develop the habit of explicitly writing the type specifier, you rarely get tripped up on a noninteger return data type from a function call. Writing the type specifier also forces you to think deliberately about the return data type from each function call. This is true when you design the function and when you use it.

Prototypes for Standard Library Functions

Clearly, it would be useful to have prototypes for all of the functions you use, including those found in the standard library. Unlike the K&R standard, the ANSI standard does define a group of functions that are expected to be found in the (ANSI) C standard library. Because a standard does exist now for the standard library, prototypes for each function also are standardized.

One result of the ANSI standard library is a list of standard header files for functions in the standard library. Table 5.1 presents a list of the standard ANSI header files and a brief description of the nature of the functions prototyped in each header file.

Each set of prototypes is found in the header file associated with those functions. For example, most I/O function prototypes are found in the stdio.h header file.

Table 5.1. *ANSI Standard Header Files*

File	Description
assert.h	Definition of the assert( ) function for expression evaluation
ctype.h	Functions for character manipulation
errno.h	Error processing functions
float.h	Mostly floating point constants
limits.h	Contains the ranges for various data types
locale.h	Specific information about how data types and functions are affected by the locale of the program. For example, many European character sets must be processed differently than the ASCII character set.
math.h	Prototypes for mathematic functions (for example, most of the trig functions)
setjmp.h	Functions for nonlocal goto-type program control
signal.h	Functions for processing signals and operating system interrupts
stdarg.h	Prototypes for functions that process variable argument lists
stddef.h	Symbolic constants and variable names reserved for use by the compiler
stdio.h	Most Input/Output function prototypes and a number of symbolic constants used with file I/O
stdlib.h	Prototypes for utility functions that don't fit nicely into some other header file
string.h	Prototypes for functions that process character arrays (or strings)
time.h	Functions that process time and date information

Some functions in the library, however, do not fit nicely into a category (for example, utility functions) for which there is a standard header file. The prototypes for the miscellaneous ANSI standard library functions are often placed in the stdlib.h header file. The name of this file is not fixed, so you should check your compiler documentation for details.

You might want to list the contents of each header file on your printer and keep it for future reference. Details on the function prototypes you find in each header file should be explained in your compiler's documentation on the standard library. You may want to review that documentation in light of what has been presented thus far in this chapter.

Definition versus Declaration (Again)

Before you begin to write functions of your own, you need to review the difference between the terms *definition* and *declaration*.

> In brief, the ANSI standard states that a *declaration* of a data item "specifies the interpretation and attributes of a set of identifiers." A data *definition*, on the other hand, "causes storage to be reserved for an object or function named by an identifier." The distinction is important.

Near the top of listing 5.3, we added the line

```
long cube_volume(long length, long width, long height);
```

This function declaration says various things about the cube_volume() function for later use in the program. (Remember that the main() function needs the information in the function declaration to work properly.) A declaration, therefore, simply passes along to the compiler information about something that is defined somewhere else.

On the other hand, near the bottom of listing 5.3, you see the *definition* for the cube_volume() function. When the compiler sees the definition of a function—warts and all—it must allocate storage to hold the code for that function. The allocation of storage also means that the definition of a data item has an lvalue. That is, the data item does have an address in memory when it is defined. This is also true for functions.

If you have written the source code for a function as part of the program, you have defined that function. When the compiler starts reading your function definition, it needs a place in memory to store the code for that function. Therefore, the compiler will pick a place in memory to store the executable code for the function. The lvalue of the function is the starting point of the executable code for the function.

You might ask, "If the compiler knows about the definition of the function, why do I need to declare the function?" If the definition of the function appears in the source code before it is ever used, the declaration would not be needed. The compiler would know about it. However, most C programmers place function definitions at the end of their programs, which means the compiler knows nothing about the function until late in the compile process. If the function is used (or called) prior to the processing of the function definition, the declaration still is necessary. This was exactly the situation in listings 5.1 and 5.2. (A more complete discussion of this is presented in Chapter 6 when the scope of variables is explained.)

One more example. A prototype for printf() appears in the stdio.h header file, but the actual code for the function is stored in a library file. Therefore, the information needed to use printf() properly is declared in stdio.h, but the code that defines printf() is in a library file. Declarations pass information to the compiler, but definitions require storage.

The ANSI specification is clear in its interpretation of the two terms. The ANSI specification says that a data definition is also a declaration, but a declaration is not a definition. You should convince yourself that prototypes for functions in the standard library are data declarations, not definitions. (Function prototypes for the standard library declare information about those functions, but storage for them is not allocated until link time.)

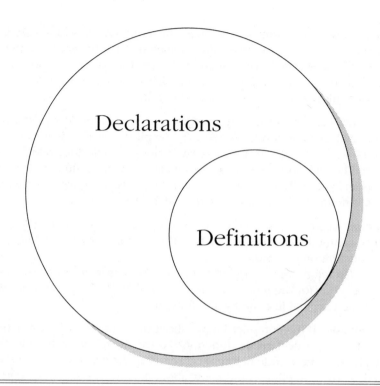

Flavors of Prototyping

Prototyping must be able to process three situations:

1. Functions with a given number of arguments
2. Functions with no arguments
3. Functions with an unknown number of arguments.

The discussion thus far in the chapter has only covered the first situation. Let's explore the remaining two alternatives.

Prototyping Functions with No Arguments

One ANSI standard library function that does not use an argument is the rand() function. The purpose of rand() is to return an integer random number. So how would you write the prototype for a function that does not use an argument? The prototype for rand() uses the C keyword void, as in

```
int rand(void);
```

> The void keyword is used to describe an empty data item.

A void data item is viewed as a data type in C; it's simply a "nothing" data item. At first blush, this may seem silly, but it really isn't. If you have prototyped rand() in your program, trying to use it with an argument will generate an error message. When used in a prototype, therefore, using the void data type in the argument list is the same as informing the compiler that no argument should be used with this function. Using void in the prototype enables the compiler to check for such errors. (Other uses for the keyword void are covered in detail in Chapters 8 and 9.)

Let's look at another example of a prototype that uses the void data type:

```
void hdestroy(void);
```

The hdestroy() function is found in the standard library for most UNIX System V C compilers. hdestroy() is declared to have no arguments and to return no useful value. That is, because the type specifier for the function is also a void, it should not be used in an assignment statement. Therefore, if you are using function declarations in your program, the statement

```
i = hdestroy();
```

should produce an error message because you are trying to assign into i a value from a function call that does not return a value. If function declarations were not used, no error message would be produced and i would contain contain some random (junk) value.

The following two examples illustrate another point about prototypes:

```
void func1(int);        /* OK    */
void func2(int, void);  /* WRONG */
```

The prototype for func1() in the preceding list is perfectly legal. The prototype simply says that func1() expects an int data type for its argument, but nothing useful is returned from the function. The prototype for func2() is incorrect because it seems to say the function wants an int argument, but the void says that no arguments are to be used with the function.

The rules for using the void type specifier are

1. Use the void type specifier in a function declaration when the function does not return a value.

2. Use a void prototype when there are no arguments used with the function.

The Ellipsis and Prototyping Functions with Variable Arguments

Some functions have a variable number of arguments, the data type and number of which cannot be known at compile time. The printf() function is the most common example. You already know that the prototype for printf() is found in the stdio.h header file. Still, there may be a time when you need to write a function that uses a variable number of arguments. If and when that time comes, how is it possible to prototype such functions?

To prototype a function with variable arguments, the ANSI committee created a new symbol called the *ellipsis*. The ellipsis consists of three periods (...). Although the comma operator is not part of the ellipsis, I have never seen a prototype with variable arguments without at least one known argument. Again, the printf() function serves as a common example:

```
int printf(char cs[],...);
```

where cs[] is an array of characters for the control string. If you think about it, you'll see that printf() will always have a string as its first argument. However, depending upon the conversion characters within that string, there can be zero or more arguments following the control string. The ellipsis gives us a way to prototype such functions that have a varying number of arguments.

A limitation exists, however, in terms of the type checking that the compiler can do when an ellipsis is used in the prototype. For example, consider the following code fragment:

```
int printf(char s[],...);           /* Prototype */

/* more code */

double x, y, z;
int i, j;

printf("%d %f %d", i, x, y);
```

The call to printf() shown above has the third argument wrong; an integer conversion character was used, but the corresponding variable (y) is a double. To correct the problem, there should either be a %f in the control string, or an integer variable should replace variable y. The compiler does not check for proper argument matches with the conversion characters in the control string (s[]). Even with prototypes, then, functions with variable arguments yield less "bulletproof" type checking than do functions with fixed argument types.

Programming Tip

Prototyping Made Simple

Obviously, it is a good idea to create prototypes for all functions that you write. As you write each function, use your editor to copy the function header (first line of the function definition, including the type specifier, function name, and prototype) to a header file. You might call the header file protos.h. After copying all of the function headers to the header file, add a semicolon at the end of each function header in the header file. Finally, place the line #include "protos.h" at the top of each program that uses the functions that are prototyped in protos.h. You then can let the compiler check the arguments in the prototypes against those you use in your program when you call the functions. This can save you a lot of debugging time down the road.

Also keep in mind that prototypes are part of a function declaration and, as such, do not cause the compiler to generate code. Although the compiler will use a little more memory to keep the prototype information available during compilation, the size of your program will not change because of prototyping. There is no reason not to use prototyping.

Function Declarations, Prototypes, and Argument Names

Function prototypes can be used in two different ways: (1) in a function declaration, and (2) in a function definition. You saw a function *declaration* using function prototypes just before main( ) in listing 5.2. You saw a function *definition* using function prototypes near the end of listing 5.2 where cube_volume( ) is defined. You will see why this distinction is important later in this section.

ANSI allows two forms for function prototypes. You have already seen the first form:

```
long cube_volume(long length, long width, long height);
```

where each argument's type is followed by its name.

> The argument names in a function declaration using function prototypes are for documentation purposes only; they do not define variables for use in the program.

That is, in the code fragment

```
#include  <stdio.h>

long cube_volume(long length, long width, long height);

void main()
{
    long i, j, k, volume;
    /* Code to assign values to i, j, k */
    volume = cube_volume(i, j, k);
}
```

variables i, j, and k will work just fine with cube_volume( ). But if you try to use length, width, or height in the fragment above, you will get an undefined variable error for each of the three variables. This happens because length, width, and height are not defined in the program. The names used in a function declaration using function prototypes exist only for documentation (that is, to give you an idea as to their purpose); they do not exist as variables in the program. If you want to use length, width, and height in a program, they must appear in a data *definition*, not a data *declaration*.

Note that the names used in a function *definition* can be used in the function. Therefore, as shown in listing 5.2, the definition of cube_volume() near the end of the program does use the variables length, width, and height. We can use the variable names in the prototype of a function *definition*, but we can't use the variable names in a function *declaration*.

You now can consider the second form a prototype can assume. The function prototype used in the preceding example could be rewritten as

```
long cube_volume(long, long, long);
```

This second form for a function prototype shows that the *type specifiers* for the function arguments are important in a prototype, not the *names* of the arguments. In fact, the compiler ignores the variable names used in a function declaration that uses function prototypes.

> You are free to use variable names that match the argument names given in function prototypes. In fact, I encourage you to do that: the result can be increased clarity of code, especially if the main purpose of the variables is to serve as arguments for the function. You must, of course, use names for prototypes in function definitions. Otherwise, there would be no way to reference the function arguments.

Of the two possible prototype forms, the one that uses argument names is preferred because it conveys more information about the arguments used in the function.

Remember that argument names used in a function *definition* can be used in the function, but argument names in a function *declaration* cannot be used. To illustrate this, you can change listing 5.1 as shown in listing 5.4.

You cannot use len, wid, or hi as variables in listing 5.4 because they appear only in a function declaration: they are not defined. On the other hand, you can use length, width, and height in cube_volume() because they are part of the function definition.

You could also use the prototype form

```
long cube_volume(long, long, long);
```

in place of

```
long cube_volume(long len, long wid, long hi);
```

in listing 5.4 without affecting how the program compiles or executes. The form shown in listing 5.4 is preferred, however, because it better describes the purpose of each variable.

***Listing 5.4.** Prototyping and Argument Names*

```
#include <stdio.h>

        /* Note argument names in prototype: */
long cube_volume(long len, long wid, long hi);

void main()
{
   long answer;
   answer = cube_volume(200L, 50L, 10L);    /* Note long modifiers */

   printf("The answer is %ld", answer);

}
/*****
                          cube_volume()

     Function determines the volume of a cube.

Argument list:      long length      length of cube
                    long width       width of cube
                    long height      height of cube

Return value:       long             volume of the cube
*****/

           /* Note argument names in definition: */
long cube_volume(long length, long width, long height)
{
   return (length * width * height);
}
```

▼ Review Questions and Exercises

1. What are the major differences between the K&R and ANSI standards with respect to function definitions and declarations?

2. What are the two forms that can be used when writing a function prototype?

3. What is the return data type when a type specifier is omitted?

4. What does the word void mean when used as the type specifier for a function? What does it mean when it appears in a function prototype?

▼ Answers

1. The primary difference between K&R and ANSI is the placement of the function arguments. In a K&R-style function definition, the function arguments are declared after the closing parenthesis of the function name, but before the opening brace of the function body. Therefore, our cube_volume() function under the K&R standard would be

```
long cube_volume(len, wid, hi)
long len, wid, hi;
{
    /* Function body */
}
```

Under the ANSI standard, the arguments are placed between the opening and closing parentheses, in prototype form. Therefore, an ANSI-style function definition would use

```
long cube_volume(long len, long wid, long hi)
{
    /* Function body */
}
```

Also, the K&R standard does not support the concept of function prototyping and does not assume argument checking for function calls.

2. The first form is

```
type_specifier function_name(type_specifier);
```

as in

```
int func1(long);
```

The second form is

```
type_specifier function_name(type_specifier  name);
```

as in

```
int func1(long customer_number);
```

Both prototypes behave in the same manner as far as the compiler is concerned. Remember that argument names in the prototype of a function declaration (for example, customer_number) do not exist for use in the program.

3. The default return data type is int. One of the most common mistakes made by beginning C programmers is forgetting to tell the calling function (for example, main( )) that a function returns a data item other than int.

4. When void is used as the type specifier in a function prototype,

```
void func1(int cycles);
```

there is no return value from the function. Therefore, if you tried to use func1( ) in an assignment statement, the compiler would issue an error message.

When void appears in the function prototype, as in

```
int func1(void);
```

the compiler knows that no arguments can be used when calling the function. Any attempt to use an argument in the call to func1( ) will cause the compiler to generate an error message.

6

Storage Classes
and Scope

The main objective of this chapter is to show you different ways you can make data available in your programs. Most programmers agree that data privacy is one of C's strong points. That is, you can limit the use of a data item to only those parts of a program that really need access to the data. Data privacy also lets you debug programs more quickly because cause-and-effect relationships are more easily narrowed down. Mastering the concepts presented in this chapter will help you take full advantage of some of the advanced features C has to offer. Take the time to understand these concepts.

Data Privacy in C: Local Scope

Before you begin writing your own functions, you need to understand the concept of *scope* and how it relates to data types in C. The scope of a data item refers to the visibility and availability of a data item. (In fact, substituting the words *availability* or *visibility* in place of scope may help you understand the material that follows.)

lvalues and Local Scope

Listing 6.1 illustrates how scope affects C data items.

Listing 6.1. Data Privacy and Scope

```c
#include  <stdio.h>

void func1(int i);

void main(void)
{
   int i;
   i = 5;
   printf("in main(), lvalue of i = %p\n",
          &i); /* Notice "address-of" operator, & */
   printf("           rvalue of i = %d", i);
   func1(i);
}

void func1(int i)
{
   printf("\n\nin func1(), lvalue of i = %p\n",
          &i); /* Notice "address-of" operator, & */
   printf("           rvalue of i = %d", i);
}
```

Listing 6.1 defines a variable named i and assigns it a value of 5. printf() and the address-of operator are then used to display the lvalue of variable i. The address-of operator (&) does exactly what you would expect it to do—it returns the memory address, or lvalue, of the variable.

A %p conversion character is used to display the memory address (lvalue) of i. (See the Programming Tip entitled "The *%p* Conversion Character.") The address-of operator (&) is used before a variable's name and tells the compiler to use the lvalue of a data item instead of the (more typical) rvalue. The second printf() is used to display what variable i holds (that is, its rvalue).

After the lvalue and rvalue of i in main() are displayed, func1() is called with i as its argument. func1() again displays the lvalue and rvalue of i. When I ran the program, the output was

```
in main(), lvalue of i = 65530
              rvalue of i = 5

in func1(), lvalue of i = 65528
              rvalue of i = 5
```

(The output you see will probably have different lvalues, but the general conclusions will be the same.) This program illustrates an important and somewhat unique feature of C: *because the* lvalues *of* i *in* main() *and in* func1() *are not the same, they are not the same variable.* That is, a *copy* of i is sent to func1() from main(), not the original i defined in main().

> Even if two variables have the same name but different lvalues, they are not the same variable.

The concept of a sending copy of a variable to a function is often referred to as "call by value." This means that the *value* of i (5) in main() is copied to some memory location (usually on the stack) and func1() has access only to that copy. Inside func1(), the copy of i can be increased, decreased, or set to zero and the change will have no effect on the "real" i in main(). Because func1() does not know where the real i in main() is stored in memory, it cannot change the value of i in main(). Because the lvalue of i in main() is unknown to others outside of main(), no other part of the program knows about the existence of i. Indeed, would func1() behave differently if we called it using

```
func1(5);
```

in main()? It would make no difference to func1().

Programming Tip

The *%p* Conversion Character

The ANSI standard for the printf() function provides a new conversion character for use in displaying lvalues. Pre-ANSI compilers may not support the new conversion character. If your compiler does not support %p, you should first try using %u. In main(), you might write

```
printf("in main(), lvalue of i = %u\n", &i);
```

If this does not appear to work properly (for example, you see a negative value), try an unsigned long int, or %lu. (If neither %u nor %lu work and %p is not provided, complain to your compiler vendor!)

The %p conversion character was created because the way in which memory is addressed varies widely among machines. It wasn't that long ago that an integer number could represent all of addressable memory—an unsigned int was "big" enough. Things are different today. If memory addressing is done with segments (as in, for example, the Intel 80x86 family of CPUs), the %p might cause printf() to display a memory address as a segment-offset value (for example, A000:1250 in hexadecimal). For a CPU with linear address space (such as the Motorola 68000 series), the %p displays a single number for the memory address. By providing the %p conversion and allowing its presentation to be implementation defined, ANSI has permitted the compiler vendor to select the representation that best suits the host environment.

You may want to modify listing 6.1 if your standard library printf() does not support the new %p conversion character. For the remainder of this chapter, we will assume that your compiler supports the %p.

Because variable i was defined within the function block named main(), its scope is limited to that function block. When program control leaves main(), variable i is "out of scope" and cannot be directly used elsewhere in the program. More formally, we would say that the scope of i is *local* to main(). Figure 6.1 illustrates the scope of i in listing 6.1.

> By default, variables defined within a statement or function block are said to have scope that is local to that statement or function block. Such default variables are said to have auto storage class because their availability "automatically" ends when program control leaves the block in which they are defined.

Fig. 6.1. The scope of variable i *in* main( ) *and* func1( ).

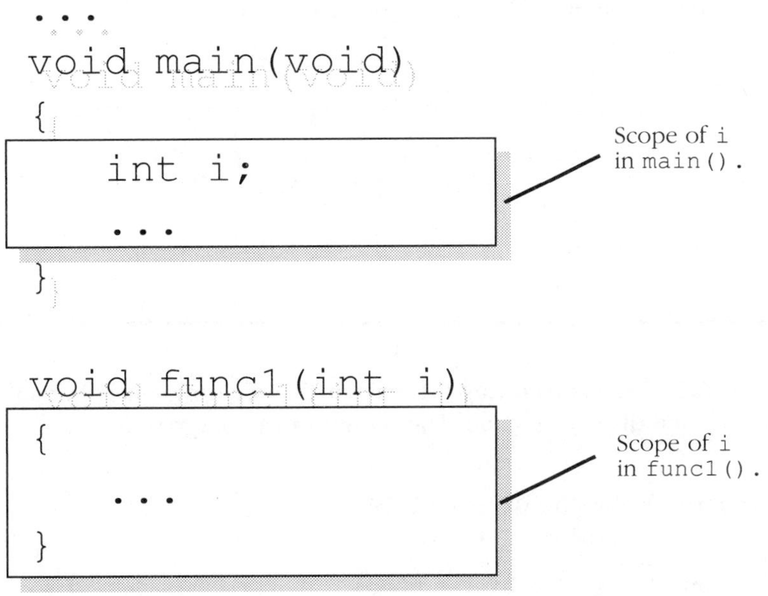

```
    . . .
void main(void)
{
        int i;

        . . .
}


void func1(int i)
{

        . . .

}
```

Scope of i in main().

Scope of i in func1().

Therefore, the i in main( ) also could have been defined as

    auto int i;

However, because the auto storage class is the default in C, programmers rarely use the auto keyword when defining a variable. (This is one of the few instances in which relying on the default seems to be acceptable.)

To reinforce the concept of local scope, consider listing 6.2.

Listing 6.2. *Local Scope of a Variable*

```
#include  <stdio.h>

void func1(int i);

void main(void)
{
    int i;

    i = 5;
    printf("in main(), lvalue of i = %p\n", &i);
    printf("            rvalue of i = %d", i);
    func1(i);
    printf("\nin main() i still equals %d\n", i);
}

void func1(int i)
{
    printf("\n\nin func1(), lvalue of i = %p\n", &i);
    printf("            rvalue of i = %d", i);
    i = i * i;
    printf("\nin func1(), i now equals %d", i);

}
```

Listing 6.2 is similar to listing 6.1, except that we now square variable i in func1() and display its value. The output of the program is

```
in main(), lvalue of i = 65530
           rvalue of i = 5

in func1(), lvalue of i = 65528
            rvalue of i = 5
in func1(), i now equals 25
in main(), i still equals 5
```

The important thing to notice is that, even though we squared i in func1(), the value of i in main() is unaffected. This should not be surprising, given that the i in func1() is stored at a different memory address than the i in main(). The program does illustrate, however, that the i in main() only "lives," or has scope, in main(). Likewise, the scope of i in func1() is limited to func1(). This is consistent with the fact that func1() received a *copy* of i in main(), not i itself.

Local Scope and Name Conflicts

Listing 6.3 will help solidify one more concept of local scope.

Listing 6.3. *Local Scope with Two Blocks*

```c
#include <stdio.h>

void main(void)
{
    int i;                                    /* Scope level 1 */

    i = 5;
    printf("in main(), lvalue of i = %p\n", &i);
    printf("            rvalue of i = %d\n", i);
    if (i == 5) {
        int i;                                /* Scope level 2 */

        i = 123;
        printf("\nin the if block: lvalue of i = %p\n", &i);
        printf("                 rvalue of i = %d\n", i);

    }
    printf("\ni after the if is still equal to %d\n", i);
}
```

Listing 6.3 defines variable i within the main() function block. A comment marks the definition of i as scope level 1. (That number was just made up; it has no real significance.) Farther down in main() is an if statement block that contains another definition for a variable also named i. We have identified this definition of i as scope level 2. The two i variables are *not* the same variables. We know this because they have different memory addresses (lvalues).

The second variable i has scope from the opening brace of the if statement block to the closing brace of the if statement. Once we leave the if statement block, the i within that block (scope level 2) is out of scope; it is no longer available for use. This is why the two definitions of i do not conflict—they exist at different scope levels. The fact that the i at scope level 2 is 123 and i at scope level 1 is 5 confirms this fact. The scope of these variables is illustrated in figure 6.2.

Fig. 6.2. *Scope of variable* i *in* main( ) *and in an* if *statement block.*

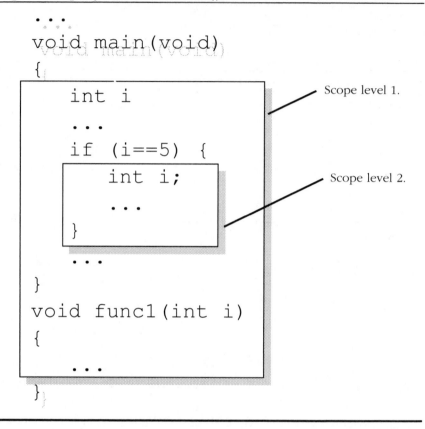

```
    · · ·
void main(void)
{
    int i
    · · ·
    if (i==5) {
        int i;
        · · ·
    }
    · · ·
}
void func1(int i)
{
    · · ·
}
```

Scope level 1.

Scope level 2.

The scope of the first variable i extends from its definition in main( ) to the closing brace of main( ). Keep in mind, however, that i cannot cross scope levels if two variables share the same name at two different scope levels. That is, the i at scope level 1 cannot cross into scope level 2 if a variable with the same name exists at the higher scope level. If no variable named i is defined at scope level 2, the i defined at scope level 1 would be available at scope level 2. To better understand this, consider listing 6.4.

In listing 6.4, variable i defined at scope level 1 would be available to scope levels 1 through 4, but not to scope level 5, because a variable by the same name is defined at scope level 5. Therefore, at scope level 5, the i defined at that scope takes precedence over all previous variable definitions that use the same variable name.

Listing 6.4. (Fragment) *Crossing Higher Scope Levels without Conflict*

```
void main(void)
{
    int i;                      /* Scope level 1 */
    if (...) {                  /* Scope level 2 */
       ...
       ...
       if (...) {               /* Scope level 3 */
          ...
          ...
          if (...) {            /* Scope level 4 */
             ...
             ...
             if (...) {         /* Scope level 5 */
                int i;
                ...
                ...
             }
             /* i at scope level 5 now out of scope */
          }
       }
    }
}
```

Likewise, variable i defined at scope level 5 "dies" when program control leaves scope level 5. Therefore, variable i defined at scope level 5 is not available at scope levels 1 through 4. But as soon as the i at scope level 5 dies, variable i defined at scope level 1 is in scope (available), as is stated in the comment line.

Rules for Local Scope

The rules for local scope are simple to remember:

1. The scope of a variable is limited to the block in which it is defined.

2. If two variables share the same name, the one in scope takes precedence over those defined at a different scope.

3. A new scope level can only begin with a statement block or a function block.

Global Scope

As discussed previously, variables defined within a block have scope that is local to the block in which they are defined. By default, such variables have auto storage class. There are times, however, when you may want to have variables that are available to all parts of the program. In other words, you would like to define variables with a scope that is global to the program, rather than local to a statement or function block.

Rules for Defining Global Scope Variables

The rule for defining a variable with global scope is simple: Any variable that is defined *outside* of a function block has global scope from the point of its definition to the end of the program source file.

This rule can be illustrated by making one change to listing 6.1. The result of the change is shown in listing 6.5.

If you compare listings 6.1 and 6.5, you will see that there are only three changes:

1. The definition of variable i has been moved from within the main() function block to a place just before main(). This changes the scope of i: in listing 6.1 it was local to main(), but in listing 6.5 it has global scope.

2. Because i now has global scope, there is no reason to pass i from main() to func1(); func1() has access to i because it has global scope. Therefore, you need to change the function prototype to show a void argument list.

3. Variable i is squared in func1() to show how its value is changed everywhere in the program.

Listing 6.5. Data with Global Scope

```
#include <stdio.h>

void func1(void);

int i;                    /* Note this was moved from main() to */
                          /* a place outside of main()          */
void main(void)
{
                          /* i used to be defined here          */
   i = 5;
   printf("in main(), lvalue of i = %p\n", &i);
   printf("           rvalue of i = %d\n", i);
   func1();
   printf("\nin main(), after func1():  rvalue of i = %d\n", i);
}

void func1(void)   /* Notice change in argument */
{
   i = i * i;
   printf("\n\nin func1(), lvalue of i = %p\n", &i);
   printf("            rvalue of i = %d\n", i);
}
```

When listing 6.5 is run, the output is

```
in main(), lvalue of i = 822
           rvalue of i = 5

in func1(), lvalue of i = 822
            rvalue of i = 25

in main(), after func1():  rvalue of i = 25
```

The output you see when you run listing 6.5 will probably have a different number for the lvalues of i, but the rvalues will be the same. The important thing to notice is that the lvalue for i in both main() and func1() is the same. This means that the same i is available to any and all functions in the program. Because i is visible to all functions, we say that i has global scope and is globally available throughout the program. This global availability is shown in figure 6.3.

Fig. 6.3. *Scope of a global variable.*

```
    . . .
int i;

void main(void)
{
    i=5;

    . . .

}

void func1(void)
{
    i=i*i;

    . . .

}
```

Scope of global variable i.

Because the definition of i is external to any statement or function block, it is said to have *external storage class*. It follows that data items with external storage class have global scope. (A section later in this chapter explains how you can change the scope of external variables.)

Global Scope and Name Conflicts

What happens when we define a local variable with the same name as a variable with global scope? Listing 6.6 shows this situation.

Listing 6.6. Global Scope and Variables with the Same Name

```c
#include <stdio.h>

void func1(void);

int i;                    /* Note this was moved from main() to */
                          /* a place outside of main()          */

void main(void)
{
   i = 5;
   printf("in main(), lvalue of i = %p\n", &i);
   printf("         rvalue of i = %d\n", i);
   func1();
   printf("\nin main(), after func1():  rvalue of i = %d\n", i);
}

void func1(void)
{
   int i;                    /* This i has local scope */

   i = 10;
   i = i * i;
   printf("\n\nin func1(), lvalue of i = %p\n", &i);
   printf("           rvalue of i = %d\n", i);
}
```

Listing 6.6 is the same as listing 6.5 except that we defined a variable named
i within the function block of func1(). When listing 6.6 is run, the output
is

```
in main(), lvalue of i = 822
          rvalue of i = 5

in func1(), lvalue of i = 65528
          rvalue of i = 100

in main(), after func1():  rvalue of i = 5
```

Notice that the two lvalues are different, which means that the two
variables named i are different variables. Note that the value of i in main()
remains unchanged even though the i in func1() has a different value. This
is as it should be because they are different variables.

Listing 6.6 shows that our rules about variables with local scope also apply to those variables with global scope. That is, if two variables share the same name, the variable in scope takes precedence. The variable defined in func1() (local scope) takes precedence over the i defined before main() (global scope). When we return from func1(), its i "dies" and is no longer in scope. This is why the i shown in main() retains its original value; it doesn't know about the i defined in func1() because that i is local to func1(). Figure 6.4 shows the scope of i in listing 6.6.

Fig. 6.4. *Precedence in scope of variable* i *within* func1().

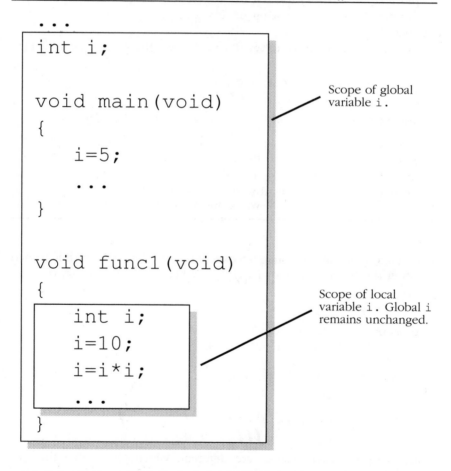

```
. . .
int i;

void main(void)
{
    i=5;
    . . .
}

void func1(void)
{
    int i;
    i=10;
    i=i*i;
    . . .
}
```

Scope of global variable i.

Scope of local variable i. Global i remains unchanged.

Why Have Scoped Variables?

If you have been programming with a language that does not support the concept of scoped variables, you may wonder why you need to bother with scoped variables. In some languages (such as BASIC) all variables have what we call global scope. While defining all variables to have global scope does away with some problems (for example, you don't have to define variables before you use them), it also creates a bunch of other problems. It is not uncommon in BASIC, for example, to fix a bug in one part of the program only to see a new bug show up elsewhere in the same program. Often, the new bug appears because your efforts to fix the first bug cause changes to variables used in other parts of the program. Because all variables have global scope in BASIC, a change made anywhere in the program has effect everywhere within the program. As shown in listing 6.2, the effect on a variable can be limited to one function or statement block when scoped variables are used.

By providing for scoped variables, C gives you a privacy of data that would not exist otherwise. Variables with local scope, for example, can be changed only within the statement or function block in which they are defined. Because the data can be localized to one function or statement block, the chances of side effects cause by program changes or debugging are minimized. (Clearly, there will come a time when you do want a local variable to have its value changed by some other function. The special means for doing this are covered in Chapters 7 and 8.)

Scoped variables also foster a "black box" approach to programming. That is, you can write functions that appear to be black boxes, whose contents and inner workings are unknown to the rest of the program. Those functions can manipulate data in whatever way is necessary, and you need not worry that those manipulations will affect other parts of the program inadvertently.

In short, scoped variables make data more private and make debugging easier.

Scope and *static* Variables

Sometimes you will want to have a variable that "lives" after you leave a function. A common example is some form of counter that is incremented each time a function is entered. If the counter's value "died" whenever program control left the function block, its value would be lost; it couldn't

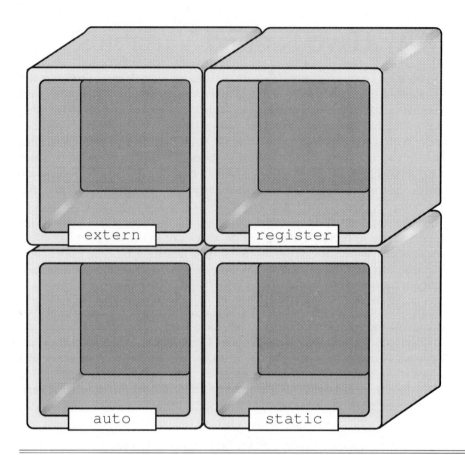

"pick up where it left off." One obvious solution is to make the variable a global. That solution, however, means that you sacrifice the data privacy that C affords to variables with local scope.

What you need is a way of defining a variable that has local scope but "lives on" even after program control leaves the function block in which it is defined, so that the value upon the next entry into the function block is the same as it was when program control last left the function block. That is, you need a way to override the default auto storage class. C provides a simple means to solve this problem.

Listing 6.7 shows how you can use the static keyword with a data-type specifier to create a variable that overrides the default auto storage class.

Listing 6.7. static *Local Variables*

```
#include <stdio.h>

#define MAXNUM  5

void func1(void);

void main(void)
{
    int i;

    for (i = 0; i < MAXNUM; i++) {
        printf("main(): i = %2d", i);
        func1();
    }
}

void func1(void)
{
    static int i = 1;               /* Notice static keyword */

    printf("     func1(): i = %2d\n", i);
    i++;
}
```

Notice how variable i is defined in func1(). The keyword static is used to tell the compiler that the integer variable i should have special storage properties. Within func1(), variable i still has scope that is local to that function. That is, the i in func1() does not "collide" with the i in main(). The keyword static, however, does cause the compiler to allocate storage for variable i in a different way than if the static keyword were not used.

When the compiler sees the keyword static, it creates storage for i in such a way that the value of i is saved when program control leaves the function. When program control is sent to the function a second time, i has the same value it had when the function was last exited.

Unlike variables of the auto storage class with local scope, variables of the static storage class with local scope continue to exist even after program control leaves the function.

The second thing to notice is that we have initialized the value of i to 1 as part of the definition of the variable:

```
static int i = 1;
```

This statement directs the compiler not only to allocate memory space for the variable i, but also to generate the necessary code to initialize its value to 1 when the program first starts to execute. Note that this initialization code is only executed once, not each time the function is executed. Therefore, when func1() is called the first time, the value displayed by the function is 1. Then variable i is incremented by 1 (it now equals 2), and control returns to main().

When func1() is called the second time, the value displayed is 2. This shows that the value of i is saved between calls to the function. Therefore, listing 6.7 simply shows that the value of i goes from 1 to 5 when the program is run. The output of the program is

```
main(): i = 0      func1(): i = 1
main(): i = 1      func1(): i = 2
main(): i = 2      func1(): i = 3
main(): i = 3      func1(): i = 4
main(): i = 4      func1(): i = 5
```

As you can see, the value of i in func1() is greater by 1 each time the function is called. This can happen only if i retains its value between function calls. The static storage class allows you to create variables that do so.

Internal Statics

Sometimes you will hear C programmers refer to variables—like the i in func1() of listing 6.7—as "internal static." The term *internal static* developed because the variable being defined is a static that is "internal" to a statement or function block.

Global Data and Multiple Files

As you gain experience with C, you will find yourself writing larger and more complex programs. As program size increases, you will also find that it is convenient to write the source code as several small files rather than one large one. Each of these smaller files will contain the source code for one or more functions. Writing functions in this way makes it easier to edit, compile, and link functions during the testing and debugging phase of program development.

Although the idea of multiple files is an excellent one, there are some problems to be solved if you use this approach, which is shown in figure 6.5.

In this example, variable i is defined as an integer with global scope and external storage class. Therefore, it is known and available throughout File 1. Now suppose that we try to compile File 2. In File 2, variable i is used in func3( ) but has not been defined. We meant to use the globally defined i in File 1, but the compiler doesn't know about File 1 when we try to compile File 2. Therefore, the compiler will tell us that i is undefined in File 2. How can we solve this problem?

Once again, C provides a simple solution to the problem, as shown in figure 6.6.

The only change between figures 6.5 and 6.6 is the statement

```
extern int i;
```

near the top of File 2. This is a data *declaration* for variable i. (It is *NOT* a data *definition* for i.) The keyword extern tells the compiler that an integer variable named i is *defined* elsewhere, but you may use i in this file and the linker will find where i is actually stored in memory (that is, its lvalue). (You may wish to review the section "Writing, Compiling, and Linking a C Program" in Chapter 1 at this time.)

The purpose of extern, therefore, is to tell the compiler the name and data type of the variable so that the variable can be used in the code of File 2. The use of extern is a data *declaration*, because no storage is allocated for the variable—storage was allocated for it when its *definition* was read at the top of File 1. In figure 6.5, the statement

```
int i;
```

Fig. 6.5. A problem with compiling multiple files.

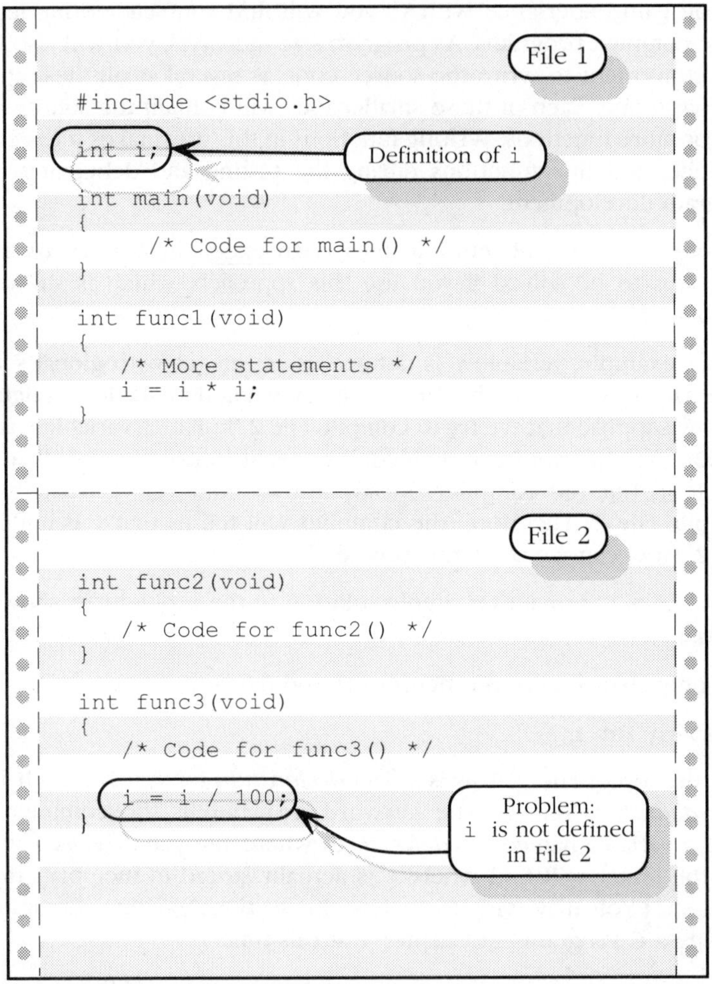

Fig. 6.6. *Compiling multiple files (Solution 1)*

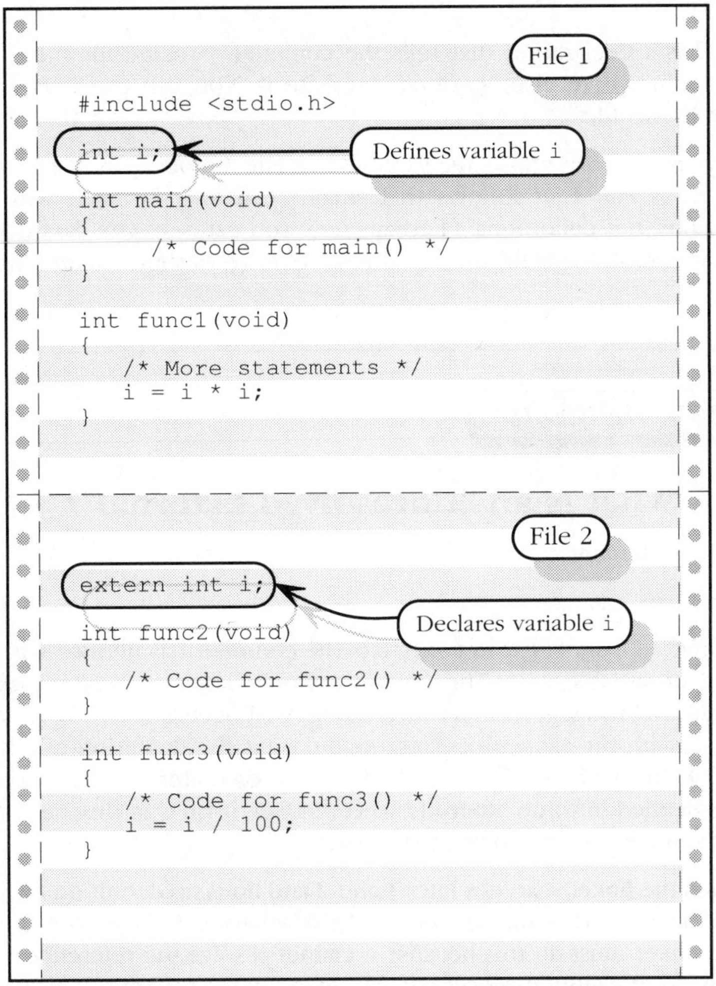

```
                                                        File 1

#include <stdio.h>

int i;              ◄———————  Defines variable i

int main(void)
{
      /* Code for main() */
}

int func1(void)
{
    /* More statements */
    i = i * i;
}


                                                        File 2

extern int i;

int func2(void)         ◄———  Declares variable i
{
    /* Code for func2() */
}

int func3(void)
{
    /* Code for func3() */
    i = i / 100;
}
```

in File 1 is the definition for variable i. This definition tells the compiler to allocate storage for i. On the other hand, the statement

```
extern int i;
```

in File 2 is a declaration that tells the compiler "Storage for i has been created somewhere else, so don't re-create it. You can use i as an int variable in this file."

The keyword extern makes the variable i in File 1 globally available in File 2 as well as File 1. It follows that extern can only be used with data declarations, not definitions. (Perhaps now you can see why data declarations and definitions really are not the same thing, as some might have you believe.)

Programming Tip

What Is an "Unresolved External"?

If the statement

```
extern int i;
```

is omitted from File 2 in figure 6.6, the compiler has no idea what kind of variable i is. The compiler would issue an "undefined variable" message. A more interesting twist occurs when we have File 2 with the extern declaration, but omit the definition of i in File 1. In this case, we have "lied" to the compiler—we told it i was defined in some other file when, in fact, it isn't. In this case, it is the linker that discovers the error.

When the linker searches Files 1 and 2 and finds no definition for i in either file, it issues an "unresolved external" error message. The linker must do this because it cannot resolve the reference to i; that is, it cannot discover where i exists in the program. This is a very common error. If you would like to see this type of error message, write a short program that includes printf(), but misspell printf() (pront(), for example). Because the linker will not find a function named pront(), it will issue an "unresolved external" type of error message.

Let's consider one more alternative to the solution shown in figure 6.7. Assume that only func3() needs access to variable i. In figure 6.7, we declare that i is external to this file by moving the external declaration from its global position as shown in figure 6.6 (File 2) into the function body of func3() as shown in figure 6.7 (File 2).

Notice that the statement

```
extern int i;
```

is no longer a global declaration of i in File 2, but is now contained within the function block for func3(). This means that *only* func3() knows about i in File 2; func2() is oblivious to the existence of variable i defined in File 1. This is a clean way to have a global variable in one file (File 1), but limit its scope in a different file (File 2).

The *make* Utility

As you gain experience with C and write larger programs, you will find yourself writing your programs as a series of multiple source files. Because C is designed for writing multiple files, many compiler vendors supply a *make* utility. The *make* utility is used to compile multiple files in an efficient manner.

For example, suppose that you are writing a program that has three modules; test1.c, test2.c, and test3.c. Suppose further that test1.c and test3.c are stable, but you're having trouble with test2.c. If you activate the *make* feature (usually with an –m switch on the compile line), each file's date and time is checked to see whether it has been edited since the last compile. If the file has changed, it is recompiled. If the file has not been changed, it is not compiled. The *make* utility, therefore, speeds up the development process because it reduces compile time. Check your compiler to see whether it supports the *make* utility.

Fig. 6.7. Compiling multiple files (Solution 2).

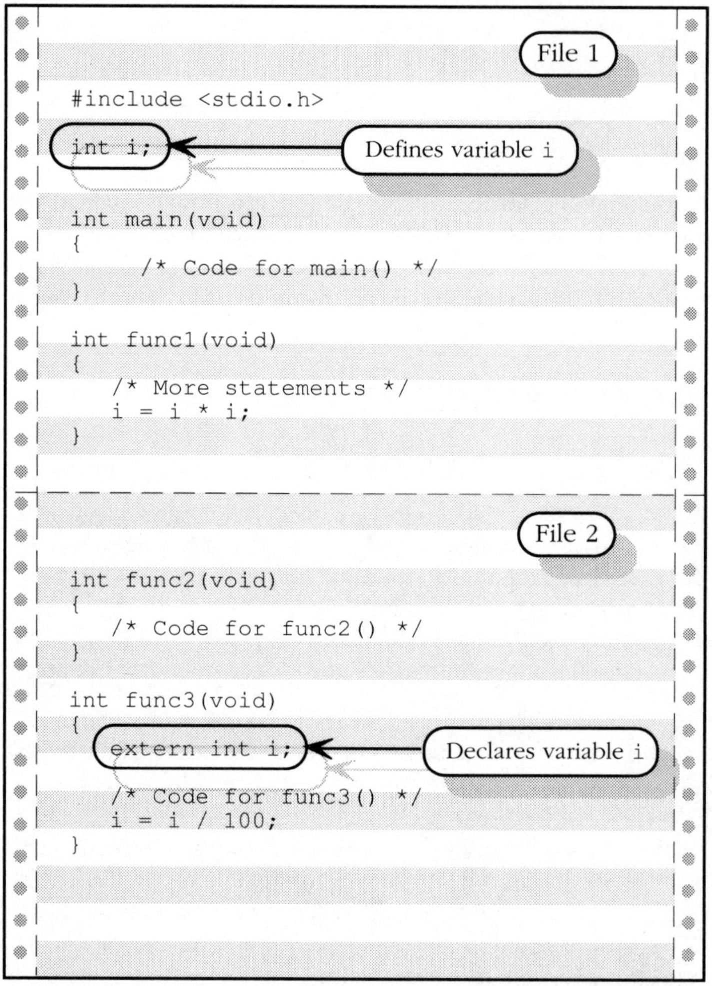

```
                                                    File 1

#include <stdio.h>

int i;              ◄──────  Defines variable i

int main(void)
{
     /* Code for main() */
}

int func1(void)
{
   /* More statements */
   i = i * i;
}
```

```
                                                    File 2

int func2(void)
{
   /* Code for func2() */
}

int func3(void)
{
   extern int i;    ◄──────  Declares variable i

   /* Code for func3() */
   i = i / 100;
}
```

Controlling Scope in Multiple Files

From time to time, you will need to use certain functions to which you do not want all other functions to have access. You might have, for example, a function that does some critical disk operation, and you want to have the function available only to selected other functions. Or you might have data that should be changed only by one or two functions.

You can accomplish any of these goals by using the static keyword for all definitions with the external storage class. Figure 6.8 shows an example of hiding data with global scope.

In figure 6.8, we are assuming that func2() should be visible in main(), but that _support2() and _support3() should only be available to func2()—no one else.

In File 2, the keyword static has been used as a storage modifier for variable i and the functions _support2() and _support3().

> All function definitions by default have global scope and external storage class; they are visible everywhere throughout the program.

Perhaps _support2() and _support3() are "dangerous" functions that you do not want visible to any function other than func2(). The appearance of the keyword static prior to the type specifier for a function definition limits the scope of those functions to the file in which they are defined. They are now said to have *external static* storage class.

In terms of figure 6.8, func2() knows about _support2() and _support3(), but nothing in File 1 can communicate with anything in File 2 other than func2(). Likewise, the definition of i in File 2

```
static int i;
```

means that i has global scope, but the keyword static tells the compiler to limit its scope to the file in which it is defined (File 2). Therefore, the static i in File 2 will not conflict with the global i defined in File 1. The i used in the _support1() and _support2() functions will be the i defined with the external static storage class in File 2. In fact, there is no way for

Fig. 6.8. Hiding data with global scope.

```
#include <stdio.h>
                                              File 1
int func2(void);

int i;
                              Defines variable i
int main()
{

    /* Code for main() */

    i = func1();
    func2();
}


int func1()
{
    /* Statements for func1() */
    i *= i;
}
                  Defines
                  variable i           File 2

    static int i;

static int _support1(void), int _support2(void);

int func2()
{
    /* Code for func2() */
    _support1();
    _support2();
    return i;
}


static int _support1(void)
{
    /* Code for _support1() that sets i up */
}


static int _support2(void)
    /* Code for _support2() to work on i*/

}
```

any of the functions in File 2 to access the global i defined in File 1; the static definition in File 2 takes precedence over the i in File 1. The i in File 1 is out of scope.

Programming Tip

Two Uses of the *static* Keyword

As you can see from the last two sections, the keyword static can be used in two different ways. An *internal static* definition, appearing within a statement or function block, uses the keyword static before the type specifier. Such a definition has two properties that make it different from the normal (default) definition in a statement or function block.

1. The value of the data item continues to exist even after the function is exited: the last value is available the next time the function is entered.

2. You can initialize an internal static variable that is an aggregate data type, such as an array. (Chapter 8 shows you how this is done.)

Therefore, you should use the internal static data definition when you need to initialize an aggregate data item or when you want its value to exist the next time you enter the function in which the item is defined.

The other use of the keyword static is with definitions of global data items, such as function definitions or data items defined outside of a function block. The purpose here is to hide the external static data item from everything outside of the file in which the item is defined. Many C programmers will use the static keyword prior to a function definition so that the name of the function will not collide with other function or variable names. (As an extra measure of protection, I also added a leading underscore to _support1() and _support2().) Therefore, the external static keyword is used to hide data items and limit their scope to the file in which they are defined.

Initializing *auto* Aggregates

Under the K&R standard, you were not allowed to initialize arrays (that is, aggregate data types) that have the auto storage class. The ANSI standard does allow initialization of auto aggregates, however.

A static array is automatically initialized with zeroes if no list of initializer values is given. An auto array, however, is not initialized with a known value in the absence of an initializer list: they will contain "garbage." Details are provided in Chapter 8.

The *register* Storage Class

One more storage class is available to you. The register keyword in a data definition tells the compiler that you want to have this variable stored in a CPU register rather than in memory. The purpose of such definitions is to provide the fastest access possible to the variable. Listing 6.8 shows a typical use for the register storage class modifier.

Listing 6.8 (Fragment). *The* register *Storage Class*

```
register int i;

for (i = Ø; i < MAXNUM; i++) {
    /* Code for loop */
}
```

The definition for i asks the compiler to place the variable in a CPU register. There is no guarantee that the request for a CPU register can or will be made by the compiler.

Obviously, there are certain limitations on register definitions.

1. There is no guarantee that any of the data items using the register keyword end up being allocated to a register.

2. It would be silly to try and use the register storage modifier for more variables than the CPU has registers.

3. The types of data items that can be placed in a register are implementation-defined. That is, using register with a double data type may or may not work with your compiler.

4. The compiler may ignore the register request and simply use the auto storage class.

5. You cannot use the address-of operator (&) with a register variable. (This makes sense because the variable has no lvalue in memory.)

Programming Tip

Save Time with *register* Variables

If your compiler supports register data types, you may be able to increase your program's speed by defining variables with the register storage class. This tip is especially useful in the case of nested loops, like these:

```
int i, j;

for (i = Ø; i  < MAXNUM; i ++) {
    for (j = Ø; j  < MAXLEN; j ++) {
        /* More loop code */
    }
}
```

Defining i and j with the register storage class will likely increase the speed of this code. If you feel that you can only get one CPU register, you are better off to make j the register variable because it is the most intensively used loop variable.

A Potential Confusion

Some people might argue that typedef should be included in a discussion of storage class. As you shall see in Chapter 9, typedefs are actually a shorthand for the attribute list of a data item—they do not "create" a new storage class. Therefore, although the compiler parses typedefs as though they are a storage class, a typedef is not a storage class in and of itself.

Some Closing Thoughts on Data Privacy

If you are new to the concept of scoped variables, you might be tempted to define all of your variables so that they have global scope. Don't!

> Although it may seem to make things easier at first (for example, you wouldn't have to contend with function arguments), the use of globals will prove costly in the future.

If you have defined all of your data as global data items, it becomes difficult to isolate which part of the program is causing a bug. All functions are potential offenders in producing the bug. If you use local variables, you will be able quickly to inject a few printf() statements before and after function calls to isolate where things are going wrong.

As you probably know, replicating and isolating a bug is the hardest task in debugging a program. Once the bug is found, correcting it is often a trivial task. Data privacy reduces the time required for you to isolate a bug.

My advice is simple: Make every effort possible to hide data between functions. This may take a little more effort at the start, but you will be rewarded many times over in the future.

▼ Review Questions and Exercises

1. What storage classes are available in C?

2. How does storage class relate to the scope of a data item?

3. If integer variable day is defined in File 1 with external storage class and you want to use it in File 2, what statement is needed?

4. Suppose that a function named brace() should only be called by a function named do_all(). How would you accomplish this limitation?

5. What is the default storage class for a function, and what is its scope?

6. How does scope change if two variables with the same name have been defined?

▼ Answers

1. There are four storage classes: (1) external (extern), (2) automatic (auto), (3) static, and (4) register.

2. The external storage class occurs when a data item is defined outside of any statement or function block. Variables with external storage class have global scope throughout the program. If multiple files are used, an extern declaration for each global is necessary in each file other than the one that contains the definition for the variables.

   The automatic (auto) storage class has scope for the block in which it is defined.

   Variables that use the static modifier come in two flavors. First, if the variable is defined within a statement or function block, it is an internal static and its scope is limited to the block in which it is defined. It also has the capability of retaining a value between function calls. Second, if the variable is defined outside a statement or function block, it has external static storage. The variable's scope is from its point of definition to the end of the file in which it is defined.

   The register storage class is limited to a function or statement block and its scope is limited to the block in which it is defined. You cannot use the address-of operator (&) with register variables.

3. If the variable is needed throughout File 2, place the following statement near the top of File 2 outside of any block:

```
extern int day;
```

If the variable is needed only in one or two functions, copy the statement into the appropriate functions.

4. Clearly, you would want to place both functions in their own file and define the brace( ) function as

```
              in File 2
static int brace(void)
{
     /* function body */
}

int do_all(int arg1)
{
     /* function body */
}
```

(We just made up the arguments for the functions.) Using the scheme shown above, do_all( ) is available to all who need it, but brace( ) is available only in File 2.

5. The default storage class for a function is external, and it has global scope by default.

6. If two variables have the same name, the one with the most-recent definition takes precedence. In listing 6.4, for example, the i defined at scope level 1 loses precedence at scope level 5 when the most-recently defined i takes precedence.

7

Introduction to Pointers

Concepts in This Chapter

- ❑ Pointer variables and how to use them
- ❑ Character arrays and the null pointer
- ❑ Incrementing and decrementing pointers
- ❑ Pointers as function arguments

O ne of the most powerful features in C is the use of pointers. In this chapter, we lay the foundation for understanding and using pointers. Chapter 8 builds on this base and examines some advanced features using pointers.

Pointers are often a stumbling block for beginning C programmers, but they need not be. Stated simply, a *pointer* is a variable that points to another variable. You also can say that a pointer has an rvalue that is the lvalue of another variable. Mastering the pointer concepts in this chapter and in Chapter 8 will help you write faster, more efficient, C programs.

Defining a Pointer

Because pointer variables can be used in ways that are different from other variables, you need a way to tell the compiler that a pointer variable is being defined. Figure 7.1 shows how you could define an integer pointer.

Fig. 7.1. *Defining an integer pointer.*

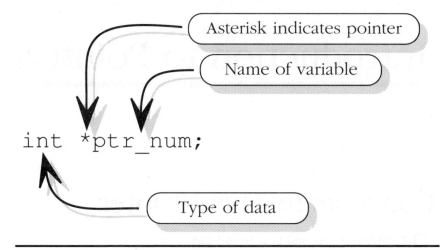

As shown in figure 7.1, the definition of a pointer has three fundamental parts:

1. An asterisk to indicate that this variable will be used as a pointer

2. The name of the pointer variable

3. The type of data to which the pointer will point

Let's examine each of these three parts in detail.

Asterisks in Pointer Definitions and Declarations

When an asterisk (*) is used in a data definition or declaration, it is a unary operator. When the asterisk is used as a unary operator, it is called the *indirection operator*. Don't confuse this operator with the multiplication operator that was explained earlier: as a multiplication operator, the asterisk indicates that two numbers are to be multiplied. In that usage, the asterisk is a binary operator—it requires two operands to perform its task of multiplication. In figure 7.1, the asterisk is the indirection operator and requires a single operand. The operand in figure 7.1 is the name of the pointer variable, ptr_num.

> The purpose of an asterisk in a data definition or declaration is simply to tell the compiler that the data item is such that we can perform indirection with it: it is a variable of type pointer. The compiler will make a note of this fact (in the symbol table) so that the variable can be used in pointer operations.

Therefore, the purpose of the asterisk in a data definition or declaration is purely informational—it tells the compiler that the variable can be used as a pointer data type.

The Name of a Pointer Variable

The second part of the pointer definition simply tells the name of the pointer variable. There is nothing special about the name given to a pointer; any valid variable name can be used. Many C programmers, however, begin the name of a pointer variable with the letters ptr (such as ptr_date, ptr_name, etc.).

Scalars and Type Specifiers for Pointer Variables

The third part of a pointer definition is critical. The type specifier in figure 7.1 is int. This means that the pointer will be used with an int data type. The *scalar* for a pointer refers to the object pointed to (not the pointer itself). Therefore, we say that the scalar for this pointer is set to that of an int. The type specifier in a pointer definition sets the scalar size for the pointer. As you will see later in this chapter, the scalar of a pointer represents an important piece of information needed by the compiler to perform pointer operations correctly.

The sizeof() operator can be used to determine the size of the scalar for a pointer. For example, if you wrote a program to find the size of a char and an int, you would probably find that

    sizeof(char)

returns a value of 1 but

    sizeof(int)

returns a value of 2. You know, therefore, that a char takes one byte of memory for storage but an int takes two bytes. This also means that if you define a character pointer as

```
char *ptr_c;        /* Scalar equals  sizeof(char) = 1 */
int *ptr_num;       /* Scalar equals sizeof(int)   = 2 */
```

the pointer variable ptr_c will have a scalar size of 1. If you have a definition of an integer pointer like the one in figure 7.1, it will have a scalar size of 2 (assuming an int is 2 bytes).

Sometimes a picture helps to solidify a concept and make it easy to understand. Think of indirection as a way of standing at one memory address (lvalue) but being able to look at the contents (rvalue) of some other memory address. To be able to see that other data item, you need to set a ruler to the proper scalar value. The analogy is presented in figure 7.2. Smaller scalars mean smaller "angles of vision," and the extent of the object "seen" is limited accordingly.

In the previous variable definitions, variable ptr_c has a scalar of 1: only character data types can be seen properly. Similarly, ptr_num has a scalar of 2 and provides the "proper perspective" only on integer data. If you tried to use a character pointer (scalar of 1) to look at an int variable, you would only "see" half of the integer, and if you tried to use an integer pointer

Fig. 7.2. *The scalar as a way of "looking" at data.*

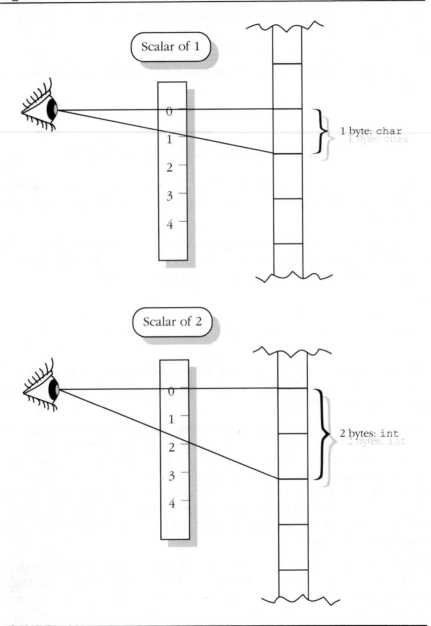

(scalar of 2) to work with character data, you would suffer "double vision" because you would see two characters rather than just one. As you will see later, trying to "view" data with the wrong scalar can cause a variety of problems.

Later in this chapter, you will see why these scalars are so important. For now, simply be aware that the type specifier for the pointer determines its scalar size.

The Concept of Indirection

Now that you know how to define a pointer, what can you do with one? An example will help explain how a pointer variable can be used. Consider listing 7.1.

The program begins with the definition of two variables: i and ptr. Next, printf() is called to show the lvalues and rvalues of the two variables. When I ran the program, the output of the first two printf()s was

```
lvalues: i = 65530   ptr = 65528
rvalues: i = 13781   ptr = 2347      *ptr = -232
```

The first line tells me that i is stored at memory location 65530 and ptr is stored at 65528. Stated a different way, the lvalue of i is 65530, and the lvalue of ptr is 65528.

The second line of output says that i contains a value of 13781 and ptr contains 2347. The values you see if you run the program will probably be different. One reason is that i and ptr are variables of the auto storage class and, as such, they are not initialized to any useful values. In this case, the rvalues for i and ptr are simply random values that just happened to be at those memory locations when the program started. The lvalues are determined by the compiler, but your compiler will probably use different values than those shown here.

Now we come to *ptr. When you use the indirection operator with a pointer variable, it tells the compiler to use indirection to get an rvalue. To see how this works, consider another view of how things presently exist (see fig. 7.3).

Listing 7.1. *Using a Pointer Variable*

```
#include  <stdio.h>

void main(void)
{
   int i, *ptr;      /* Define an integer and a pointer to int. */

   /* Right now, you will only see junk: */
   printf("lvalues: i = %p    ptr = %p\n", &i, &ptr);
   printf("rvalue:  i = %d    ptr = %p       *ptr = %d\n",
          i, ptr, *ptr);

   i = 5;             /* Set i equal to some known value.      */

   /* i is set, but ptr is still junk: */
   printf("\n\nAfter i is assigned:\n\n");
   printf("lvalues: i = %p    ptr = %p\n", &i, &ptr);
   printf("rvalue:  i = %d    ptr = %p       *ptr = %d\n",
          i, ptr, *ptr);

   ptr = &i;          /* Now make ptr point to variable i.     */

   /* Now ptr has meaningful data in it:  */
   printf("\n\nAfter ptr is assigned:\n\n");
   printf("lvalues: i = %p    ptr = %p\n", &i, &ptr);
   printf("rvalue:  i = %d    ptr = %p       *ptr = %d\n",
          i, ptr, *ptr);

   *ptr = 1Ø;         /* Use indirection to change value of i. */

   /* Show how i is now changed: */
   printf("\n\nAfter ptr uses indirection:\n\n");
   printf("lvalues: i = %p    ptr = %p\n", &i, &ptr);
   printf("rvalue:  i = %d    ptr = %p       *ptr = %d\n",
          i, ptr, *ptr);
}
```

Fig. 7.3. rvalues *and* lvalues *for listing 7.1.*

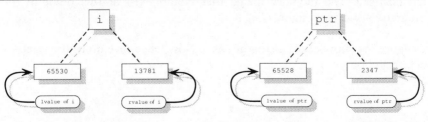

As you can see, the rvalue of ptr is 2347. Also remember that pointer variables are supposed to have rvalues that represent memory addresses. Whenever the compiler sees the indirection operator (*), it knows that it is supposed to get the rvalue of the pointer variable (2347), go to that memory address, and get "scalar-bytes" of data. This is the process of indirection.

> Indirection involves using the rvalue of a pointer variable as a memory address, going to that address, and reading scalar bytes of data.

Recall that the size of the scalar is set by the type specifier when the pointer is defined. Let's assume that your computer uses 8 bits per byte and that an integer is two bytes. Because ptr is an int pointer and has a scalar of 2 (that is, 16 bits for an integer), the indirection operator causes program control to go to memory address 2347 and reads two bytes (2347 and 2348, or two bytes for an int) to form the data type it points to—which is an int for ptr.

Unfortunately, things haven't worked too well thus far, because neither i nor ptr have "useful" rvalues yet. They simply contain random values in memory. With this in mind, let's examine the next line of output.

After the program statement

```
i = 5;
```

in listing 7.1, two more calls to printf() show the following results:

```
lvalues: i = 65530    ptr = 65528
rvalues: i = 5        ptr = 2347      *ptr = -232
```

Because of the assignment statement, the rvalue of i is now 5. Nothing else has changed. The memory image that would exist at this point in the program is shown in figure 7.4.

As figure 7.4 shows, the rvalue of i is 5. Now let's move on to the next set of printf()s.

Fig. 7.4. rvalues *and* lvalues *for listing 7.1 after* i *assignment.*

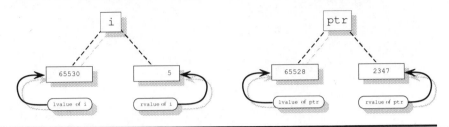

After the program statement

    ptr = &i;

the third set of calls to printf( ) yields an output of

    lvalues: i = 65530   ptr = 65528
    rvalues: i = 5   ptr = 65530   *ptr = 5

Recall from Chapter 6 that the ampersand (&) is the address-of operator. It tells the compiler to use the lvalue of the data item rather than the rvalue. The assignment statement says "Take the lvalue of i (&i) and place it into the rvalue of ptr." Or, you could also verbalize the ptr assignment statement as "Take the address where i is stored in memory and assign it into ptr." As the output of printf( ) shows, the rvalue of ptr does indeed now hold the lvalue of i. In other words, ptr now knows the memory address where i is stored because we have used the assignment statement in conjunction with the address-of operator to initialize ptr to i's memory address.

There is another result of all this. Because ptr does know i's location in memory, the indirection should now work. Indeed, the printf( ) using indirection (*ptr) now shows a value of 5, suggesting that things are working as they should. That is, the expression *ptr says, "Use indirection to form a data item that is the size of ptr's scalar." Therefore, the compiler gets the rvalue of ptr (65530), goes to that address, grabs scalar-bytes of data (2 bytes because it is an int pointer), and forms an int from those two bytes of data. Obviously, this will have the same value as i because we grabbed the two bytes from i's memory address. The memory image now appears as shown in figure 7.5.

Fig. 7.5. rvalues *and* lvalues *for listing 7.1 after* ptr *is initialized.*

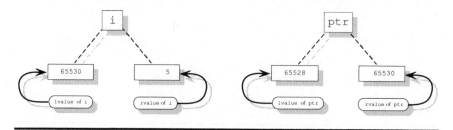

It is important to note that in figure 7.5, the rvalue of ptr is the lvalue of i.

The last set of printf()s shows how you can use a pointer to change the value of what it points to. The statement

    *ptr = 1Ø;

tells the compiler "Using indirection, get the rvalue of ptr (65530), go to that memory address (65530), and store the value of 10 into those scalar-bytes of memory." This should have the effect of changing the value of i to 10. The output of the last two printf()s (after ptr uses indirection) is

```
lvalues: i = 6553Ø    ptr = 65528
rvalues: i = 1Ø       ptr = 6553Ø    *ptr = 1Ø
```

Notice that i and *ptr both have a value of 10. The memory image becomes that shown in figure 7.6.

Fig. 7.6. rvalues *and* lvalues *for listing 7.1 after* ptr *indirection.*

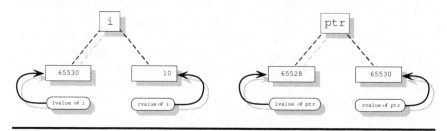

If you reverse the positions of the variables, you can show the intimate relationship between ptr and i (see fig. 7.7).

Figure 7.7 shows that ptr has an rvalue that is equal to the lvalue of i. The process of indirection using ptr simply reads figure 7.7 from left to right. For example, in the call to printf()

```
printf("%d", *ptr);
```

the *ptr tells the compiler (follow figure 7.7 from left to right as you read) "go to the lvalue of ptr (65528), get its lvalue (65530), go to that memory address (actually, variable i), and get its rvalue (10)." The printf() will display a 10 on the screen.

Fig. 7.7. Reversing i *and* ptr.

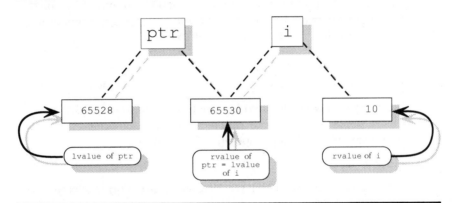

Using a Pointer in an Assignment

Using figure 7.7 and assuming you have a third integer variable named j, what would the following statement do?

```
j = *ptr;
```

From figure 7.7 and its earlier discussion, you know that *ptr resolves to the value 10. That is, indirection causes the compiler to fetch the rvalue of ptr (65530), go to that memory address, grab scalar-bytes of data (2 because ptr is a pointer to int), and use those 2 bytes to form the value stored there (10). The result of the statement above, therefore, is that j now equals 10.

Summary of Pointer Rules

Let's summarize the rules about pointers discussed thus far:

1. An asterisk in a definition or declaration such as

    ```
    int *ptr;
    ```

    simply indicates that you want to use a pointer variable.

2. The scalar of a pointer is determined when the pointer is defined. Ignoring data arrays for the moment, the scalar is determined by the type specifier for the pointer. For example,

    ```
    double *ptr;
    ```

    would have a scalar of sizeof(double), which is typically 8 bytes.

3. Pointers never point to anything useful until they are initialized. This requires an assignment statement for the pointer variable, often using the address-of operator. For example,

    ```
    ptr = &i;
    ```

4. After a pointer is initialized, you can use indirection to change what the pointer points to, such as

    ```
    *ptr = 1Ø;
    ```

    You also can read a value by using indirection, such as

    ```
    printf("%d", *ptr);
    ```

We will add a few things to the list of rules later in this chapter. For now, however, you have enough information to write some useful programs.

Programming Tip

Initializing Pointers

No matter how many times we say it, programmers will always use a pointer before it points to something useful. Consider the following code fragment:

```
static int *ptr;

*ptr = 1Ø
```

Because we have made ptr a static integer pointer, it is initialized to zero by default. When we assign 10 into ptr, we are actually writing an integer 10 into memory location 0. Often, this is the base address for the operating system, causing your system to "go to lunch."

The moral is simple: Initialize a pointer *before* you use it.

Why Pointers Are Useful

A good question at this point is "Why use a pointer?" If you remember program 6.2 in Chapter 6, we showed that variables with local scope could not be directly changed by a function call. A shortened form of program 6.2 is presented in listing 7.2.

When I ran listing 7.2, the output was

```
i: lvalue = 6553Ø    rvalue = 9
in func1()  i: lvalue = 65528    rvalue = 9
in func1()  i: lvalue = 65528    rvalue = 81
after func1()  i: lvalue = 6553Ø    rvalue = 9
```

This illustrates how data defined in one function block is out of scope for a different function block. How do we know this? We can tell this at a glance, because the lvalue of i in main() is not the same lvalue for i in func1().

Listing 7.2. Data Privacy and Scope

```c
#include <stdio.h>

void func1(int integer);

void main(void)
{
    int i;

    i = 9;
    printf("i: lvalue = %p    rvalue = %d\n", &i, i);
    func1(i);
    printf("after func1() i: lvalue = %p    rvalue = %d\n", &i, i);

}

void func1(int i)
{
    printf("in func1() i: lvalue = %p    rvalue = %d\n", &i, i);
    i = i * i;
    printf("in func1() i: lvalue = %p    rvalue = %d\n", &i, i);
}
```

This agrees perfectly with the discussion in Chapter 6 of variables with local scope.

But suppose that you want func1() to be able to change i in main() so that the changes func1() makes to i are still in effect after program control returns to main(). You can do this by making two small changes to listing 7.2, as shown in listing 7.3.

There is only one change in main(). Instead of calling func1() with i as its argument, we use the address of i instead. Notice that we can use the address-of operator to send the address of i to func(). This means that we are sending an lvalue to func1(), not the rvalue as is done in listing 7.2.

Now look at the definition for func1(). In the function prototype, the argument has been changed to be an int pointer. This tells the compiler to create an integer pointer named ptr and place the value sent to the function into the rvalue of ptr. Because rvalues of pointer variables are supposed to be memory addresses, what comes into func1() should be an lvalue. We can tell from the argument of func1(&i) in main() that we are sending the lvalue of i to func1().

Listing 7.3. *Using Pointers to Change Values Out of Scope*

```
#include <stdio.h>

void func1(int *integer);      /* Prototype using integer pointer */

void main(void)
{
    int i;

    i = 9;
    printf("i: lvalue = %p    rvalue = %d\n", &i, i);

    func1(&i);                          /* Note the address-of operator here */

    printf("after func1() i: lvalue = %p    rvalue = %d\n", &i, i);}

void func1(int *ptr)
{
    printf("in func1() ptr: lvalue = %p    rvalue = %p\n", &ptr, ptr);
    *ptr = *ptr * *ptr;
    printf("in func1() ptr: lvalue = %p    rvalue = %p\n", &ptr, ptr);
}
```

The statement

```
    *ptr = *ptr * *ptr;
```

looks intimidating, but it need not be so. The intent is clear if you use parentheses to group things a bit, such as

```
    *ptr = (*ptr) * (*ptr);
```

This statement says, "Use indirection to get whatever ptr points to, square that value, and reassign it back into whatever ptr points to." That is, each *ptr expression goes to the memory address of i in main() and gets the value stored there (the scalar is 2 bytes because ptr is defined as an integer pointer). Because the rvalue of ptr is the memory address of i back in main(), the net effect is that we are using indirection to square the value of i in main(). The last printf() in main() should prove this.

When I ran listing 7.3, the output was

```
    i: lvalue = 65530    rvalue = 9
    in func1()  ptr: lvalue = 65528    rvalue = 65530
    in func1()  ptr: lvalue = 65528    rvalue = 65530
    after func1()  i: lvalue = 65530    rvalue = 81
```

The first line doesn't change between listings 7.2 and 7.3. Note that i is stored at memory location 65530. The next two lines tell us that ptr is stored at memory address 65528, but its rvalue is 65530—the same address as i in main(). Therefore, using indirection on ptr (that is, *ptr) means that you are actually manipulating variable i in main()! The final printf() proves that you did, in fact, square i in func1(). This is pretty powerful stuff!

> Pointers provide a means by which you can still hide data if you want to (as shown by the local scope and auto storage class of i in main(), listing 7.3), yet you can use indirection to change its value if you need to, even though the variable is not in scope.

Changing i outside its own scope, however, must be done in a purposeful manner. You must use indirection to communicate i's value to a different scope level. Only when you use a pointer in a deliberate way can "outsiders" have access to variables with local scope. This means that you can protect such variables from outside forces, yet allow those outside forces to change data if need be. All of this is possible because of pointers and the process of indirection.

Implications of Using Pointers

One of the major strengths of C is the privacy it can afford to data items. As you saw in Chapter 6, variables defined within a function or statement block are private to that block. This data privacy reduces the chance of altering a data item by mistake. Some languages such as BASIC have all items globally available: there is no data privacy. Inadvertent changes to a data item are a serious problem for such languages.

C, on the other hand, gives you a choice of local or global scope. Although global scope eliminates the need for passing arguments to functions or using pointers, the price paid is that your data is wide open to contamination throughout the program. "Side-effect" bugs become a real problem.

Things are different in C. Chapter 6 showed that a function does not have direct access to data items defined in some other function. Even when you pass the value of a data item to that function, it receives a *copy*—not the actual data item itself. This permits us to use data in the privacy of a function without the fear of affecting it elsewhere by mistake.

Yet there are many situations in which one function needs to alter a data item defined in another function. As you saw in listing 7.3, you can use pointers and indirection to make variables defined in one function available to another function.

Pointers provide you with a nice middle ground. You can define a data item with local scope, and then use a pointer to let some function that is not in scope alter the value of the data item as required.

A second reason for using pointers is that they often are the most efficient way of accomplishing a given task. As you will see later in this chapter and in Chapter 8, pointers often result in faster programs that use less memory.

Pointers and Arrays

As you probably know, an array is a collection of identical data items that can be treated as a unit. Suppose, for example, that we define a character array

```
char day[5]
```

and that the compiler places the beginning of one array at memory location 50,000. The memory image would be as shown in figure 7.8.

Fig. 7.8. Memory image of an array.

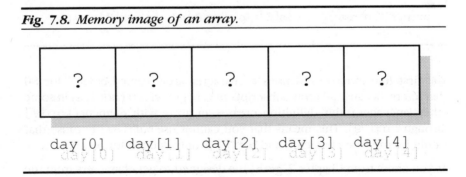

Notice that arrays in C begin with element 0. Because arrays do begin with element 0, the last usable element in the array is day[4], not day[5] as would be the case in other languages. Also, because C does not check array boundaries, you must pay attention to the index numbers used when working with arrays. We will have more to say about arrays later in this and other chapters.

Using Arrays of *char*

An intimate relationship exists between pointers and array variables in C. Listing 7.4 shows how you might use a character array in a program.

Listing 7.4. Character Arrays and Pointers

```
#include <stdio.h>

void func1(char *s);

void main(void)
{
   char buff[80];

   printf("Enter up to 75 characters:\n");
   gets(buff);
   printf("\n&buff=%p     &buff[0]=%p   buff=%s\n",
          &buff, &buff[0], buff);
   func1(buff);
}

void func1(char *s)
{
   printf("\n\n&s=%p     &s[0]=%p   s=%s\n", &s, &s[0], s);
}
```

The first line in main() defines a character array named buff[] for 80 characters. Because all array subscripts in C begin with 0 (not 1, as in some other languages), this definition creates an array with elements buff[0] through buff[79]. This means that you cannot use buff[80] because that would be the 81st character, and buff[] is only defined for 80 characters.

As you know from Chapter 2, gets() is designed to get characters from the keyboard and place them sequentially in the buff[] array until a carriage return (the Enter or Return key on most keyboards) is read. When gets() sees the carriage return character, it assumes this is the end of data entry. It then replaces the carriage return with a special character called the *null* character.

Character Arrays and the Null Character

The null character is special in C because it marks the end of a string. For example, if gets() is called and you type "Hello", the memory image of buff[] would look like figure 7.9.

Fig. 7.9. Memory image of a string, with a null character marking the end.

buff[0] buff[1] buff[2] buff[3] buff[4] buff[5]

H	e	l	l	o	'\0'

Notice that the null character appears at the end of the string typed in by the user. (Although they are not shown here, there are also 74 bytes of junk in buff[] after the null, even though we did not use those bytes.)

The character representation for the null character is

'\0'

When printf() wants to display a string, it does so by putting characters to the screen until it encounters the null character. Therefore, the null character is taken to mean "end of string" in C. (In this way C differs from other languages like Pascal and BASIC, in which the first byte of the string holds a count of the number of characters in the string.) Keep in mind that the null character is a single character in memory even though it looks like a backslash-zero pair of characters.

Another useful thing to know about the null character is that a logical test using the null character will always return logical False. For example,

```
if ('\0') {
   printf("Logical True");
} else {
   printf("Logical False");
}
```

Programming Tip

Finding the Length of a String

A common task in working with character strings is determining the length of a string. A function named strlen() from the standard library provides a simple solution to the task. The function prototype for strlen() is

```
int strlen (char str[]);
```

which says that strlen() returns an integer number equal to the length of string held in str[].

There are two important facts about strlen() to keep in mind. First, the null character is *not* counted when computing the length of the string (that is, the string "Mary" has a length of four). Only the characters are counted; not the null.

The second fact to remember is that the definition of a character array, such as

```
char buff[5Ø];
```

does not mean that strlen() always returns 50 as the length of the string. If "Mary" is presently in buff[], strlen() would return a value of four, not 50.

---

would print Logical False because a logical test on the null character results in a logical False condition. It also follows that a pointer to a null character also produces a logical False result when used in a logical test. As you shall see later in this chapter, this can be useful when you are processing character strings.

Returning to listing 7.4, printf() displays the lvalue for buff and buff[Ø] and then uses the %s conversion character to display buff[] as a string. Lastly, func1() is called, using buff as its argument.

In the definition of func1(), we have prototyped the argument passed to the function as a character pointer. Then printf() is called to display the same information shown in main(). When I ran the program, the output was

```
Enter up to 75 characters:
Hello

&buff=65452     &buff[Ø]=65452     buff=Hello

&s=6545Ø     &s[Ø]=65452     s=Hello
```

You can learn several interesting things from the output of listing 7.4. First, buff and buff[Ø] have the same lvalue. This means that the name of an array variable is viewed by the compiler as the lvalue for the array. The name of an array without the array subscript is the same as the name of the array with a subscript of zero (that is, the address of buff and buff[Ø] are the same). The memory image of buff[] looks as it did before, except that the memory addresses actually used by the compiler have been added (see fig. 7.10).

Fig. 7.10. *Equivalence of* &buff *and* &buff[0].

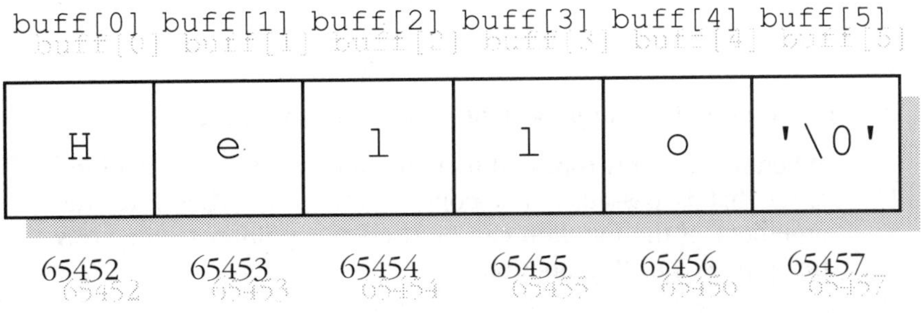

```
buff[0] buff[1] buff[2] buff[3] buff[4] buff[5]
```

H	e	l	l	o	'\0'
65452	65453	65454	65455	65456	65457

The second important thing to notice is what happens when func1() is called, using buff as its argument. We define the argument passed to func1() as a character pointer (char *s). In the function body, we print out the lvalue and rvalue of the character pointer being passed to func1() (s). Notice that the lvalue is a different value, but the rvalue of s is the lvalue of buff[] from main(). The memory image is shown in figure 7.11.

The result is as expected: A new pointer variable (s) contains the address at which buff[] is stored in main(). This means that s has been initialized to point to buff[] in main(). The variable s can be used to reference buff[] via indirection.

Fig. 7.11. Pointer s *in* func1( ) *vs.* buff[] *in* main( ).

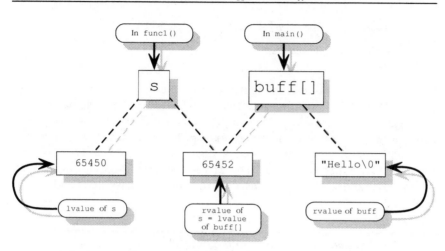

You can now draw an important conclusion about arrays:

> Whenever an array is passed to a function, it is the lvalue of the array that is passed, not a copy of the array. Therefore, the argument of the function can be used as a pointer to the array being passed to the function.

The Define-Declare Debate and Arrays as Function Arguments

Given the rule above about passing arrays to functions, we could change the first line in the function definition of func1( ) to

```
void func1(char s[])
```

and it would make no difference to func1( ). In fact, you could use any one of the following for the first line of the definition of func1( ):

```
void func1(char *s)
void func1(char s[80])
void func1(char s[])
```

and the program would behave exactly as before. This is because func1() is receiving a pointer to char, and all three forms of func1() above resolve the function argument as a pointer to char.

The first example of the argument to func1() (char *s) was just explained by listing 7.4. The second example (char s[80]) should have intuitive appeal, because it looks much the same as buff[] in main(). The third one may seem strange at first glance.

Why can we omit the subscript size of the array in func1()? The reason is that the storage for the array has already been defined in main(). All we are doing in the prototype for func1() is telling the function what type of data is being passed to it. Because C does not perform boundary checking on arrays, the function need not know anything about the size of the array, only that it is an array. This is a classic example of the difference between defining a variable and only declaring it. The storage for the array passed to func1() was allocated in main(). We have declared in func1() what the data item is, not its size.

The empty brackets after the array name are viewed in the same manner as a pointer. This means we are declaring a pointer data type. All we are doing in func1() is telling the compiler what type of data is being passed into func1() so that the function knows how the argument can be used in the function body of func1().

Figure 7.11 verifies what the output of the program tells us. That is, the rvalue of s[] in func1() is the lvalue of buff[] in main(). Therefore, s is a pointer that points to buff[].

Null Pointers

You will hear programmers refer to something as a "null pointer." There is one exception to the rule that pointers are not the same as integers: when the pointer has a value of zero. If a pointer has a value of zero as its rvalue, it is said to be a *null pointer*. A null pointer can never point to valid data.

Pointers in Logical Tests

A common use of a null pointer is in a function call to request additional memory storage from the operating system. The ANSI standard library function for a request for storage is the calloc() function. (This is explained further in Chapter 8.) If the operating system can supply more memory, the function returns a pointer to that additional storage. If all available memory is used up, the function returns a null pointer.

Because a null pointer equates to the value zero, you might see something like the following in a program:

```
ptr = calloc(100, sizeof(char));
if (ptr) {
    printf("More memory available");
} else {
    printf("Out of memory");
    abort_now();
}
```

If we can get 100 bytes of storage from the operating system, the rvalue of ptr will be the memory address of that 100 bytes of storage. If 100 bytes are not available, a null pointer is returned. Many functions use the fact that a null (zero) pointer is guaranteed not to point to valid data. A pointer can be used in a test condition; if the pointer is null, its value equates to a logical False. The preceding code fragment shows how a null pointer might be used with an if statement.

You can, therefore, use a pointer in a logical test, using a null pointer to indicate an exception or error condition.

Incrementing and Decrementing Pointers

Often you will want to "march through" an array, performing some operation on each element as you go. This section explains how you can do this by using pointers.

Suppose that you want to write a program that simply displays a character string on the screen. (This would be similar to the puts( ) function in the standard library.) Listing 7.5 shows how this might be done.

Listing 7.5. Incrementing a Pointer

```c
#include <stdio.h>

#define MAXBUF  128

void show_string(char *s);

void main(void)
{
    char buff[MAXBUF];

    printf("Enter a string: ");
    gets(buff);
    show_string(buff);
}

void show_string(char *s)
{
    while (*s) {
      printf("%c", *s++);
    }
}
```

The function show_string( ) does all of the work. We use buff[ ] as an argument to show_string( ) and define its argument as a character pointer s. The while loop uses indirection to examine each character pointed to by s. As long as a non-null character is read, the while loop continues to execute.

Notice that a post-increment operator is used in the printf() statement. You need to use the post-increment so that you display the character first and then move on to the next character. If you use a pre-increment operator, you would never see the first character in the string. Think about it.

Eventually, *s will point to the null character at the end of the string. Because the null character equates to a logical False condition, the while loop terminates after all of the characters have been displayed.

Pointers as Arguments to Functions

Let's re-examine the output that was produced by listing 7.3. Figure 7.12 shows the same output values, but in an lvalue-rvalue format.

Fig. 7.12. *The output of listing 7.3.*

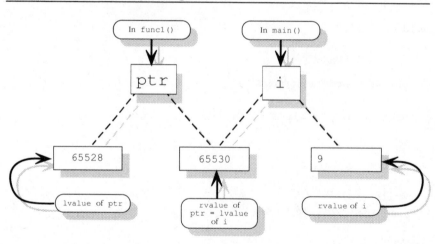

As you would expect, the lvalue of i in main() is the rvalue of ptr in func1(). The other thing to note is that ptr has a different lvalue than i, but its rvalue *is* the lvalue of i in main(). Therefore, passing an lvalue in a function call is the same as initializing the pointer. That is,

```
void main(void)
{
```

```
    ...
    func1(&i);
    ...
}
void func1(int *ptr)
{
```

has the same effect as executing the statement

```
ptr = &i;
```

The func1(&i) call in main() causes the pointer argument defined in

```
func1(int *ptr)
```

to be initialized to the lvalue of i (that is, &i). It is important to remember that func1() does create a new variable called ptr but its rvalue is the lvalue (address) of i in main(). Because ptr points to i, we can use indirection to change the rvalue of i. Under no circumstances can you change the lvalue of i in main().

In this chapter, we have called some functions with the variable name preceded by the address-of operator (for example, func1(&i)), and other calls have simply used the variable name without the address-of operator (for example, func1(name)). In both cases, however, func1() is defined to receive a pointer data type (for example, the function definition might be void func1(char *ptr)). How do you know when to use the address-of operator when passing a pointer to a function?

The rule is simple:

> If a function expects a pointer data type as its argument,
> use the address-of operator in front of the variable name if
> the data item being passed is not an array or pointer.

To illustrate, consider the following code fragment:

```
int i, vals[10];

i = 10;
vals[0] = 10;

printf("%u   %p", i, vals);
```

If you used this code fragment in a program, it would display something like

```
10    65530
```

which says that using `i` without the address-of operator gives you the rvalue of `i`. On the other hand, using the name of an array variable by itself in an expression gives you the lvalue of the array variable. Extending the code fragment,

```
int i, vals[1Ø];

i = 1Ø;
vals[Ø] = 1Ø;

printf("%u    %p", i, vals);
func1(i);
func2(vals);
```

the call to `func1()` would pass the rvalue of `i` to the function. Because the function expects a pointer data type, however, `func1()` will think that the value passed to it (that is, 10) is a memory address. This probably means that the pointer in `func1()` points into the operating system! Usually, this doesn't work too well.

The call to `func2()` also uses the variable name without the address-of operator. However, we know that array names equate to the memory address of the first element of the array (`vals = &vals[Ø]`) which is an lvalue. Because `vals` is an lvalue, `func2()` can use the argument as a pointer, and the program will behave as expected.

When you pass a variable that is not an array or pointer to a function that expects a pointer as its argument, you must use the address-of operator in front of the variable name. If both functions in the example expect to receive a pointer data type, the proper calls to the functions would be

```
func1(&i);
func2(vals);
```

Both these calls pass an lvalue to their respective functions and would allow them to perform their tasks in the correct manner.

▼ # Review Questions and Exercises

1. What steps are required to use a pointer correctly?

2. Write a function that determines the length of a string that is typed in by the user.

3. Is the following code fragment syntactically "legal"?

```
int func1(int s[])
{
    while (*s + +) {
        /* Do something here */
    }
    return *s;
}
```

What value is returned from the function?

4. Suppose that you have a purchase order number that always consists of three letters (for example, the initials of the person buying the item) followed by digits that represent the date (for example, JJP010188). Write a function that copies the letter component of the purchase order into a character array and the date component into an integer. The original purchase order array, the character array to hold the letters, and the integer should be passed as arguments to the function.

▼ # Answers

1. You must (1) define the pointer (for example, int i, *ptr;), (2) initialize the pointer to point to something (ptr = &i;), and (3) use indirection on the pointer (*ptr = 5;). These steps will assign 5 into i via indirection.

2. The function slen() behaves much the same way as strlen() in your standard library.

```
#include <stdio.h>

#define MAXBUF   128

int slen(char *s);
```

```
void main(void)
{
    char buff[MAXBUF];

    printf("Enter a string: ");
    gets(buff);
    printf("\nThe length of the string is %d", slen(buff));
}

int slen(char *s)
{
    int i = 0;

    while (*s ++)
      i ++;

    return i;
}
```

The program is pretty simple. The only strange part might be

```
while (*s ++)
```

which first examines what s points to and then increments the pointer.
If s points to the null string-termination character, the while views the
result of the test on s as logical False and terminates the loop. This
means that i will contain the number of non-null characters, and that
number is the length of the string.

3. Because s[] resolves to a pointer data type in the argument list of a
   function definition, the code fragment is perfectly legal. Note that the
   following is not legal:

```
void main()
{
    int s[10];

    s ++;                     /* Not legal */
}
```

This is an attempt to change the address at which s[] is stored in
memory (its lvalue) because s is simply an abbreviation for where the
array is stored in memory. That is, s is equivalent syntactically to &s[0].
If you think about it, you'll see that the compiler should never let you
change an lvalue. Only rvalues can be manipulated in a program. If the
compiler allowed you to change lvalues directly, it could never find the
data item again.

In func1(), the while loop continues to increment pointer s until the null statement is read. However, because we use a post-increment on s in the while loop, when the loop ends, s points to the character stored after the null character. Therefore, the return value will be the character stored after the null at the end of the string. This will probably be whatever random junk was at that memory location when the program started.

4. The program could be written as

```
#include <stdio.h>
#include <stdlib.h>
#include <string.h>

#define MAXINIT  3                    /* Always 3 initials */

void separate(char s[], char *initials, int *date);

void main(void)
{
   char buff[5], po[15];
   int date;

   printf("Enter the purchase order number: ");
   gets(po);

   separate(po, buff, &date);

   printf("\n\nP.O.=%s, initials = %s, date = %d\n",
          po, buff, date);
}

void separate(char s[], char *initials, int *date)
{
   strncpy(initials, s, MAXINIT);
   initials[3] = '\0';    /* Make it a string */


   *date = atoi(&s[3]);  /* Start with the first date char */
}
```

Because we expect the initials to consist of three characters in all cases, we #define a constant named MAXINT for three characters. The program asks the user to enter a PO number, which is placed in the character array po[] by the call to gets(). We call separate() with the arguments necessary to complete the task. Because the name of an array equates to an lvalue, we do not use the address-of operator (&) before the array variables. However, because you want to assign the date value in separate( ) and it is not an array, you must use the address-of operator in front of its name (that is, &date) so that you can use indirection to change its value.

In separate( ), you use the standard library function strncpy( ) to copy the first three characters of the purchase order into the initials[ ] array. You then assign initials[3] to the null terminator so that you can treat the array as a string.

You know that atoi( ) converts the character digits of the date to a numeric value. Note that you tell atoi( ) to start with element four (which is actually s[3] because arrays start with element zero) of the purchase order character array. Because an array name by itself equates to element zero of the array (that is, s is the same as &s[Ø]) and you want to start with the fourth element, you must use the address-of operator in front of the array element (atoi(&s[3])).

Program control then returns to main( ), prints out the results, and ends.

8

Using Pointers Effectively

Concepts in This Chapter

- ❑ Valid pointer operations
- ❑ Pointer arithmetic
- ❑ How pointers can save memory space
- ❑ Why pointers are often faster than array indexes
- ❑ How to use pointers to function
- ❑ The Right-Left Rule for deciphering complex data definitions

This chapter builds on what you learned in Chapter 7. You should be comfortable with the contents of that chapter before you read this one. In particular, you should know how to define a pointer variable, initialize it, and use indirection to change what the pointer points to. The concepts presented in this chapter build on those concepts.

Using Equality and Relational Operators with Pointers

Variables of the pointer data type can be tested for equality (==) and inequality (!=) when both operands are pointers (ptr1 == ptr2) or when one operand is a null pointer (ptr != NULL or ptr != '\Ø'). Obviously, it makes little sense to perform an equality test if the pointers point to different data types.

Relational tests (such as >=, <=, >, and <) on pointers are acceptable only when both operands are pointers. That is,

```
if (ptr1  < ptr2) {
    . . .
}
```

is acceptable, but

```
if (ptr1 > 1Ø) {
    . . .
}
```

is not. The second form is not acceptable because constants are not a pointer data type. (You can get around this by using the cast operator, which is explained in a later chapter.) The first form is acceptable because both operands are pointer data types.

Programming Tip

Invalid Pointer Comparisons

Do not compare two pointers if they do not point to the same data item. In other words, you cannot compare two pointers if those pointers do not point to the same variable. Some compilers do not detect this type of error, and it can be difficult to track down bugs caused by incorrect pointer comparisons.

Pointer Arithmetic

Listing 8.1 shows how the compiler uses pointer arithmetic in a program.

Listing 8.1. *Pointer Arithmetic*

```c
#include <stdio.h>
#include <string.h>

void func1(char *s);

void main(void)
{
    char buff[8Ø];
    int i, len;

    printf("Enter up to 75 characters:\n");
    gets(buff);

    len = strlen(buff);
    for (i = Ø; i < len; i++) {
        printf("%c", buff[i]);
    }
    printf("\n\ngoing into func1()\n\n");
    func1(buff);
}

void func1(char *s)
{
    int i, len;

    len = strlen(s);

    printf("First, we use an index:\n");
    for (i = Ø; i < len; i++) {
        printf("%c", *(s + i) );
    }

    printf("\n\nNow for the pointer version:\n");
    for (i = Ø; i < len; i++) {
        printf("%c", *s++);
    }

}
```

In listing 8.1, we #include the string.h header file because we use the strlen() library function to find the length of the string held in buff[]. In main(), the user is asked to enter a string of up to 75 characters. (A good test string to enter is "1234567890".) The program then proceeds to print the string out character by character in a for loop using variable i as an array index.

The program then calls func1() with buff[] as its argument. Once again, we have defined the argument passed to func1() as a char pointer (char *s). The program then uses a for loop and pointer arithmetic to display the contents of the string whose address is passed from main().

So what does the following expression do?

    *(s + i)

Its purpose is to yield the character "i bytes after" the character at s[Ø]. If you look at table 3.7 in Chapter 3, you will see that the indirection operator has higher precedence than does the addition operator. Because you want to add the offset i to s before performing indirection on the pointer, the parentheses are necessary. If they were omitted, the program would perform the indirection and then add i to the character pointed to by s—not what we want to do!

Now let's look at what's inside the parentheses:

    s + i

You already know that a variable name by itself in an expression asks for the rvalue of the variable. Because s is a pointer that points to the buff[] defined in main(), the rvalue of s is the lvalue of buff[]. Suppose that buff[] is stored in memory starting at location 50,000. If you look at buff[], you might see something similar to the diagram shown in figure 8.1.

Fig. 8.1. *Memory image of* buff[].

| '1' | '2' | '3' | '4' | '5' | '6' | '7' | '8' | '9' | '0' | '\0' |

50,000   50,010

In the first `for` loop in `func1()`, when `i` equals 0, the expression

    s + i

is converted to

    5Ø,ØØØ + Ø

We now can write

    *(s + i) = *(5ØØØØ)

The indirection operator tells the program to go to address 50,000 and display what is stored there as a character. (The program knows to use only one byte because s is defined as a character pointer, which has a scalar of one.) The program then displays a '1' on the screen. On the next iteration of the `for` loop, the program would solve the expression

    *(s + i) = *(5ØØØØ + 1) = *(5ØØØ1)

and display the character '2'.

The program continues to do this operation until the entire string has been displayed (len is used to control the number of characters displayed). The output in func1() becomes

    1234567890

In the second for loop in func1(), s is incremented on each pass through the loop, showing what it points to. The output is the same as that of the first loop.

The Importance of Scalars

What is not obvious in listing 8.1 is that the compiler automatically adjusts i for the scalar size of the pointer. You can think of the scalar for s as a "scaling factor" for i (that idea was illustrated in figure 7.2): the compiler generates code so that whenever we add i to s in the expression s + i, i is adjusted to the size of a char before it is added to s.

To the compiler, the expression

    *(s + i)

actually looks like

    *(s + (i * sizeof(char))

Because the size of a character is usually one byte, it appears that nothing special is being done by the compiler when s and i are added together. The expression becomes

    *(s + (i * sizeof(char)) = *(s + (i * 1))

which has no effect on i.

To prove that such scaling is being done, make the following change to func1():

```
void func1(int *s)              /* Notice the int now */
{
    int i, len;

    len = 5;                        /* Notice the constant */

    printf("First, we use an index:\n");
    for (i = 0; i < len; i++) {
        printf("%c", *(s + i) );
    }
```

```
    printf("\n\nNow for the pointer version:\n");
    for (i = 0; i < len; i++) {
        printf("%c", *s++);
    }

}
```

The only changes are (1) we have "lied" to func1() and told it that the argument being passed to it is an *integer pointer*, not a character pointer, and (2) we removed the call to strlen() and set len to 5. (We assume you enter the same string as before—"1234567890".)

When you compile the program, you may get a warning about mixing an integer pointer with a character pointer. Just ignore the warning for now; you're lucky enough to have a compiler that pays attention to details! Now when you run the program, the output becomes

    13579

Why? Because of the changed definition of s in func1(), func1() thinks it has been passed a pointer to int rather than a pointer to char. With these changes, the compiler generates code that sets the scalar for i to that of an int.

Assuming that an integer is two bytes, the expression

    *(s + i)

now becomes

    *(s + (i * sizeof(int)) = *(s + (i * 2))

On the first pass through the loop in func1(), the expression is

    *(s + (i * sizeof(int)) = *(s + (0 * 2)) = *(50000 + 0)

which displays a '1' on the screen.

On the next iteration of the for loop, the expression becomes

    *(s + (i * sizeof(int)) = *(s + (1 * 2)) = *(50000 + 2)

which displays a '3' on the screen. This shows why the character '2' is not printed and leads us to an important conclusion about pointers.

> Pointer arithmetic is always scaled by the size of the data item being pointed to.

Because the scalar for an int is twice as large as the scalar for a char, we will skip over a character on each pass through the loop. Because we use a character conversion in the printf( ), we still see the data displayed as a character.

Notice that this "skipping" behavior is consistent. That is, in the second for loop in func1( ), the increment operation on s is also scaled by the size of an int. The second loop will display the same information as the first loop ("13579").

The concept of scalars also can help you understand why you must define pointers in a way that agrees with the object pointed to. That is, defining a char pointer and then initializing the pointer to a double isn't going to work too well. The conclusion should be clear: All pointer arithmetic is scaled by the size of the object being pointed to, and pointers should be initialized to point to variables of the proper data type with the same scalar.

Programming Tip

A Common Problem with Pointers

It's not uncommon to define a data item in one function as a char, and then define a function to receive the data item as some other data type. That is what was done by the modification of func1( )s argument in listing 8.1: it created a mismatch between the true size of the elements in buff[ ] as defined in main( ) and the size of the item referenced by pointer s defined in func1( ).

Mistakes like this often show themselves as a "skipping" behavior followed by "junk" values. (In listing 8.1, the call to strlen( ) was removed and len was set equal to 5 so that junk was not displayed on the screen. Why would junk be displayed if len were not changed?)

Any time the first value of a pointer is correctly displayed, but subsequent output seems to skip the value expected or to display junk, chances are good that there is a mismatch between the pointer being used to reference the data (for example, an int) and the size of the actual data (for example, a char).

Two-Dimensional Arrays and Pointers

Two-dimensional arrays are used often in programming, especially when working with tabular data. For example, if we want to define a two-dimensional character array for the days of the week, we would use

```
char days[7][1Ø]          /*   C    */
```

Similar definitions in Pascal and BASIC would be

```
days [Ø..7, Ø..1Ø]        {Pascal}
```

```
days (7, 1Ø)              'BASIC
```

All three state that there are seven elements in the array, each of which can hold up to 10 characters.

Listing 8.2 shows one way that you can use a two-dimensional array of characters.

Listing 8.2. *Two Dimensional Array of Characters*

```
#include  <stdio.h>

#define DAYS    7
#define LEN     1Ø

void main(void)
{
   static char days[DAYS][LEN] = {
       "Monday", "Tuesday", "Wednesday","Thursday",
       "Friday", "Saturday","Sunday"
       };

   int i, j;

   for (i = Ø; i  < DAYS; i + +) {
      printf("\n%p ", &days[i][Ø]);
      for (j = Ø; days[i][j]; j + +) {
         printf("%c", days[i][j]);
      }
   }
}
```

Data item days[] is defined as a two-dimensional array of characters. Symbolic constants were used to specify the size of the array. DAYS is 7 and LEN is 10. (LEN must be 10 because "Wednesday" is the longest element in the array, requiring 9 characters plus one character more for the null terminator for a character string.) days[] was defined with the static storage-class modifier so that the array can be initialized with either a K&R or ANSI compiler. (ANSI allows auto storage class variables to be initialized, while K&R does not.)

Listing 8.2 uses two for loops to display the characters in the array. On the first pass through the loop, the first printf() displays where days[0][0] is stored in memory.

Program control now enters the for loop controlled by j. Notice how the second expression is written by using

    days[i][j]

When the j loop begins, we reference days[0][0] (that is, i and j are both equal to 0). This means we are looking at the 'M' in "Monday," which we print out using the %c conversion character in printf(). We then increment j to 1 and look at days[0][1] in the second expression of the for. Because days[0][1] is 'o,' not zero, we display the letter 'o' and increment j again. This continues this until we see "Monday" displayed on the screen. The 'y' in "Monday" corresponds to days[0][5] in the loop.

Notice what happens on the next pass through the j loop, when we examine days[0][6]. Because "Monday" was initialized as a double-quoted string constant, the compiler has added the null termination character '\0' to the end of the string. Because the null character equates to a logical False, the second expression of the inner for loop (that is, days[i][j] or days[0][6]) evaluates to logical False and the j loop terminates. Program control then passes back to the third expression of the for loop controlled by i, which increments i (i++).

Once again, the program displays the address of days[1][0] and falls into the j loop. Because days[1][0] is where the 'T' in "Tuesday" is stored, the program displays the next day of the week. The program continues in this manner until all of the days of the week are displayed.

When I ran the program, the output was

    39 Monday
    49 Tuesday
    59 Wednesday
    69 Thursday
    79 Friday
    89 Saturday
    99 Sunday

The output of listing 8.2 confirms two important facts:

1. Each element of the days[ ][ ] array is allocated 10 bytes of storage even though the only day that requires that much storage is "Wednesday."

2. *It is the second dimension (LEN) in the* days[ ][ ] *definition that determines the scalar size for an increment operation.*

You can prove this last point by modifying the for loop in listing 8.2 to be

```
for (i = Ø; i < DAYS; i++) {
    printf("\n%p  %s", &days[i][Ø], days + i);
}
```

Notice that we have removed the loop controlled by j and added a %s (string) conversion to the printf(). To print out the string, we reference

```
days + i
```

The %p tells us where the days[i][ ] element is stored. Using the memory addresses from the first run, we have

```
days[Ø][Ø] = 39
days[1][Ø] = 49
    .
days[6][Ø] = 99
```

Because the program works as before, we now know that

```
days + i  = 39 +  Ø = 39 = "Monday"
days + i  = 39 + 1Ø = 49 = "Tuesday"
    .
days + i  = 39 + 6Ø = 99 = "Sunday"
```

Notice that each time i is incremented (that is, i++), the address is increased by 10. This is exactly the value of LEN. This tells us an important fact about two-dimensional arrays:

The scalar for a two-dimensional array is equal to the size of the object (as set by the type specifier) times the second dimension in the array definition.

All pointer arithmetic on two-dimensional arrays follows this rule. In terms of listing 8.2, the scalar size is

```
sizeof(char) * LEN = 1 * 1Ø = 1Ø
```

or a scalar size of 10. This is why the expression days + i always increases by 10 each time i is incremented (for example, 39, 49, 59, etc. for the lvalues).

Programming Tip

Determining the Scalar for Two-Dimensional Arrays

Remember that the scalar of a two-dimensional array is determined by two factors, not just one as we have seen in so many earlier examples:

1. The type specifier determines the basic scalar size.

2. The type specifier then is multiplied by the size of the second element of the array to arrive at the final size of the scalar.

The compiler, of course, does all of this for you. However, you still must keep in mind the importance of the second dimension and the type specifier when working with double-dimensioned arrays.

To make sure that you understand the relationship between a scalar and the data definition, figure out the scalar for the following item:

```
long int big[5][5Ø];
```

Assuming that each long requires 4 bytes of storage, the scalar size becomes

```
sizeof(long) * 5Ø = 4 * 5Ø = 2ØØ
```

Therefore, if you look at the addresses of big[Ø][Ø] and big[1][Ø], you will find they are 200 bytes apart. Listing 8.3 confirms this.

Listing 8.3. *Scalar Size*

```
#include <stdio.h>

#define FIRST    5
#define SECOND   50

void func1(long int b[][SECOND]);

void main(void)
{
    long int big[FIRST][SECOND];

    printf("The size of each long is %d\n", sizeof(long));
    printf("\nThe address of big[0][0] is %p", &big[0][0]);
    printf("\nThe address of big[1][0] is %p", &big[1][0]);
    func1(big);

}

void func1(long int b[][SECOND])
{
    printf("\n\n\nThe address of b is %p", b);
    printf("\nThe address of b + 1 is %p", (b + 1) );
}
```

The size of the scalar is best demonstrated in func1(). Note that you can leave the size of the first dimension empty in defining the function argument to func1(). You must, however, supply the second dimension of the array—SECOND in listing 8.3—because the compiler needs to be able to compute the size of the scalar for b[][] and it cannot perform that calculation without the second dimension. If you use a three-dimensional array, you would need to supply the second and third dimensions. Only the first dimension can be left empty. (The first dimension tells *how many* elements there are, not *how big* each one is. To perform pointer arithmetic, however, we must know *how big* each element is, but not *how many* there are.)

Running the program produced the following output:

```
The size of each long is 4

The address of big[0][0] is 64532
The address of big[1][0] is 64732
The address of b is 64532
The address of b + 1 is 64732
```

You can see that moving from big[Ø][Ø] to big[1][Ø] is a 200-byte change—the scalar is 200. In func1(), adding 1 to the lvalue of b[][] also causes a 200-byte change—again, the scalar is 200 (200 = 64732 – 64532).

Programming Tip

The Rule for Scalar Calculations

If you get involved with arrays of three (or more) dimensions, the rules for the size of the scalar are the same. Simply take the basic size of the object as determined by the type specifier and multiply it by the second and third (or more) dimensions. Using the earlier example,

```
long b[5][5Ø];
```

the scalar becomes

```
scalar = sizeof (type specifier) * dimension_list
```

where the dimension_list is the subscript dimension for all but the first dimension. The scalar becomes

```
scalar = sizeof(long) * 5Ø
       = 4 * 5Ø
       = 2ØØ
```

If the definition were

```
long b[5][5Ø][1Ø];
```

the scalar becomes

```
scalar size = sizeof(long) * dimension_list
            = 4 * 5Ø * 1Ø
            = 2ØØØ
```

Notice that the first element in the list is not used.

More on Pointers and Arrays

Listing 8.4 shows how you can use a pointer to reference any element in an array.

Listing 8.4. Using a Pointer To Reference a Two-Dimensional Array

```c
#include <stdio.h>
#include <stdlib.h>

#define FIRST    3
#define SECOND   10

void show_one(int *ptr);
void display(int b[][SECOND]);

void main(void)
{
    char buff[20];
    int b[FIRST][SECOND], i, j, k;

    k = 0;
    for (i = 0; i < FIRST; i++) {
        for (j = 0; j < SECOND; j++) {
            b[i][j] = k;
            k++;
        }
    }
    display(b);
    printf("First index? ");
    index1 = atoi(gets (buff));
    printf("Second index? ");
    index2 = atoi(gets (buff));
    show_one (&b[index1][index2]);
}

void show_one(int *ptr)
{
    printf("\n\nptr points to %d", *ptr);
}


void display(int b[][SECOND])
{
    int i, j;

    for (i = 0; i < FIRST; i++) {
        for (j = 0; j < SECOND; j++) {
            printf("%3d ", b[i][j]);
        }
        printf("\n");
    }
}
```

The for loop in main() simply stuffs the b[][] array with some values that we can examine. The call to display() shows us those values.

The program now asks the user to enter two index numbers that can be used to examine a user-specific element of the array. (To keep things simple, we do no boundary checking on the values entered by the user.) When show_one() is called, the address-of operator is used to pass the memory address (lvalue) of where the user-defined element is stored.

When show_one() is called, the address-of operator (&) is used to pass the memory address where [1][5] is stored. In the definition of show_one(), we have declared that it is being passed a pointer to an int. This is fine because we have passed an lvalue to the function. We can use that lvalue as a pointer as long as we remember that it points to the proper data type (an int in listing 8.4).

As a small exercise, you might want to add the following lines after the printf() in show_one():

```
--ptr;
printf("\nNext lower value is: %d\n", *ptr);
```

You could add a for loop to increment or decrement the pointer to view other elements of the b[][] array in main().

Using Arrays of Pointers

You can make some minor changes to listing 8.2 that will illustrate how you can use an array of pointers to char. This is shown in listing 8.5.

The most significant change in listing 8.5 as compared to listing 8.2 is that days[] is now defined as an array of pointers to char. The effect of the change is best discussed in terms of the output of listing 8.5. The output is for my system is

```
83 Monday
85 Tuesday
87 Wednesday
89 Thursday
91 Friday
93 Saturday
95 Sunday
```

Listing 8.5. *An Array of Pointers to* char

```c
#include  <stdio.h>

#define DAYS      7

void main(void)
{
    static char *days[DAYS] = {
        "Monday",  "Tuesday",  "Wednesday","Thursday",
        "Friday",  "Saturday","Sunday"
        };

    int i;

    for (i = Ø;  i  < DAYS;  i ++) {
        printf("\n%u ", &days[i]);
        printf("%s", days[i]);
    }
}
```

In the output of listing 8.2, on the other hand, the numbers were in increments of 10, not 2. This is because each element in the array had to be as large as the day of the week with the most characters in it ("Wednesday") plus one character for the null terminator. In listing 8.5, the numbers are in increments of 2 because my compiler uses two bytes of storage for each pointer. In all other respects, the output of this program is the same as the output of listing 8.2.

In memory, the days[] arrays might look like figure 8.2.

Fig. 8.2. *Memory image for an array of pointers.*

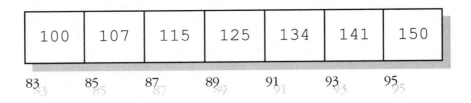

100	107	115	125	134	141	150

83   85   87   89   91   93   95

Figure 8.2 points out a subtle difference between listing 8.2 and listing 8.5. In listing 8.2, the days[][] array required 70 bytes of storage (that is, 10 bytes for each day times seven days). In listing 8.5, only 56 bytes of storage are required. The pointer version does not waste space padding the array to accommodate the largest element in the array. With listing 8.5 using an array of pointers to char, the compiler only allocates exactly the storage required to hold the data; there is no padding. This example shows how pointers can save memory space over double-dimensioned arrays, yet still accomplish the same task.

Allocating Memory Space at Run Time

At times, you will need to allocate storage for a variable after the program has begun execution. For instance, the size of a variable might be determined by user input or some other value that is not known until run-time. Listing 8.6 uses the Magic Square problem to illustrate how this is done.

A magic square is a square in which the rows, the columns, and the diagonals all sum to the same number. For example, figure 8.3 shows a magic square in which the common sum is 15. That is, in the top row 4 + 9 + 2 = 15; in the first column 4 + 3 + 8 = 15, and diagonal 4 + 5 + 6 = 15. The algorithm presented in listing 8.6 only works for matrices with a size that is an odd number greater than 1. (Solving magic squares for even-sized matrices is considerably more complex.)

Although listing 8.6 is longer than most programs you've seen so far, it really isn't difficult to understand. The function get _size( ) asks the user to enter the size of the matrix to be used. Because the matrix must be odd, the function will only accept an odd number that is greater than 1.

Fig. 8.3. *A 3×3 magic square.*

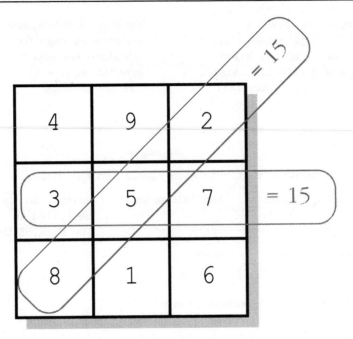

Listing 8.6. *Magic Square with Dynamic Memory Allocation*

```
#include  <stdio.h>
#include  <stdlib.h>

int magic(int row, int col, int n),
    get_size(void),
    *get_room(int);

void show_magic(int *matrix, int n),
     do_magic(int *s, int n);

void main()
{
   int *matrix, size;
```

Listing 8.6 continues

Listing 8.6 continued

```
    size = get_size();          /* How Big is the square    */
    matrix = get_room(size);    /* Get some storage for it  */
    do_magic(matrix, size);     /* Calculate the square     */
    show_magic(matrix, size);   /* Show the square          */
    free( (void *) matrix);     /* Free the storage         */
}


/*****
                            do_magic()

        Function that sets each element in the matrix.

        Argument list:      int *elements       pointer to the matrix to
                                                be filled in
                            int n               the size of the matrix

        Return value:       void
*****/

void do_magic(int *elements, int n)
{
    int i, j;

    for (i = 0; i < n; i++)
        for (j = 0; j < n; j++, elements++)
            *elements = magic(i + 1, j + 1, n);
}


/*****
                            show_magic()

        Function that displays the magic square.

        Argument list:      int *elements       pointer to the matrix to
                                                be filled in
                            int n               the size of the matrix

        Return value:       void
*****/

void show_magic(int *elements, int n)
{
    int i, j;
```

```
    for (i = Ø; i < n; i++) {
        for (j = Ø; j < n; j++, elements++) {
            printf("%4d", *elements);
        }
        printf("\n");
    }
}
/*****
                            get_room()
```

Function that allocates enough space to hold the magic square.

Argument list:	int n	the size of the matrix
Return value:	int *	pointer to the storage for the matrix.

```
*****/

int *get_room(int n)
{
    int *ptr;

    ptr = (int *) calloc( (unsigned) n, sizeof(int));
    if (ptr == NULL) {
        printf("Out of memory. Abort.\n");
        exit(1);
    }
    return ptr;
}

/*****
                            get_size()
```

Function that finds out how big the magic square will be.

Argument list:	void	
Return value:	int	the size of the matrix.

```
*****/

int get_size(void)
{
    char buff[2Ø];
    int n;
```

Listing 8.6 continues

Listing 8.6 *continued*

```
    for (;;) {
       printf("Enter the size matrix desired (must be odd and > 1): ");
       n = atoi(gets(buff));
       if (n % 2 == 1 && n > 1)
          break;
    }

    return n;
}

/*****
                              magic()

        Function that finds the value for each element of the magic
    square.

        Argument list:      int row       the row of the matrix to be
                                          filled in.

                            int col       the column of the matrix to be
                                          filled in.

                            int n         the size of the matrix (one
                                          side).

        Return value:       int           the magic number for element
                                          row-col of the matrix.
*****/

int magic(int row, int col, int n)
{
   int term1, term2;

   term1 = col - row + (n - 1) / 2; /* Set initial term values */
   term2 = col + col - row;
   if (term1 >= n)                  /* If term is too large... */
      term1 -= n;
   else
      if (term1 < 0)                /* Or if it's too small... */
         term1 += n;
   if (term2 > n)                   /* Now adjust second term  */
      term2 -= n;
```

```
    else
       if (term2 <= Ø)
          term2 += n;
    return term1 * n + term2;        /* Return magic number      */
}
```

The *calloc()* Function and the Cast Operator

After the size of the matrix is given, the function get _room( ) attempts to get enough storage to hold the matrix. The statement

```
    ptr = (int *) calloc( (unsigned) n, sizeof(int));
```

calls the ANSI standard library function calloc( ) to gain storage for the matrix from the operating system. The first argument tells how many items we want, and the second argument tells how large each item is.

The return data type from calloc( ) is a pointer to void. However, because you need a pointer to int, you must *cast* the return value.

A *cast* is an operator that converts one data type to another type. The general form is

```
    (data_type) expression
```

The cast operator is nothing more than an opening parenthesis followed by the name of the data type desired, followed by a closing parenthesis. The value of expression is converted to the data type enclosed by the parentheses.

In the example, expression is the return value from calloc(). That function returns a pointer to void. Because you need a pointer to int, the calloc( ) call (shortened to omit unneeded detail) is

```
    ptr = (int *) calloc();
```

We can verbalize this statement as "Take the pointer to void returned by calloc(), use a cast operator to force it to be a pointer to integer, and assign that integer pointer into ptr." Without the cast operator, we might draw an error message from the compiler because we would be trying to assign a void pointer into an int pointer. (Technically, a void pointer does not need a cast. However, because omitting the cast might promote sloppy coding practices and the cast helps document the program, you should always cast the pointer returned by calloc().)

After the value returned from calloc() is cast to an integer pointer, we test the pointer (ptr) to see whether the return value was non-null. A null pointer means there is not enough memory to hold the array, and the program aborts. If the pointer is non-null, the pointer is returned to main() and assigned into matrix.

Next we call do_magic(). Its arguments are matrix and the size of the square. In do_magic(), notice how we simply increment the pointer to the matrix and call magic() to set each value in the square.

After the magic square has been filled in with the appropriate values, show_magic() is called to display the square. The call to free() releases to the operating system the storage that was given to us by the call to calloc(). This lets us reuse the storage if need be. The pointer to the storage (matrix) is cast to a void pointer because that is the type of argument that free() expects.

Always remember that your program should have a matching call to free() for each call to calloc().

Pointer Arithmetic and Double-Dimensioned Arrays

In listing 8.6, we called several functions that used double-dimensioned arrays. Let's explore an alternative way to work with such arrays. Suppose that you constructed a 3 × 3 magic square and that calloc() returned a pointer to memory address 60,000 for the square. In memory, the magic square might look like figure 8.4.

Programming Tip

Use Casts To Avoid Type Mismatches

Many compilers will produce error messages that include the words "Type mismatch". The most common cause of this is attempting to assign one data type into another one without using a cast. For example, compiling the code fragment

```
long big;
float x;

...
...
x = big;
```

would produce a type-mismatch error message because big and x are not of the same data type. Note that this would occur even if a long and a float both require the same amount of storage. The solution to the mismatch problem is to use a cast, such as

```
x = (float) big;
```

In most cases, the cast operator will contain the data type of the variable to the left of the assignment statement.

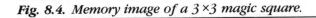

Fig. 8.4. *Memory image of a 3×3 magic square.*

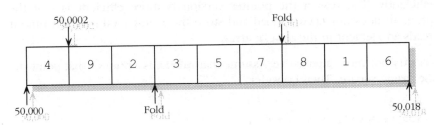

As you can see, a double-dimensioned array is stored as a linear vector in memory. If we had used a data definition statement for the matrix

```
int matrix[3][3];
```

the second dimension sets the scalar for the matrix. The scalar tells where the matrix is "folded" in memory. In figure 8.3, the 3 ×3 matrix would be folded at memory address 50006. This agrees with our rule that the scalar is the size of the type (that is, int = 2) times the second element size (3). Because 2 ×3 = 6, the offset for the first fold is 6 bytes from the start of the array (50,006). This also means that moving from matrix[Ø][Ø] to matrix[1][Ø] involves moving a total of six bytes down the vector stored in memory.

In listing 8.6, a pair of for loops was used to set and display the matrix. These had a form similar to

```
for (i = Ø; i  < 3; i + +) {
   printf("\n");
   for (j = Ø; j  < 3; j + +) {
      printf("%4d", matrix[i][j]);
   }
}
```

Using a pointer to the matrix, we might have

```
for (i = Ø; i  < 3; i + +) {
   printf("\n");
   for (j = Ø; j  < 3; j + +, matrix + +) {
      printf("%4d", *matrix);
   }
}
```

which will process the array exactly as before, although somewhat more efficiently. The reason the pointer version is more efficient is that the program does not need to load and store the i and j values each time it reads an element in the matrix array.

Let's try one more alternative. Assume that matrix is a pointer that points to the magic square. Then consider

```
n = 3;
for (i = Ø; i  < n; i + +) {
   printf("\n");
   for (j = Ø; j  < n; j + +) {
      printf("%4d", *(matrix  + n * i  + j) );
   }
}
```

In this example, pointer arithmetic is used to display the proper element in the array. An integer expression is used to calculate the address of the array element. The address can be broken down into two parts: the base address, plus an offset. That is,

```
*(matrix + n * i + j)
```

has two parts, a base and an offset:

```
base = base address of the matrix (its lvalue) = matrix
offset = n * i + j;
```

Or

```
*(matrix + offset);
```

If you want to examine the element matrix[1][1], all you need is the base address, which equates to the array name, plus an offset. Therefore, the proper pointer address becomes

```
*(matrix + n * i + j)
*(50,000 + 3 * 1 + 1)
*(50,000 + 3 + 1)
*(50,004)
```

This doesn't look like the right memory address. What went wrong? Don't forget that pointer arithmetic uses a scalar on the data. Because we are using a pointer to int, the scalar is 2. Even though the compiler makes the adjustment automatically, we need to restate the offset calculation as

```
offset = (n * i + j) * scalar;
```

Now the calculation becomes

```
*(matrix + (n * i + j) * scalar)
*(50,000 + (3 * 1 + 1) * 2)
*(50,000 + (3 + 1) * 2)
*(50,000 + 4 * 2)
*(50,008)
```

If you examine the memory image for the magic square, you will find that memory address 50,008 does in fact have the correct value of 5 for element matrix[1][1]. Fortunately, we need not worry about multiplying by the scalar. The compiler uses the scalar automatically in all pointer arithmetic.

Programming Tip

"Hand-Optimize" Your Code

In the previous section, the code fragment

```
for (i = 0; i < n; i++) {
   printf("\n");
   for (j = 0; j < n; j++) {
      printf("%4d", *(matrix + n * i + j) );
   }
}
```

is not as efficient as it could be. If you look at the pointer arithmetic, you find two terms that cannot change within the j loop. That is, in the expression

```
*(matrix + n * i + j)
```

neither n nor i change within the j loop. This is an example of *loop invariant* code. Although some compilers will optimize loop invariant code, many don't. In this example, it causes the program to multiply n times i on each pass through the j loop. If you changed the loop slightly, such as

```
int temp; /* New variable here */

for (i = 0; i < n; i++) {
   printf("\n");
   temp = n * i;                    /* New code here */
   for (j = 0; j < n; j++) {
      printf("%4d", *(matrix + temp + j) );
   }
}
```

you get rid of n − 1 multiplications on each pass through the j loop. If n is large, this could save considerable processing time. Can you think of a way to reduce the calculation of temp to a simple add on each pass through the i loop? Would temp += n do it if temp starts at 0? Think about it.

Pointer to Function—A Special Case

A pointer to function is a special case for the pointer data type. If you have defined a pointer to function and initialized it to point to a function, that pointer holds the lvalue of where the function is located in memory. Given what a pointer to function is, therefore, it is not surprising that there are only a few valid things you can do with a pointer to function. You may

❑ Assign into a pointer to function
❑ Invoke a function via a pointer to function
❑ Pass a pointer to function as a function argument

Everything else is illegal (for example, you cannot increment or decrement pointers to functions, add an offset, etc.).

Listing 8.7 shows a simple example of using a pointer to function.

Listing 8.7. *Using a Pointer to Function*

```
#include <stdio.h>

int func1(int val);

void main(void)
{
    int i, func1();
    int (*ptr)(int i);

    i = 123;
    ptr = func1;              /* No parentheses      */
    i = (*ptr)(i);            /* Invoke the function */
    printf("\ni = %d", i);
}

int func1(int val)
{
    printf("\nval is %d", val);

    return (321);
}
```

The definition of the pointer to function:

```
int (*ptr)(int i);
```

appears strange because of the parentheses. The parentheses are necessary, however, to properly define a pointer to function and its argument. If we omitted the first set of parentheses, such as

```
int *ptr(int i);
```

we would be declaring that ptr() is a function returning a pointer to int—not that ptr is a pointer to function.

The next odd statement is

```
ptr = func1;
```

If you think about it, the name of a function all by itself resolves to an lvalue—its address in memory. The statement above simply takes where func1() is stored in memory (an lvalue) and assigns it into ptr. The parentheses must not be used. (If they were present, we would call func1() rather than assign its lvalue into ptr.)

The next line,

```
i = (*ptr)(i);
```

invokes the function that ptr points to using variable i as its argument. That is, the statement is the same as calling func1(), except that we are using a pointer to invoke the function call. We assign the return value from func1() into i and display its new value. When I ran the program, the output was

```
val is 123
i = 321
```

which is exactly what we would expect to see.

The steps in using a pointer to function are the same as those mentioned earlier: define the pointer to function, initialize the pointer, and then use indirection to invoke the function.

Using a Pointer to Function as a Function Argument

Several functions in your standard library use a pointer to function as a function argument. One example is the bsearch() function to perform a binary search. The function prototype for bsearch() is

```
char *bsearch(char *k, char *b, unsigned n, unsigned w,
              int (*comp)(void *indexy, void *indexz));
```

where k is what you are searching for, b is the start of the list, n is the number of elements in the list, w is the size of an item in the list, and comp is a pointer to a compare function.

Listing 8.8 shows how to use bsearch().

Listing 8.8. *Using* bsearch() *Library Function*

```
#include <stdio.h>
#include <stdlib.h>

int table[] = {11, 22, 33, 44, 55, 66, 77, 88, 99};
int func1(int *ptrl, int *ptrz)

void main(void)
{
   char buff[20], *ptr;
   int key, n, w;

   printf("Enter a value: ");
   key = atoi(gets(buff));

   w = sizeof(table[0]);
   n = sizeof(table) / w;
   ptr = bsearch(&key, table, n, w, func1);
   if (ptr != NULL) {
      printf("Match on %d and %d\n", key, *ptr);
   } else {
      printf("No match found in list for %d\n",key);
   }
}

int func1(int *ptr1, int *ptr2)
{
   return (*ptr1 - *ptr2);
}
```

The only difficult thing about using bsearch() is setting up the variables that need to be passed to it. First, we defined table[] as an array of integers and initialize it with a list of values. (The values must be in order for a binary search to work properly.) Next, we define some working variables and declare that func1() returns an integer.

The user then types in the value to be found. The next two statements

```
w = sizeof(table[Ø]);
n = sizeof(table) / w;
```

give you a portable way of determining the number of elements in an array. Variable w gives the size of one element in the array, and sizeof(table) gives the total size of the array. You should convince yourself that n is the number of elements in the table[ ] array.

The program now calls the bsearch( ) function, supplying appropriate arguments. Because bsearch( ) requires a pointer to the item being compared, we must pass the address of key (that is, &key) to bsearch( ).

Because the comp argument of bsearch( ) must be a pointer to function, we use the function name func1 without parentheses. That expression resolves to a pointer to function. The comparison routine, func1( ), does nothing more than return the difference of the two values its arguments point to. If the return value is zero, there is a match. Any other value means no match was found on the two data items passed to func1( ).

If bsearch( ) finds a match, the function returns a pointer to the matching item. If no match is found in the list, a null pointer is returned. The if statement tests ptr to see whether a match was found and displays the appropriate message based on ptr.

Why does bsearch( ) use a pointer to the comparison function? By using a pointer to function, we can define the comparison routine to compare any type of data. This feature makes bsearch( ) data-nonspecific—it can perform a binary search on any list of data regardless of whether the list is of type char, double, or anything else. All you have to do is write a compare routine that uses pointers for the correct data type.

If a pointer to the compare function was not used, we would have to code a "fixed" compare routine, or a fixed function name, within the bsearch( ) function. Either way, we would lose the generality of the function. As it's written, we have a generalized black box that can be made to work with whatever data type is dictated by the task at hand.

If you look through your standard library, you will find several other functions that use pointer to function as one of the arguments (for example, qsort( )). Pointers to functions are a powerful feature of C, and it's well worth the effort to understand how they work.

Arrays of Pointers to Function

Pointers to function can provide an efficient way of calling a series of functions based upon some value. For example, a friend of mine was writing a computer version of a popular board game. The action of each position on the board was performed by a function call for that board position. Rather than use a switch or some other control structure to decide which function to call based on the player's current position, he simply created an array of pointers to functions and used the player's position to index into the array.

An array of pointers to functions is an efficient way of invoking a certain function based on some indexing value. Listing 8.9 is a simple example of how to use an array of pointers to functions.

Listing 8.9. Program Using an Array of Pointers to Function

```
#include <stdio.h>

void func1(void), func2(void), func3(void);

void (*array[])() = {func1, func2, func3};

void main(void)
{
   int i;

   for (i = Ø; i  < 3; i ++)
     (*array[i])();
}

void func1(void)
{
   printf("\nIn func1()");
}

void func2(void)
{
   printf("\nIn func2()");
}

void func3(void)
{
   printf("\nIn func3()");
}
```

The program begins with a declaration of the functions that will be used in the array of pointers. The statement

```
void (*array[])() = {func1, func2, func3};
```

defines an array of pointers to functions that return void, each of which returns no value (that is, void). We can leave the dimension size of the array empty because we have an initializer list of the functions used in the array. In the example, enough space will be allocated to hold three pointers for the three functions in the list. Remember that a function name by itself (without parentheses or arguments) resolves to the lvalue of that function. Therefore, the definition of array[] fills in the three pointers with the lvalues of func1(), func2(), and func3(). That finishes the hard part of the program.

The for loop in main() simply calls each of the three functions in order, and the appropriate message is displayed on the screen.

Arrays of pointers to function provide an alternative means of changing program control without using conventional program control structures.

Pointer Summary

This section provides a summary of some of the important aspects of using pointers.

❑ **Defining a pointer**

Use a data definition with an asterisk before the name of the pointer. For example,

```
int *ptr;
```

The type specifier sets the size of the scalar for all pointer operations using ptr.

❏ Initializing a pointer

Pointers must point to valid data before they are used. To make ptr
point to i, use

```
ptr = &i;
```

When a pointer is initialized, the lvalue of a variable becomes the
rvalue of the pointer. If the variable being pointed to is not an
aggregate data type (for example, an array), the address-of operator
must precede the name of the variable.

❏ Use pointers to alter auto variables via function calls

Because auto variables only have scope in the statement block in which
they are defined, use a pointer in the function to change the auto. Pass
the address of the variable to be changed, and tell the function it has a
pointer by using

```
        int i;

        func1(&i);
        . . .

        . . .
    void func1(int *ptr)
    {
        . . .
    }
```

Notice that passing the address of i to func1() has the same
affect as

```
ptr = &i;
```

❏ Use indirection

Any time you want to see what the pointer is pointing to, use the
indirection operator. For example,

```
int *ptr, i = 12;

ptr = &i;
printf("%d", *ptr);
```

would display 12 on the screen.

❏ Pointer arithmetic

Only subtraction should be used with pointers. (You may use the
increment and decrement operators, of course.) You can add an
offset to a pointer, but you cannot add two pointers.

Pointer arithmetic is not guaranteed if the pointers do not point to the same data item. That is, if you try to subtract ptr1, which points to weeks[], from ptr2, which points to days[], as in

```
ptr1 = ptr2 - ptr1;
```

you may get very strange results.

❑ **Arrays and pointers**

A compiler uses a base address and an offset to find an array element. That is, an offset is added to the lvalue of the array. Before the addition, however, the offset is multiplied by the scalar size of the array data type. Therefore,

```
*(array + i);
```

takes the lvalue of array (the memory address of array[Ø]) and adds i times its scalar to find the address of array[i].

Also remember that only an integral data type can be added to the pointer (for example, don't use a double as an offset).

❑ **Pointer to function**

First, define the pointer to function, such as

```
int (*ptr)(int i);
```

Next, initialize the pointer to point to a function, such as

```
ptr = func1;
```

Then call the function

```
(*ptr)(i);
```

where i is the arguments passed to the function.

Complex Data Definitions and the Right-Left Rule

You have now studied all the basic data types that C has to offer. You should also know, however, that you can create new data types from the basic data types. For example,

```
int (*ptr[1Ø])(void);
```

Programming Tip

Common Pointer Mistakes

Perhaps the most common mistake is forgetting to initialize a pointer before you use it. Although some compilers warn you of such errors, most do not. Another common mistake is something similar to the following:

```
char grade[1Ø];

grade = 'A';
```

You often will hear people who know better saying "Arrays and pointers are the same." Well, not quite. The name of the array does equate to an lvalue, but that does not mean you can assign into the lvalue. In the example, the programmer is trying to assign the letter 'A' as the lvalue of grade[ ]. If you try to change the lvalue of an array, the compiler will lose track of where the array is stored. What the programmer means to do is

```
grade[Ø] = 'A';
```

which causes the letter 'A' to become the rvalue for the first element of the array.

Another common mistake is trying to initialize a character array with a string constant, such as

```
char NAME[] = "FRED";
```

which is not legal. However, if a pointer is used

```
char *name = "FRED";
```

no complaint is issued by the compiler because this form is valid C syntax.

---

is an example of a complex data definition built up from basic data types. What is ptr? In other words, what are the attributes that ptr will have in the program?

We can decipher complex data definitions by using the Right-Left Rule. Simply stated, the RIght-Left Rule for verbalizing a complex data definition says that you first locate the name of the variable (or identifier), and then spiral your way outward in a right-to-left manner.

To decipher the data definition

```
int (*ptr[1Ø])(void);
```

you first locate the name of the variable; ptr, in this example. Now look at what is immediately to the right of the variable name. In the example, you see brackets, which tells you that ptr is an array of ten "somethings." To find out what the "somethings" are, look to the left of the variable name. In this case, you see an asterisk (*), so you know ptr is an array of pointers.

However, pointers must point to something. To find out what the pointers point to, look to the right again. You will see void surrounded by two parentheses. This means that the pointers are pointing to functions which require no arguments. Because functions return a value when they are called, look to the left to find the next attribute. The only thing left is the type specifier int.

You now know the full attribute list for the variable ptr. Variable ptr is "An array of pointers to functions that return integers." Notice that each time you move right or left, you add a new data attribute to the list. A summary of this right-left movement is shown in figure 8.5.

Fig. 8.5. The Right-Left rule.

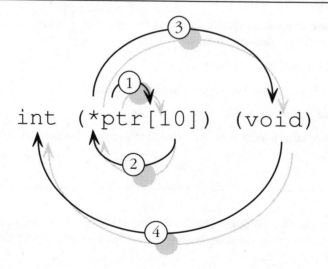

If you follow the arrows in figure 8.5 and verbalize each attribute, you will construct the complete attribute list for ptr.

Review Questions and Exercises

1. What do each of the following define?

   a. `int (*ptr)[10];`
   b. `int *ptr[10];`
   c. `int (*ptr)(void);`

2. If `s[]` is an integer array with external storage class, what does the following code fragment do? What is the value of `k`?

   ```
   int k;

   k = s[0] + +;
   ```

3. The prototype for a function you want to use is

   ```
   char *search(char *s);
   ```

   Assume that you want to search a character array named `data[]`, starting with the 10 element. How would you call the function?

4. Modify the `show_magic()` function in listing 8.6 to use pointer arithmetic.

Answers

1. a. `int (*ptr)[10];`   ptr is a pointer to an array of 10 ints
   b. `int *ptr[10];`   ptr is an array of 10 pointers to int
   c. `int (*ptr)(void);`   ptr is a pointer to function returning an int

2. Because `s[]` is defined outside of any function block, all elements are initialized to zero. Therefore, the statement

   ```
   k = s[0] + +;
   ```

   will cause a 0 to be assigned into `k` and the value of `s[0]` will equal 1 because of the post-increment operation on `s[0]`.

3. You would call the function as

```
ptr = search(&data[9]);
```

You must use the address-of operator prior to the array name because you want to start the search in a place other than the beginning of the array. The function call shown above passes the lvalue of the tenth element of the data[] array as an argument to search().

If you called the function like this:

```
ptr = search(data[9]);
```

thus omitting the address-of operator, you would pass the rvalue of data[9] to search(). Chances are that the contents of data[9] will not be a memory address that search() can use properly.

4. One alternative might be

```
void show_magic(int *elements, int n)
{
    int i, j, temp;

    for (temp = i = Ø; i < n; i++) {
        for (j = Ø; j < n; j++) {
            printf("%4d", *(elements + temp + j));
        }
        temp += n;
        printf("\n");
    }
}
```

In this version, we have avoided the loop invariant code of the form:

```
*(elements + n * i + j)
```

by moving the n * i calculation outside the j loop. The variable temp replaces the n * i. We further simplified the calculation of temp to simple addition rather than a multiply because i always increases by 1 (that is, the i++ expression in the outer for loop). If the matrix being manipulated is large, removing all of the extraneous multiplications could save considerable time.

9

Structures, Unions, and Other Data Types

Concepts in This Chapter

- ☐ Structures
- ☐ Unions
- ☐ enum data type
- ☐ typedefs
- ☐ const and volatile
- ☐ cast operator

This chapter discusses several new data types available in C that can simplify your programming tasks. Once you've mastered these data types, you'll wonder how you got along without them.

What Is a Structure?

You probably have experienced a programming problem where you wanted to keep a group of dissimilar data types together. Your first impulse was probably to use an array. But, because arrays require that all data items be of the same data type, you probably were forced to solve the problem by selecting variable names that "tied" the data items into a group.

The problem of grouping dissimilar data items in C is solved by using a structure. The concept of a structure is similar to that of a record in other languages and not too different from a FIELD statement in BASIC. A *structure* organizes different data items so that they may be referenced as a single unit. A structure usually contains variables of two or more different data types (although nothing prevents you from using a single variable).

Declaring a Structure

An example will help show how you create a structure for use in a program. Suppose that you have a stamp collection and you want to create a data item that contains information about a given stamp. Specifically, you want to keep track of five things: (1) the year the stamp was issued, (2) the denomination of the stamp, (3) the "theme" of the stamp, (4) the date you purchased the stamp, and (5) how much you paid for the stamp.

First, you must declare the type of structure you want to create. The data item is declared as shown in figure 9.1.

There are several things to note about this structure declaration. First, the keyword struct tells the compiler the type of data being declared: a structure. Second, because an identifier (that is, stamp) has been placed before the opening brace, this particular structure has a name (tag) associated with it. In other words, this fragment is creating a structure named stamp. In the example, stamp is the *structure tag* for this structure. Later in the program, when a variable is defined using this type of structure, it is the structure tag that tells the compiler which structure you want to reference.

The third thing to note is that the stamp structure consists of five different variables; two ints, two char arrays, and one double. Each of these variables is called a *structure member*. It follows, therefore, that any structure will have one or more members.

The fourth thing to note is that, so far, you have only *declared* a structure named stamp; you have not yet *defined* a variable that can be used. (If you need to review the distinction between a data declaration and data defini-

Fig. 9.1. Parts of a structure declaration.

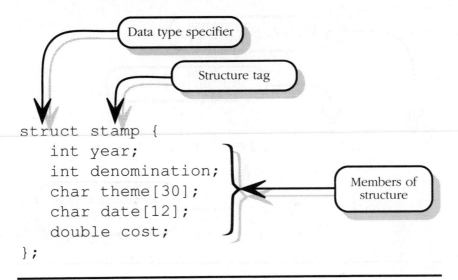

tion, see the section "Defining Data Types" in Chapter 2.) The declaration of a structure simply tells the compiler what is in a structure. A structure declaration creates a "mold" or "cookie cutter" that describes the contents of structure, but does not create a variable that you can use.

Finally, the structure tag is not a variable. It is simply a name, or label, that you gave to the structure so the compiler knows which cookie cutter to use when a variable of that type of structure actually is defined.

Defining a Structure Variable

Obviously, structures would be of little value if we could not create structure variables that could be used in our programs. To define a structure variable, you can use the statement shown in figure 9.2.

The structure definition causes the compiler to follow three steps to define a structure variable: (1) go to the structure list, (2) find the structure named stamp, and (3) create storage (that is, define a variable) for a structure of type stamp and call it collection. As you can see, the stamp structure tag is used by the compiler to determine which structure "mold" to use when defining the collection structure variable.

Fig. 9.2. *Definition of a* struct *variable.*

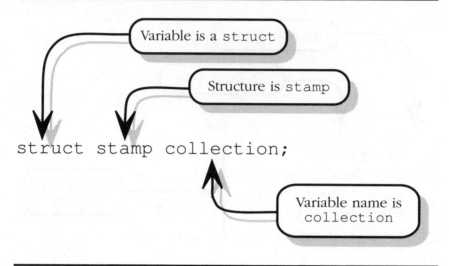

Variable is a struct

Structure is stamp

```
struct stamp collection;
```

Variable name is collection

Declaring and Defining a Structure in One Step

If you want to, you can declare and define a structure variable in one step, as shown in figure 9.3.

The only difference is the addition of the structure variable name (collection) before the closing semicolon of the structure declaration.

Structure Definitions without Structure Tags

The normal convention is to use a structure tag when you expect to create several structure variables of the same type. If you expect to use only a single structure variable in a program, you can use the form

Fig. 9.3. Declaring and defining a struct *variable.*

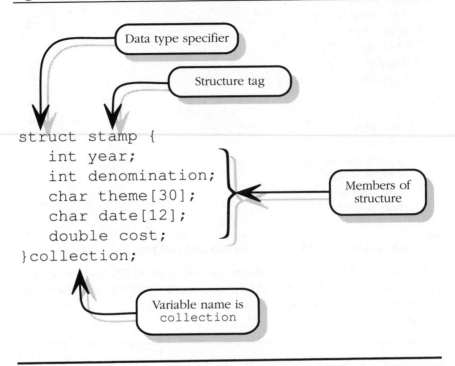

```
struct {
    int year;
    int denomination;
    char theme[3Ø];
    char date[12];
    double cost;
} collection;
```

Notice that there is no structure tag in the structure definition of collection. We can get away with this without confusing the compiler because
the declaration and definition of the structure appear together in the
program. If you need two structure variables, you could use either of the
following two forms:

```
struct {
    int year;
    int denomination;
    char theme[3Ø];
    char date[12];
    double cost;
} US_collection, Canada_collection;
```

or

```
struct stamp {
    int year;
    int denomination;
    char theme[3Ø];
    char date[12];
    double cost;
};
```

```
struct stamp US_collection, Canada_collection;
```

Either form will define two structure variables named US_collection and Canada_collection. The second form requires a structure tag because the structure declaration and definition are not combined.

Programming Tip

When To Use Structure Tags

How do you decide whether to use a structure tag or not? There are no hard and fast rules. However, if you plan to use more than one variable of a given structure type or pass structure variables to functions or return them from functions, you should use a structure tag. Also, a structure tag can help to document the purpose of a structure. Most C programmers use structure tags even when they are not necessary in a strict syntactical sense.

Referencing a Structure Member

Now that you have created a structure variable, you need to know how to reference the members of a structure. Suppose that you want to assign the value 1988 to the year member of the collection variable. The proper syntax is

```
collection.year = 1988;
```

Notice how the dot (.) operator separates the structure variable name from the structure member's name. To the compiler, this statement means "Get the collection structure variable, find the member named year, and assign the value 1988 into that member of the collection structure." Listing 9.1 shows how you might do this in a program.

Listing 9.1. Referencing a Structure Member

```
#include <stdio.h>
#include <stdlib.h>

struct stamp {
    int year;
    int denomination;
    char theme[3Ø];
    char date[12];
    double cost;
    };

void main(void)
{
    struct stamp collection;
    char buff[2Ø];

    printf("\nEnter the year: ");
    collection.year = atoi(gets(buff));

    printf("\nYear = %d", collection.year);

}
```

Listing 9.1 declares a structure by using the stamp structure tag. In main(), a structure variable named collection of type stamp is defined. The program then asks the user to enter the year that the stamp was issued. As you will recall, in the statement

```
collection.year = atoi(gets(buff));
```

gets() is called first to get the input from the user. The atoi() function then uses whatever the user entered into buff[] to form an integer value. Finally, the value is assigned into the year member of collection (note the dot operator). The call to printf() then displays the year as held in collection.year.

Returning a Structure from a Function Call

Suppose that you want to use a function call to fill in the year value. The new ANSI standard allows you to pass an entire structure to and return a structure from a function. (Pre-ANSI compilers may not allow this. You will see how to address this problem later in this chapter.)

One way to design the program would be to write a function that would prompt the user to enter the year, return the value for the year from the function call, and then just assign it into collection.year. Another design alternative is shown in listing 9.2.

Listing 9.2 uses the same structure used in listing 9.1, but also defines a function named get_year() to get the value of the year from the user. Because you want to return the entire structure back to main(), you need to define the return data type from get_year() (that is, its type specifier) to be of type struct stamp. Also notice how the program declares the argument to get_year() (that is, c) also to be of type struct stamp.

Keep in mind that the program is sending a *copy* of collection to get_year(); it is not the same structure defined in main().

Because K&R C does not provide for structure passing and assignment, the get_year() description in listing 9.2 includes a caution. If your compiler

Listing 9.2. Passing a Structure to a Function

```
#include <stdio.h>
#include <stdlib.h>

struct stamp {
    int year;
    int denomination;
    char theme[3Ø];
    char date[12];
    double cost;
    };

struct stamp get_year(struct stamp);

void main(void)
{
    struct stamp collection;

    collection = get_year(collection);

    printf("\nYear = %d", collection.year);
}
/*****
                            get_year()

        Function prompts the user to enter a value for the year
    and assigns it into the structure that was passed to the
    function.

    Argument list:      struct stamp c      the stamp structure to
                                            be filled in.

    Return value:       struct stamp c

    CAUTION:  K&R compilers may not allow structure passing and
              assignment. ANSI compilers will.
*****/
struct stamp get_year(struct stamp c)
{
    char buff[2Ø];

    printf("\nEnter the year: ");
    c.year = atoi(gets(buff));
    return c;
}
```

does not support the ANSI feature of structure passing and assignment, simply get the value for the year from the user and return it as an int. The line in main( ) would change to

```
collection.year = get_year();
```

and get_year( ) would become

```
int get_year()
{
    char buff[20];

    printf("\nEnter the year: .");
    return ( atoi(gets(buff)) );
}
```

Notice the changes in the type specifier and prototype for get_year( ).

Using Pointers with Structures

As mentioned in the last section, K&R C did not allow passing of an entire structure to a function. You could only pass a pointer to the structure. This meant that you had to use indirection to change any member of the structure during a function call. Listing 9.3 is similar to 9.2 except that it uses pointers to the structure for setting the year.

Because you are passing a pointer to the collection structure, the declaration for get_year( ) at the top of the program is changed to

```
void get_year(struct stamp *);
```

Notice that the type specifier is changed from struct stamp in listing 9.2 to void in listing 9.3 because you are using pointers and there is no need to return the structure. Also notice that the program uses the form of declaration for get_year( ) that does not use a variable name in the prototype.

The call to get_year( ) also changes because you are now using pointers. That is,

```
get_year(&collection);
```

uses the address-of operator (&) to pass the address (lvalue) of collection to get_year( ). The prototype for get_year( ) also has been changed to use a pointer to a struct stamp pointer.

The statement

```
(*c).year = atoi(gets(buff));
```

Listing 9.3. Pointer to Structure

```
#include <stdio.h>
#include <stdlib.h>

struct stamp {
    int year;
    int denomination;
    char theme[3Ø];
    char date[12];
    double cost;
    };

void get_year(struct stamp *);

void main(void)
{
    struct stamp collection;

    get_year(&collection);

    printf("\nYear = %d", collection.year);

}

void get_year(struct stamp *c)
{
    char buff[2Ø];

    printf("\nEnter the year: ");
    (*c).year = atoi(gets(buff));
}
```

looks strange, but really is no different than what you saw in Chapters 7 and 8. The indirection operator (*) must be used because the function now uses a pointer to a struct stamp.

The parentheses around the structure name and the indirection operator are necessary because the dot operator has higher precedence than does the indirection operator. (Table 3.7 presents a complete list of operators and their precedence.) If the parentheses were omitted, the statement

```
    *c.year = atoi(gets(buff));
```

would take the integer value returned from atoi() and store it at the address contained in c.year. Because c.year is not a pointer, you should get an error message from the compiler. If an error is not given, you would end up writing the value for the year at some unknown place in memory (that is, whatever address might result from the contents of c.year). This probably is not going to work too well!

In fact, using pointers to structures is so common in C programming (and programmers got so tired of typing in the parentheses) that C provides a special indirection operator called the *arrow operator* for use with pointers to structures. The statement

```
(*c).year = atoi(gets(buff));
```

may also be written as

```
c->year = atoi(gets(buff));
```

Either form will produce the same results. (To verify this fact, you might want to modify listing 9.3 so that it uses the arrow operator.) The latter form uses the "arrow" operator (->), which indicates indirection on a structure pointer and is formed from the hyphen (–) immediately followed by the greater-than sign (>). No character or space can appear between the minus sign and the greater-than sign.

Of the two forms for referencing pointers to structures, the one using the arrow operator is the most common. (It's pretty easy to remember the arrow operator: "arrows point to structures.")

Initializing a Structure

As you may recall from the discussion of storage classes in Chapter 6, external and static data items may be initialized. (The ANSI standard implies that aggregate data types with the auto storage class can also be initialized. This was not allowed under the K&R standard.) If you want to initialize the collection structure, you might use the code shown in listing 9.4.

Because you have now defined collection as a variable of the static storage class, you can initialize its members to whatever values you want to use. If you are using an ANSI compiler, you could delete the static keyword from the definition of collection and the program would still work. In listing 9.4, the values indicate that the stamp was issued in 1847 and has a five cent face value. The picture on the stamp is of Ben Franklin, and the stamp was purchased on December 1, 1988 for $650.00.

Listing 9.4. Initializing a Structure

```
#include <stdio.h>
#include <stdlib.h>

struct stamp {
    int year;
    int denomination;
    char theme[30];
    char date[12];
    double cost;
    };

void main(void)
{
    static struct stamp collection = {
            1847,
            5,
            "Ben Franklin",
            "12/01/88",
            650.0
        };
    printf("\nYear = %d    denomination = %d\n",
            collection.year, collection.denomination);
    printf("\ntheme = %s    date = %s",
            collection.theme, collection.date);
    printf("\ncost  = $%10.2f\n", collection.cost);

}
```

The rule for initializing a structure is simple: The comma operator separates elements in the list of initializers.

Arrays of Structures

Clearly, a stamp collection will consist of more than a single stamp. You need to create an array of structures, each element of which will hold one

Programming Tip

Use Structures To Group
Function Arguments

In some programming situations, you will find that you are consistently calling a function with a fairly large number of arguments. In such situations, it is often easier to define the function arguments as members of a structure and pass the structure to the function. Often the meaning of

```
get_data(collection);
```

is more clear than the meaning of

```
get_year(year, denomination, theme, date, cost);
```

Not only does the structure help document the program (structures have an intuitive appeal when used as function arguments), but it can also save a lot of typing if the function is called frequently in a program.

stamp in the collection. The definition for an array of structures is no different from the definition of any other array. Listing 9.5 shows how you can use arrays of structures.

Listing 9.5 is much the same as listing 9.4, except the definition

```
static struct stamp collection[MAXSTAMPS] = /* rest of code */
```

defines an array of MAXSTAMPS (that is, 100) stamp structures. You can initialize members of the array because collection[] is defined with the internal static storage class. This will work with K&R and ANSI compilers. (If you are using an ANSI compiler, the static keyword could be omitted from the definition.) Notice that each element in the initializer list must be enclosed by braces and that another pair of braces is used to delimit the entire initializer list for the structure array. Finally, notice that the values for the structure members are separated by the comma operator.

Listing 9.5. *Arrays of Structures*

```
#include <stdio.h>
#include <stdlib.h>

#define MAXSTAMPS     100

struct stamp {
   int year;
   int denomination;
   char theme[30];
   char date[12];
   double cost;
   };

void show_one(struct stamp);

void main(void)
{
   int i;

   static struct stamp collection[MAXSTAMPS] =
   {                               /* Opening brace for entire list  */
      {                            /* Opening brace for first element */
        1847,
        5,
        "Ben Franklin",
        "12/01/88",
        650.0
      },                           /* Closing brace for first element */
      {                            /* Opening Brace for 2nd element   */
        1847,
        10,
        "George Washington",
        "12/05/88",
        1250.0
      }                            /* Closing Brace for 2nd element   */
   };                              /* Closing brace for entire list   */

   for (i = 0; i  < MAXSTAMPS; i++) {
      if (collection[i].year == 0)
         break;
      show_one(collection[i]);
   }
}
```

```
void show_one(struct stamp c)
{
    printf("\nYear  = %d    denomination = %d", c.year, c.denomination);
    printf("  theme = %s\ndate = %s", c.theme, c.date);
    printf("  cost  = $%10.2f\n\n", c.cost);
}
```

If the size of an array is omitted and an initializer list follows, the compiler only allocates enough space to hold the values in the list. Therefore, if you had defined collection[] as

```
static struct stamp collection[] = /* rest of code */
```

with the initializer list shown in listing 9.5, the compiler would have allocated enough memory for only the two initialized values for the structure.

The call to show_one()

```
show_one(collection[i]);
```

illustrates how an element of an array of structures is referenced. Also, the printf() calls in the show_one() function show how the members of a structure array are referenced.

If a function needed to change an element of an array of structures, you would have to pass the address (lvalues) of that element in the array to the function. To do this, you would use the address-of operator in the function call

```
func1(&collection[i]);
```

and then use indirection in func1() to change the data in that element of the structure.

Unions

A *union* is a small chunk of memory that can hold different data types. The advantage of a union is that it allows you to place different sized data items in the same data space. In fact, you can think of a union as a small buffer that can hold data items of different sizes. When a union is defined, it is allocated enough storage to hold the *largest* data item in the list of union members.

Programming Tip

Structure Members Are Ordinary Variables

Keep in mind that you may use members of a structure in the same manner as though they were defined outside of a structure. That is, if name[] is a character array in a structure named mail_list, then

    strcpy(mail_list.name, "John Adams");

is perfectly acceptable C syntax.

Although it takes a while to get used to structures, they are an extremely powerful feature of C, and you will find them very useful.

The syntax for defining and using a union is the same as the syntax for a structure (see fig. 9.4).

Fig. 9.4. A union definition.

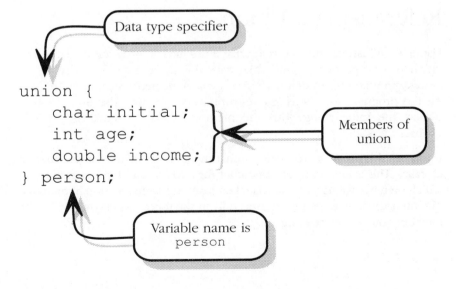

The definition in figure 9.4 defines a union data type named person with sufficient storage to hold the *largest member* in the union. Because a double uses more storage than either a char or an int, person will end up being the size of a double (that is, typically 64 bits, but perhaps up to 80 bits).

If you need more than one union, you can use a union tag, such as

```
union demograph {                        /* Union declaration */
   char initial;
   int age;
   double income;
};

union demograph person1, person2;        /* Union definition  */
```

The union declaration named demograph establishes what may reside in the union, but no union variables yet exist. As you saw earlier with structures, a union declaration with a union tag simply tells the compiler the size of the union, what can reside within the union, and the name by which that union will be referenced. On the other hand, the definition

```
union demograph person1, person2;
```

allocates enough storage for two unions named person1 and person2, each of which is of type demograph.

Referencing a Union

Listing 9.6 illustrates how to reference a union. The program declares a union of type demograph and then uses the union keyword with the demograph union tag to define a union variable named person in main(). All the program does is assign appropriate values into the union and display the value along with the memory addresses (that is, their lvalues).

If you run this program, you will see that the memory address is the same in all cases. This is important to remember for two reasons. First, regardless of which member we use, the data is taken from the same location in memory. The number of bytes of data retrieved from the union is determined by the member you are referencing.

Listing 9.6. Using a Union

```
#include <stdio.h>
#include <stdlib.h>

union demograph {
    char initial;
    int age;
    double income;
    };

void main(void)
{
    union demograph person;

    person.initial = 'A';
    printf("initial = %c   address = %u\n",
            person.initial, &person.initial);

    person.age = 40;
    printf("    age = %d   address = %u\n",
            person.age, &person.age);

    person.income = 18500.0;
    printf(" income = %-10.2f   address = %u\n",
            person.income, &person.income);

}
```

The second important thing to remember is a logical conclusion of the first: It's up to the programmer to retrieve meaningful information from a union. For example, if you had the following two lines in listing 9.6,

```
    person.age = 50;
    printf("Income = %-10.2f", person.income);
```

you probably will see garbage for the income value. This happens because the union contains a valid integer value, but not a valid double value.

> The programmer is responsible for keeping track of union contents.

How Unions Differ from Structures

Suppose that a program contained the following two definitions:

```
struct {
    char initial;
    int age;
    double income;
} s;

union {
    char initial;
    int age;
    double income;
} u;
```

If you examine the size of the structure named s, you would find that it uses 11 bytes (one byte for the char, two bytes for the int, and eight bytes for the double). If you check the size of the union, it will only use eight bytes because its size is determined by the largest member of the union. Therefore, the size of a structure is the sum of the sizes of *all* of the members of the structure while the size of a union is the size of the *largest single member* of the union. (By the way, the compiler would not confuse the members of the structure and union even though they have identical member names.)

A union can be quite handy when you want a single data item capable of holding more than one data type. (For additional examples of using unions and structures together, see listing B.2 in Appendix B.)

Bit Fields

One of the primary motivations for creating C was to have a high-level language that could perform "bit fiddling." One way this can be done is with the bit field data type. A bit field simply allows you to give a name to one or more bits within an int, signed int, or unsigned int. (The actual type of integer used for bit fields may vary among compiler vendors and, hence, is implementation-defined. Consult your compiler's documentation.) The general form of a bit field is

```
type-specifier identifier : constant_expression
```

where constant_expression specifies the number of bits used for identifier.

Suppose, for example, that you wanted to create a series of flag variables. Let's further assume that one flag can only have a True-False value, but the second and third flags could have values between 0 and 7. You could create three separate variables, or you could use a bit field. You might do this with the following code fragment:

```
struct flags {
    int flag1 : 1;
    int flag2 : 3;
    int flag3 : 3;
} test;
```

This defines a variable named test with three bit fields. The first bit field uses only one bit because it only needs a 0 or 1 value. The second two bits fields each use 3 bits because they can assume values between 0 and 7. (Three bits allows us to count up to 7 in binary.)

If the number of bits needed would overflow the bit limit for a single integer, the compiler will automatically allocate another integer for the bit field. (Not all compilers handle this problem gracefully.)

Once the bit fields are defined, they are referenced just as any other structure-type data item would be referenced. The following code fragment shows how the sample fields might be used:

```
test.flag1 = status_ready();
test.flag2 = device1();
test.flag3 = device2();
```

It should be clear that the function status_ready() should only return a value of 0 or 1, although functions device1() and device2() could each return values between 0 and 7.

> If you try to assign into a bit field a value that is larger that the field can hold, behavior is implementation defined (which is a polite way of saying that anything can happen).

Although the syntax for using bit fields is similar to that of structures, they are not the same data type. Technically, what appear to be structure members in a bit field should be referred to as *fields*. Also, the size of the data item in the preceding code fragment is one int, whereas a struct with three int members would be three times as large.

enum Data Type

The ANSI standard has formally added the enumerated (enum) data type, although enum has been available for some time. This data type evolved as part of a desire for stronger type checking in C. The primary purpose of the enumerated data type is to provide for named integer constants in a program. Unlike a #define for a symbolic constant, enum is a true data type for a named constant. Further, because an enum is a data item, it has an lvalue which can be useful for debugging purposes.

Declaring *enum* Types

Examine figure 9.5, which shows the declaration of an enumerated data type. This statement declares an enum data type called sex. The only legitimate values that can be used with variables of this type are female and male. The names appearing between the opening and closing braces are called the *enumeration list*.

Fig. 9.5. *Declaration of an* enum *data type.*

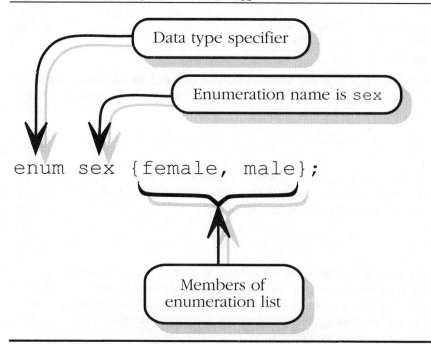

The declaration only creates a type of enumerated variable, in much the same way that a structure declaration only creates a mold for a structure variable. To *define* an enumerated variable for use in a program, you would now write

```
enum sex school_age, college, adult;
```

This statement defines three variables of enum type sex: school_age, college, and adult. (Notice the parallel between sex and a structure or union tag.)

You can also combine the declaration and definition of an enumerated variable into a single statement, such as

```
enum sex {female, male} school_age, college, adult;
```

Values for Enumerated Data Types

So what values are associated with female and male? By default, the names in the enumeration list begin with 0 and increase by one for each item in the list. Therefore, female is associated with the value of 0 and male assumes the value of 1.

The default values can be overridden when enum types are declared. For example,

```
enum speeding {city_usa = 55, rural_usa = 65, canada = 62};

enum speeding arrest;
```

creates an enum variable named arrest that can assume the values of 55, 65, and 62. If a fourth name followed canada in the enumerator list, it would be assigned the value of 63: 1 greater than the last value in the list.

To use the enumerated data type, you might include something like the following in a program:

```
arrest = get_speed();
switch (arrest) {
   case rural_usa:
       /* Code to issue a ticket */
}
```

> Although the intent of the enumerated data type is to provide tighter type checking, the ANSI standard does not define what happens if you attempt to assign a value into an enumerated variable that is not within the set specified in the enumerator list.

*typedef*s: Shorthand for Data Definitions

A typedef allows you to consolidate a complex data declaration into a single word. Simply stated, a typedef is a shorthand notation for a previously declared attribute list. For example, suppose that you need three integer arrays of 5 elements each to hold status information about a program. Using a typedef, you can do the following:

```
typedef int STATUS[5];              /* Establish the typedef */

STATUS port1, port2, port3;         /* Define the variables  */
```

The attribute list for STATUS is "an array of five ints." (The Right-Left Rule from Chapter 8 can be used to construct this attribute list.) To determine the complete attribute list for port1, port2, and port3, simply add the typedef to the end of the variable name. Therefore, port1, port2, and port3 are each five-element integer arrays. The preceding STATUS typedef and definitions are the same as the following definition:

```
int port1[5], port2[5], port3[5];
```

Often, typedefs are used when the attribute list for a data type is fairly long and complex (for example, when you are defining structure variables). You will see less trivial examples of typedefs in Chapter 10 when file input and output are discussed.

Advantages of *typedef*s

A typedef has three important benefits. First, it allows you to consolidate complex data types into a single word that can be used in subsequent data definitions. This helps minimize typing errors when long data definitions are used many times in a program. The second benefit is that typedefs can help document the purpose of a variable in a program. For example,

```
typedef char *STRING;
...
...
STRING message, prompts;
```

The STRING typedef helps to make clear what the purpose of message and prompts are in the program. The third benefit is that if the attribute list needs to be changed in the future, a single change to the typedef fixes every use of the typedefed variables throughout the program.

ANSI Standard *typedefs*

The ANSI standard discusses a header file named stddef.h which contains a number of typedefs for specific uses. For example, size_t is a typedef for type of data returned by the sizeof operator. Another example is ptrdiff_t which is a typedef for the data type used when performing pointer arithmetic.

Type Qualifiers: *const* and *volatile*

The ANSI standard provides two new type qualifiers for data items. Both type qualifiers supply information to the compiler about the "variability of a variable."

The const keyword says that a variable cannot be changed after it is initialized. For example,

```
const double pi = 3.14;
```

says that pi is a variable whose value should not be changed in the program. The only value a const variable can assume is the value that appears as its initialized value in the data definition.

Another common use for const is in function definitions. For example, if you were writing your own version of the standard library string copy function, you might use

```
char *strcpy(char *destination, const char *source)
{
    /* The code */
}
```

The use of the keyword const tells the compiler that the contents pointed to by source should not be altered by the program. Any attempt to change to change a const variable should produce an error message by the compiler, the contents of which are implementation-defined.

The keyword volatile has a slightly different meaning. If your program has the definition

```
volatile char *ioport;
```

you are telling the compiler that no optimizations should be used when an expression involving variable ioport is used. Although most people don't give it much thought, optimizing compilers can generate code that is substantially different than your program source code. Indeed, some compilers can "optimize away" variables that you placed in the program because they may not appear to change. (This is especially true when pointers are used to reference a data item.) The volatile keyword in a variable definition prevents such optimizations from being performed on expressions that use the variable. It forces the volatile data item to be loaded each time it is referenced.

The Cast Operator

You have now been introduced to all of the fundamental data types that C has to offer. Although the cast operator was introduced in Chapter 8, it is discussed here in a little more detail. If you are mixing data types in an expression such as

```
int i;
long int j, k;

. . .
. . .
k = j + i;
```

some compilers will issue a warning that you are trying to add two data items of different types. This is not a true syntax error, however, because C automatically adjusts the contents of variable i to that of a long prior to adding it to j. This "automatic scaling" of the data in an expression is convenient, albeit a bit messy. Fortunately, C provides the *cast* operator to let you force data types to match. The general form of the cast operator is

```
(data_type_desired) expression
```

Programming Tip

The Danger of Mismatched Argument Types

When you use a new library function for the first time, a common mistake involves using the wrong data type as an argument to the function. For example, you might want to take the square root of a variable that has been defined as an int, such as

```
int i;
double answer;

/* Some code to set things up */
answer = sqrt(i);
```

If you do this, i is placed on the stack and sqrt() is called. The sqrt() function assumes that a double is sitting on the stack. If you assume a double uses eight bytes of storage and an int takes two bytes, the sqrt() function grabs eight bytes; but you've only placed two bytes on the stack. The result is that things aren't going to work too well. The necessary change simply involves a cast on i, such as

```
answer = sqrt( (double) i);
```

which will expand i to eight bytes prior to calling sqrt(). Now things will work properly.

In terms of the example

```
k = j + (long) i;
```

we have cast the *value* of variable i into a long data type prior to its addition to j. This statement will pass through a compiler without a warning. Keep in mind that i is *not* changed by the cast; only a copy of i is cast to a long.

A more useful illustration involves pointers. Suppose that your program asks the user to enter a number (for example, wants) that will determine how many double data types will be used in a program. You might see something like

```
int wants;
double *dptr;

dptr = calloc(wants, sizeof(double));
```

However, if you look up calloc() in the documentation, you will find that calloc() returns a pointer to void (pre-ANSI form is pointer to char); but you want to assign the pointer into dptr, which is a pointer to double. Although a void pointer can be assigned into any type of pointer, good coding style would cast the void pointer to a double pointer. The proper way to do this would be

```
dptr = (double *) calloc(wants, sizeof(double));
```

which forces the pointer returned from calloc() to be a pointer to double. This means that the scalar size will be adjusted to the correct value and that pointer arithmetic (for example, an increment) will perform correctly.

A cast, therefore, is used to force the data type of the expression following the cast to be the type of data appearing within the parentheses of the cast operator. In fact, if you strip away the parentheses of the cast operator and the assignment into dptr in the example above, you would have

```
double *calloc(wants, sizeof(double));
```

which looks very much like a declaration in which calloc() returns a pointer to double (which is exactly what you want when used with dptr).

If standard library functions seem to return the wrong values, check to make sure you are passing the proper data type. If the data types are not correct, use a cast to force them to the proper type.

The important thing to keep in mind that the primary purpose of a cast is to change the current attribute of a variable to some new attribute list.

▼ Review Questions and Exercises

1. What reason could some people have for calling structures "arrays for adults"?

2. Given the following structure,

```
struct crt {
     char clear_screen[1Ø];
     int lines;
     int width;
};
```

how would you initialize the members of the structure?

3. Using the structure from Question 2, how would you reference the clear_screen[] array in a program? What changes would have to be made if a pointer is used?

4. What is the difference between a structure and a union?

5. Some writers have suggested that typedefs offer nothing that cannot be done with a #define. Do you agree?

6. The printf() does return an integer value, although programs rarely use this value. In the strictest sense, something must be done with this return value. What would you suggest?

7. Write an input function that could be used to fill in each structure member of the stamp collection example in this chapter. Then write two output functions; one that would pass the structure to the function for displaying the structure data, and a second version that would pass a pointer to the structure for display.

▼ Answers

1. Arrays are composed of elements, or units, of identical data types; all elements are homogeneous. Structures permit the programmer to process data comprised of dissimilar data types as a single unit. Obviously, with this increased flexibility comes a little more complexity, hence the allusion to "arrays for adults."

2. First, there is no structure variable defined, only a template for the structure. The first step must be to define a variable of type crt. If you assume the structure has external storage class, you could initialize it as

```
struct crt terminal = {
     "\033[2J",                    /* ANSI clear-screen code */
     25,
     80
};
```

If the definition of terminal is within a function block and you are using a K&R compiler, you will have to use the keyword static prior to the definition to be able to initialize the structure.

3. The ANSI device driver uses the character sequence shown in the answer to Question 2 to clear the screen and home the cursor. To use this feature, you would write

```
printf("%s", terminal.clear_screen);
```

If terminal were defined as a pointer to structure, the syntax would change only slightly, as in

```
printf("%s", terminal->clear_screen);
```

4. Although structures and unions use similar syntax, they are different in terms of what they are designed to do. A structure is usually comprised of several different data types called members. Each member is allocated enough storage to hold that member. This means that using sizeof on a structure will yield a byte count that is equal to the sum of the storage requirements for all members in the structure. The sizeof a union, on the other hand, will equal the size of the largest member of the union, not the total of the members.

Therefore, structures are used to hold data for each of its members and all values are available at one time. With a union, only one member can reside in the union at one time and it is the responsibility of the programmer to know what is currently in the union.

5. Remember that a #define is a textual substitution for a string in a program. A typedef is an attribute list used by the compiler for defining variables in the program. We purposely picked the array example for discussing the typedef because a #define cannot handle dimensioned arrays.

6. If you are not going to use the return value (and using the answer from Question 3), the statement

    ```
    (void) printf("%s", terminal.clear_screen);
    ```

    would be the proper solution. In this example, we have cast the return value to void which tells the compiler it is safe to ignore the return value from printf().

7. This is left as an exercise for the reader.

10

Disk File Operations

Concepts in This Chapter

- ❑ High and low-level open, read, and write file operations
- ❑ Sequential and random file access
- ❑ I/O functions from the standard library
- ❑ Using command line arguments

In this chapter, you will learn how disk data files are used in C. You will also learn about the two basic ways in which you may use disk data files and the advantages and disadvantages of each.

Any useful programming language must be able to communicate with disk data files. The mechanics for this communication depends on the disk operating system (or DOS) under which the language is used. C was born under the UNIX operating system, and its input/output (I/O) functions reflect that birth.

C has now found a home on every major operating system available for computers. Although not all UNIX operating system facilities are available to all operating systems, most of C's I/O functions behave in a consistent fashion across operating systems. This chapter concentrates on these functions.

High-Level versus Low-Level Disk I/O

Reading and writing data stored on disk can be accomplished at two levels in C: high and low. (Sometimes you will hear high-level file I/O referred to as "buffered" I/O and low-level file I/O as "unbuffered" I/O.) Low-level disk I/O under UNIX is accomplished through calls to the operating system. Because some operating systems do not have the same facilities, C compilers for those operating systems must implement low-level I/O in a different manner. Some of these low-level functions are either "built up" from the I/O facilities that do exist or are simply omitted. MS-DOS, for example, is a single-user operating system and does not need to provide some of the multi-user facilities provided by UNIX.

Low-level disk I/O reads the data from the disk in chunks convenient for the operating system (often 512 bytes for UNIX and MS-DOS, but 128 bytes for CP/M). Usually the size of the chunk is determined more by hardware considerations than anything else.

In many situations, however, programs need to work with the data in smaller, more manageable chunks, often as small as one byte. The high-level disk I/O functions are designed to work with the data in a form that is convenient for the task at hand. Usually, the high-level disk functions are built up from the low-level functions.

In its specification of the standard library functions, the ANSI committee has omitted all library functions that use low-level file routines. A detailed discussion of the reasons for not including the low-level routines in the standard is presented in the Input/Output section (4.9) of the draft. Simply stated, the committee felt that unbuffered I/O often duplicated existing system facilities, offered little or no performance improvement over buffered I/O, and may be inappropriate for some environments. Still, because there is a large body of code out there that uses the low-level file operations, they are also discussed in this chapter.

Opening a Disk File

A disk file must be opened before anything else can be done with it. In order to work with a disk file, the program and the operating system must share certain information about the file. That is, specific overhead informa-

I/O Streams

If you read articles about C programming, you may find the words *I/O stream* used. Stated simply, a *stream* refers to a collection of data that can be written to or read from an I/O device. Streams come in two flavors: (1) text, and (2) binary.

A text stream is simply a sequence of text characters (often ASCII) grouped into lines. Each line consists of zero or more characters terminated by a newline character. A text stream may have zero or more lines in the stream.

A binary stream is a sequence of "row" data. That is, it does not have to be represented in the host character set. A binary stream might represent hexadecimal numbers, floating-point numbers in BCD (Binary Coded Decimal) or any other form that might be useful.

The C standard library functions provide I/O functions to process both types of streams.

tion on each file must be available before a program can access the file. This overhead information usually is stored in a structure.

The declaration of this structure is contained in the stdio.h header file supplied with your compiler. If you examine your stdio.h header file, you will probably find something similar to that shown in listing 10.1.

Listing (Fragment) 10.1 The FILE *Structure*

```
#define OPEN_MAX 1Ø

struct _buffer {
     int _fd;                /* File descriptor          */
     int _left;              /* Characters left in buffer */
     int _mode;              /* How we will use the file  */
     char * _nextc;          /* Next character location   */
     char * _buff;           /* Base of file buffer       */
};

typedef struct _buffer FILE;
extern FILE _iob[OPEN_MAX];
```

The overhead information for a particular file is available through a structure named FILE (as created by a typedef). Because each file needs similar information, stdio.h declares an array of such structures called _iob[].

The symbolic constant OPEN_MAX determines the maximum number of files that can be open at one time in a program. The specific number for OPEN_MAX (as defined in stdio.h) depends upon the compiler's design considerations and any related constraints dictated by the operating system. Your compiler's documentation should tell you what the limit is, or you can find out by inspecting the stdio.h header file.

Fortunately, the programmer does not have to worry about the specific contents of the members of a FILE structure. Your immediate concern is to open a file so that you can work with it. The function that does this is fopen().

The fopen() function performs two essential tasks. First, it fills in the FILE structure with the information needed by both the operating system and the program so that they can communicate with each other. Second, fopen() returns a FILE pointer to the location in memory where the FILE structure is stored (the lvalue).

This pointer to FILE is used in nearly all high-level disk I/O functions. The definition might be

```
FILE *fpin, *fpout;
```

Variables fpin and fpout, therefore, are pointers to structures of type FILE.

Each disk file used in a program needs its own FILE pointer. If you expect to use several files in a program, but only one file will be open at a time, you can "reuse" a single FILE pointer for a second file after you have finished (that is, closed) the first file. As a general rule, you must define enough FILE pointers to equal the number of files that will be open at the same time.

Ways To Open a File

To generate code for opening a file, the compiler needs to know three things: (1) the name of the file you wish to use, (2) the way in which you want to work with the file, and (3) where to store the relevant information about the file. The statement

```
fpin = fopen("test.txt", "r");
(3)             (1)         (2)
```

specifies the three required pieces of information. Specifically, (1) the file is named test.txt, (2) we want to read ("r") information from the file, and (3) the file information is stored at the address contained in the FILE pointer variable fpin. Therefore, it is fpin that becomes your communication link between the structure with the file information in its members and your program.

The first argument to fopen() is the name of the file as it appears on the disk. The second argument determines how the file can be accessed. The three general modes are

"r" for reading
"w" for writing
"a" for appending

Two modifiers are available for the file mode. The letter "b" is used when binary data is stored in the file (that is, a binary stream). In most cases, if a file does not contain ASCII characters, or text data, the file consists of binary data (for example, numeric values). A plus sign (" +") is used when a file already exists and you want to update the file. Therefore, a mode of

"rb +"

says that you want to open this file for binary updating (reading and writing a binary data file).

If no modifier (such as "r") is present, the file is opened as a text stream—it contains data that is representable in the host character set. If you used "r +", you would be opening a text (for example, ASCII) file for updating. A complete list of the options for the fopen() file mode strings is presented in table 10.1.

Notice that each mode is a character string (pointer to char). Also, you can write "rb +" as "r +b" with the same effect.

Errors in Opening a Disk File

An error can occur when fopen() is called. Possible reasons include a disk full condition when writing, a disk drive door open, or perhaps some form of media or hardware failure. If an error condition is detected, a NULL pointer is returned from the fopen() function call. As you may recall from the discussion about pointers, a null pointer is guaranteed not to point to anything useful. Therefore, you will often see code similar to the following in a program:

```
if ( (fpin = fopen("test.txt", "r") ) == NULL) {
    printf("Cannot open file. Abort.");
    exit(EXIT_FAILURE);
}
```

Table 10.1 *High-Level Modes for Opening a File*

Mode	Interpretation
"r"	Open for reading
"w"	Truncate to zero length or create for writing
"a"	Open for writing at the end of the file or, if the file does not exist, create for writing
"r +"	Open existing file for reading-writing
"w +"	Truncate to zero length or create for updating
"a +"	Open for appending or (create and) open for updating at the end of file
"rb"	Open binary file for reading
"wb"	Create and open binary file for writing
"ab"	Open binary file for writing at the end of the file or, if the file does not exist, create for writing
"rb +"	Open existing binary file for reading and writing
"wb +"	Create and open binary file for updating
"ab +"	Open binary file for appending or (create and) open for updating at the end of file

It is common for the null pointer to be #defined in the stdio.h header file as a symbolic constant NULL. Because of the parentheses, the expression

```
(fpin = fopen("test.txt", "r"))
```

is evaluated first, so the call to fopen() is performed first and the return value assigned into fpin. fpin then is tested against NULL to see if a non-null pointer was returned. If the pointer is null, we know the file was not opened successfully, and an error message is issued. The call to exit() is usually called to abort the program when the call to fopen() fails. The exit() function often is called with a symbolic constant defined in stdlib.h (EXIT_FAILURE or EXIT_SUCCESS) header file. If fpin is non-null, the file was opened successfully, and the program proceeds to the next phase.

Reading a Disk File One Character at a Time

You can read data from a file in several ways. The first method we will discuss uses the fgetc() function. Assuming that fpin is a FILE pointer to an open disk file that you want to read, the call would be

```
int c;
...
...
c = fgetc(fpin);
```

The fgetc() function reads one character from the FILE structure pointed to by fpin and assigns it into variable c.

Listing 10.2 is an example of how you might read an ASCII text file using the fgetc() function.

The program first calls get_filename() so the user may enter the name of the data file to be listed. The input by the user is held in filename[]. Because file names may vary among operating systems, this program does not include any error checking to see that the input by the user constitutes a valid file name. You may want to add these checks yourself.

Next, open_file() uses the file name stored in filename[] and attempts to open the data file entered by the user. If the file is opened successfully, fpin will be non-null and the file is opened. If fpin contains a null pointer, the call to fopen() failed. An error message is issued and the program terminates.

Assuming the file is open (otherwise, the program would have aborted in open_file()), the call to show_and_tell() reads the file one character at a time. The call to putchar() is used to display the character on the screen. You could also use

```
printf("%c", c);
```

if you wish. Eventually, all of the data will have been read and c will read the end-of-file (EOF) mark. At that point, the while loop ends and the program calls fclose().

The EOF symbolic constant is used to signal that the end of the file has been read. The value for EOF is a negative integral constant, the specific value for which is defined in the stdio.h header file. (Because EOF is defined as part of the ANSI standard, it should be available for all compilers and, hence, we need not concern ourselves with its actual value.)

Listing 10.2. Reading an ASCII Text File One Character at a Time

```c
#include <stdio.h>
#include <stdlib.h>

void show_and_tell(void),
    open_file(char *filename),
    get_filename(char *s);

FILE *fpin;

void main(void)
{
   char filename[256];

   get_filename(filename);
   open_file(filename);
   show_and_tell();
}
/*****
                              show_and_tell()
      Reads the data file one character at a time.

*****/

void show_and_tell(void)
{
   int c;

   while ((c = fgetc(fpin)) != EOF) {
      putchar(c);
   }
   fclose(fpin);
}
/*****
                              open_file()
      Attempts to open a data file for reading.

*****/

void open_file(char *filename)
{
   if ((fpin = fopen(filename, "r")) == NULL) {
      printf("Cannot open %s. Abort", filename);
      exit(EXIT_FAILURE);
   }
}
```

```
/*****
                        get _filename()

    Gets the name of the data file to be read. WARNING: This
is a very dumb function that does not check to see whether
the file name entered is of the form expected by the operating
system.

*****/

void get _filename(char *s)
{
    printf("Enter file name: ");
    gets(s);
}
```

Closing a Disk File

When you are finished with the file, you should close it. The function that closes a disk file is named fclose(). The call is

```
    fclose(fpin);
```

The call to fclose() does any cleanup that might be required and frees fpin for reuse with another file if needed.

Another function that closes *all* open disk files is the exit() function. (You can see an example of this in the open _file() call.) The exit() function is different from fclose() in several ways. First, exit() closes all data files. The argument to exit() is implementation defined, but is usually 0 if a normal program termination is desired and non-zero for abnormal program termination.

A second difference is that the exit() function also terminates the program. A call to fclose() simply closes the data file associated with the FILE pointer used as the argument to fclose(). The exit() function closes all files and returns control to the host environment (usually the operating system).

Programming Tip

Be Careful in Testing for *EOF*

Notice that variable c is defined as an integer in listing 10.2 even though we are reading a character. This is because we must eventually read the end-of-file (EOF) marker. Often the EOF marker has a value of –1 which may not be sensed properly if a char data type is used. The code fragment

```
while ((c = fgetc(fpin)) != EOF) {
    putchar(c);
}
```

may not sense the EOF mark properly if c is defined as a character. If c is defined as an unsigned char, the test may work properly, but a cast should then be used. The safest way to test for EOF is to assign the return value into an int prior to the test.

By the way, don't assume that reading a file one character at a time is a slow way of doing things. You might be surprised at how fast fgetc() actually is.

Keep in mind that the end-of-file marker can be different for different operating systems. The actual value for EOF could be anything. Because it can be different, always use EOF in your programs when testing for end-of-file. Using magic numbers (for example, –1) instead of EOF could cause problems if you move the program to another operating system.

Reading a File One Line at a Time

If you want to read a text file one line at a time, use the fgets() function in the form

```
char *fgets(char *buffer, int n; FILE *fpin);
```

The fgets() function reads one line (with a maximum of n minus one characters) from a file and places the line into buffer. Either a newline character ('\n') or EOF terminates the read. A null string terminator is added to the line (or to the n characters) held in buffer. (Full details on the fgets() function can be found in your compiler's documentation for the standard library.) A pointer to buffer is returned on successful reads and a null pointer is returned on error or end of file.

You may remember gets() from earlier program examples. Obviously, fgets() and gets() are related functions, but with several important distinctions. First, gets() receives input from the keyboard, while fgets() reads disk files. Second, gets() terminated when a newline character was read from the keyboard (the user pressed the Return or Enter key). The newline character then was overwritten with the null character to end the input string. The fgets() function, however, does not overwrite the newline character. Instead, a null character is added after the newline character.

If you retain most of listing 10.2, you can modify the show_and_tell() function to use the fgets() function quite easily.

```
#define MAXSTR   81
void show_and_tell(void)
{
    char buff[MAXSTR + 1];
    while (fgets(buff, MAXSTR, fpin) != NULL) {
        printf("%s", buff);
    }
    fclose(fpin);
}
```

Near the top of listing 10.2, a #define was inserted for the maximum line length expected. Because the program will be displaying its output on the screen, the length was set to 81. That is, 80 characters for the screen plus the null string termination character at the end. Within the function body of show_and_tell(), we define a character array buff[] of size MAXSTR plus 1. A while loop then is used to read the input file.

fgets() returns a character pointer to the string read from the file. Because fgets() adds a null terminator to whatever is read, we can test the pointer to see whether we have a null (empty) string. If fgets() returns a null string, we know that we have read the file completely. This means that end-of-file is sensed differently when fgets() is used versus fgetc().

We use a "%s" control string to print buff[] because buff[] could contain conversion characters a in string causing the program to expect arguments to follow in the printf() call. That is, if buff[] held a double-quoted string like

```
"value is %d"
```

using printf() as

```
printf(buff);
```

would cause printf() to look for an argument to match the %d in the string. By using printf() with a %s instead, we avoid this problem.

Reading a File in Convenient Chunks

If you are reading a binary file, it may not make sense to read the file one character or line at a time. If, for example, the file contains structures whose members are all binary data, you may want to read the file one structure at a time. The proper function to use would be

```
fread(char *buff, size_t big, size_t num, FILE *fpin);
```

Recall from Chapter 9 that size_t is a typedef for the data type returned by the sizeof operator. Therefore, fread() reads num items each of size big from the file associated with fpin; the data is stored in buff.

> It is your responsibility to ensure that buff points to a storage area large enough to hold the data to be read.

The return value from fread() is the number of items (num) read. The return value will be less than num if an error occurs or end-of-file is read.

Programming Tip

puts(), *printf()*, and Program Size

In a seminar, I once presented a program similar to listing 10.2, using fgets() to read the file. One attendee told me that it would be much more efficient to use the puts() (that is, put string) function instead of printf() to do the output to the screen. His reasoning was that using the puts() function would produce smaller code size for the program. Well, he was sorta right and sorta wrong.

It is true that puts() is a much smaller function than printf() and it may even execute slightly faster. However, because printf() is already used once in the get_filename() function, the printf() code is already "in" the program; get_filename() and open_file() both call printf(). In fact, using puts() in show_and_tell() would actually increase the code size of the program. The rule is simple: If function a() is already in the program and can also do the work of function b(), inclusion of function b() will increase code size.

One other difference about puts(); it automatically sends a newline character to the screen after the string is printed. In the modified listing 10.2, this has the effect of double spacing the output on the screen. Think about it.

Once again, you can modify listing 10.2 to use the fread() function as follows:

```
#define MAXSTR   81
/*****
                                    show_and_tell()
        Reads the data file one character at a time.
*****/
void show_and_tell(void)
{
    int num;
    char buff[MAXSTR + 1];
```

```
        while ((num = fread(buff, sizeof(char), (unsigned) MAXSTR, fpin)) != 0) {
            buff[num * sizeof(char)] = '\0';
            printf("%s", buff);
        }
        fclose(fpin);
}
```

You need to pay a little more attention to detail when using fread(), because it knows nothing about newlines or null termination characters. It is the programmer's responsibility to keep everything in sync. First, we changed the definition of buff[] so that it has an extra character. Because fread() will read MAXSTR characters at a time, we need room for the null termination character at the end of those MAXSTR characters; hence the increase of MAXSTR from 80 to 81.

Variable num holds a count of the actual number of elements read by fread(). (Although it probably will not make a difference on most systems, we multiplied num times the sizeof(char) to compute the proper index into buff[].) If fread() reads MAXSTR characters from the file, num will equal 81. The statement

```
    buff[num] = '\0';
```

places a null at position buff[81]. Because arrays begin with 0 in C, we have actually written the null into the 82nd position in the string. That is, a count of 81 characters is equivalent to buff[80]. Because it is unlikely that a file will always have an even multiple of 81 bytes in it, num ensures that we place the null at the end of the actual number of characters read from the file. The call to printf() then prints out the contents of buff[] as a string.

Program control stays in the while loop until EOF is read, at which time we close the file and end the program.

A Read-Write Example

Now that you know something about how disk files are opened and read, you are ready to write a simple program. Listing 10.3 takes a C program source file and writes out the same file, but with line numbers.

Listing 10.3. Reading-Writing a Disk File

```
#include <stdio.h>
#include <stdlib.h>

FILE *fpin, *fpout;
void open_files(void), process_files(void);

void main(void)
{
    open_files();
    process_files();
    fclose(fpin);
    fclose(fpout);
}

/*****
                            process_files()

        This function reads an input file one line at a time by calls
    to fgets(). A line number is written to the output file, followed
    by the line just read from the input file.

    Argument list:      void

    Return value:       void

*****/

void process_files(void)
{
    char buff[8Ø];
    int line_count;

    line_count = 1;
    while (fgets(buff, 8Ø, fpin) != NULL) {
        fprintf(fpout, "%4d  ", line_count++);
        fputs(buff, fpout);
    }
}
```

```
/*****
                        open _files()

    Function that attempts to open both the input and
    output disk data files. If either fopen() call fails,
    the program aborts.

*****/
void open_files(void)
{
    if ((fpin = fopen("test.c", "r")) == NULL) {      /* Open input */
        printf("Cannot open test.c. Abort\n");
        exit(EXIT_FAILURE);
    }
    if ((fpout = fopen("test.cl", "w")) == NULL) {    /* Open output */
        printf("Cannot open test.cl. Abort\n");
        exit(EXIT_FAILURE);
    }
}
```

The program begins by defining a character array to hold the file names and two FILE pointers: one each for the input and output files because both files must be open at the same time. Because the FILE pointers were defined with external storage class, we will not have to pass them as function arguments.

The function open_files() in listing 10.3 is a little more flexible than the earlier version in listing 10.2. Because we want to be able to use the same function to open files for different purposes (for example, reading instead of writing) open_files() simply calls fopen(), using the file names and mode supplied as the arguments. If the call is successful, fpin and fpout will both contain valid FILE pointers (that is, non-null) when control returns to main().

The process _files() function does all of the work. The call to fgets() reads one line (79 characters maximum) from the input file into buff[]. fprintf() is similar to printf(), except the output is sent to fpout rather than the screen. Because the first argument to fprintf() is the line count and the call to fprintf() is the first output function called, each line in the output file has a line number at the beginning.

The call to fputs( ) simply writes out the contents previously read into buff[ ] to the file pointed to by fpout. As long as fgets( ) continues to read valid data (as evidenced by a non-null character pointer returned by fgets( )), the program will continue to read and write lines from the input file to the output file.

Eventually, fgets( ) will have read all of the data from the input file and a null character pointer will be returned. When this happens, the while loop ends and control returns to main( ). Both files are then closed by the two calls to fclose( ); one call for each of the two open files.

Although listing 10.3 doesn't perform any fancy error checking and some formatting problems are not addressed properly, the program is simple and easy to understand, yet useful.

Command Line Arguments

Listing 10.3 would be even more useful if you could enter the input and output file names at the time you invoke the program. This is exactly what command line arguments allow us to do.

A *command line argument* is a parameter supplied to main( ) when the program is invoked from the operating system's command line. For example, suppose that listing 10.3 is called LINEFILE and you want to read an input file named TEST.C and output the file with line numbers as TEST.CL. When you run the program, you would type

```
LINEFILE TEST.C TEST.CL
```

and then press the Return key. In this example, there are three command line arguments: (1) the program named LINEFILE, (2) the input file named TEST.C, and (3) the output file named TEST.CL. Each command line argument is separated by a blank space.

The first command line argument is always the program name. Because it is always first, a copy of it is stored at the memory address stored in argv[Ø]. The second command line argument is the input file name (TEST.C), and it would be stored at the memory address held in argv[1]. Finally, the third command line argument (TEST.CL) would be stored at the memory address pointed to by argv[2]. With this information in mind, consider listing 10.4.

Listing 10.4. *Command Line Arguments*

```
#include <stdio.h>
#include <stdlib.h>

FILE *fpin, *fpout;
void open_files(int argc, char *argv[]), process_files(void);

void main(int argc, char *argv[])
{
    open_files(argc, argv);
    process_files();
    fclose(fpin);
    fclose(fpout);
}

/*****
                            process_files()

        This function reads an input file one line at a time by calls
    to fgets(). A line number is written to the output file, followed
    by the line just read from the input file.

    Argument list:      void

    Return value:       void
*****/

void process_files(void)
{
    char buff[80];
    int line_count;

    line_count = 1;
    while (fgets(buff, 80, fpin) != NULL) {
        fprintf(fpout, "%4d ", line_count ++);
        fputs(buff, fpout);
    }
}

/*****
                            open_files()
```

Function that attempts to open both the input and output disk data files. If either fopen() call fails, the program aborts.

*****/

```c
void open_files(int argc, char *argv[])
{
    if (argc != 3) {
        printf("Usage: program inputfile outputfile:");
        exit(EXIT_FAILURE);
    }

    if ((fpin = fopen(argv[1], "r")) == NULL) {      /* Open input */
        printf("Cannot open %s. Abort\n", argv[1]);
        exit(EXIT_FAILURE);
    }

    if ((fpout = fopen(argv[2], "w")) == NULL) {     /* Open output */
        printf("Cannot open %s. Abort\n", argv[2]);
        exit(EXIT_FAILURE);
    }
}
```

If you study listing 10.4, you will see that main() looks a bit different now:

```c
void main(int argc, char *argv[])
```

main() has two arguments: argc and argv[]. The first argument is called the *argument count*. It holds a number that is equal to the number of command line arguments that were typed on the command line when the program began execution. In the preceding example, argc would equal 3 (that is, one for the program name, another for the input file name, and a third for the output file name).

The second argument to main(), called the *argument vector*, is argv[]. argv[] is an array of pointers to char. To help explain how this works, suppose that the operating system has provided memory location 100 for the argument counter (argc) and that an integer requires two bytes of storage. Let's further assume that the argument vector (argv[]) is stored immediately after argc and that each pointer also requires two bytes of storage. Figure 10.1 shows how the (hypothetical) memory image might look.

Fig. 10.1. *Memory image for* argc *and* argv[].

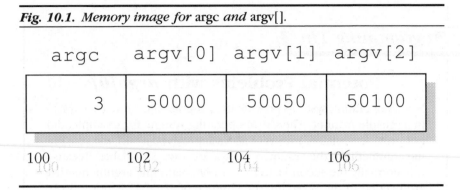

As you can see from figure 10.1, argc is simply an integer and argv[] is an array of pointers to char. Because argv[] is an array of pointers to char, the rvalues for argv[] should point to some useful data. Figure 10.2 shows what argv[] points to.

Fig. 10.2. *What* argv[] *points to.*

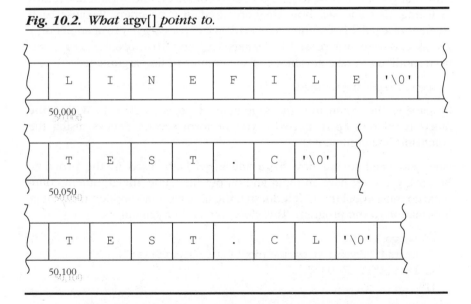

Figure 10.2 shows that the rvalue of argv[Ø] points to the program name, argv[1] points to the input file name, and argv[2] points to the output file name. Because argc and argv[] are passed into the program as arguments to main( ), you can use this information to add flexibility to a program. The command line arguments provide you with an easy way of passing information into a program from the command line prior to executing the program.

Programming Tip

Potential Problems with *argv[0]*

Not all operating systems provide the program file name (argv[Ø])
in a reliable manner. The CP/M operating system, for example, did
not provide a reliable means of accessing argv[Ø]. Still, the remaining arguments in the argument vector are always available. Because
it is normally the second and higher command line arguments that
are needed in the program, the absence of argv[Ø] is not a problem in most circumstances. However, using argv[Ø] may not be
portable across operating systems.

Now that you know how to gain access to command line arguments, return
to listing 10.4 and see how they are used in a program. Because each
element of argv[] is a pointer to char, you can pass argv[] to open_file()
just as filename was passed in listings 10.3 and 10.4. open_files() has
been modified to take advantage of the command line arguments

```
open_files(argc, argv);
```

by passing the command line arguments to open_files(). Within the
function body of open_files(), you perform several checks, using the
command line arguments.

Now you need to see how argc and argv[] are used in the program.
Because you must have an input and output file name, the argument counter argc must equal three. If it doesn't, the user has not supplied the proper
information to the program. Therefore, the code fragment

```
if (argc != 3) {
    printf("Usage: program inputfile outputfile:");
    exit(EXIT_FAILURE);
}
```

gives the user a brief message of what the command line arguments must be
in order to use the program properly.

Assuming that argc does equal 3, you can proceed to open the input and
output files through calls to open_file(), which is the same as in listings
10.2 and 10.3. The code sequence is similar for both files:

```
if ((fpin = fopen(argv[1], "r")) == NULL) {      /* Open input */
   printf("Cannot open %s. Abort\n", argv[1]);
   exit(EXIT_FAILURE);
}

if ((fpout = fopen(argv[2], "w")) == NULL) {      /* Open output */
   printf("Cannot open %s. Abort\n", argv[2]);
   exit(EXIT_FAILURE);
}
```

This fragment looks almost identical to the file open statements in listing 10.3 except that argv[1] was used to provide the input file name. Using figures 10.1 and 10.2, you should be able to convince yourself that fpin will open the correct input file. Similar reasoning applies to the way the output file is opened using argv[2]. Once the files are opened, the program performs in a manner similar to listing 10.3.

Alternative Definitions for *argv[]

You may also see *argv[] defined as

```
void main(int argc, char **argv)
```

which says that argv is a "pointer to pointer to char." If you recall the discussion of pointers from Chapters 7 and 8, you know that when array names are used as arguments to functions, those names equate to a pointer. Therefore, if argv[] resolves to *argv, then it follows that *argv[] can also be written as **argv. Either form may be used.

Reading and Writing Binary Data Files

All of the file examples presented thus far have used ASCII data files. Although there isn't much difference with binary files, Listing 10.5 shows one example of how they might be used.

Listing 10.5. Reading-Writing Binary Files

```c
#include <stdio.h>
#include <stdlib.h>

#define MAXVALS 100

FILE *fpout;
void open_files(int argc, char *argv[]),
    write_doubles(void),
    open_file(char **argv),
    show_doubles(void);

void main(int argc, char *argv[])
{
    open_files(argc, argv);
    write_doubles();
    open_file(argv);
    show_doubles();
    fclose(fpout);
}
/*****
                            show_doubles()

    This function shows a sequence of random doubles
    as read from a file.

    Argument list:      void

    Return value:       void
*****/
void show_doubles(void)
{
    int i;
    double temp;

    for (i = 0; i < MAXVALS; i++) {
        if (i % 10 == 0)
            printf("\n");
        fread( (void *) &temp, sizeof(double), (size_t) 1, fpout);
        printf("%5.0f ", temp);
    }
}
```

```
/*****
                            open_file()

        This function reopens the file holding the random doubles.

    Argument list:      char **argv    pointer to filename

    Return value:       void
*****/
void open_file(char **argv)
{
    if ((fpout = fopen(argv[1], "rb")) == NULL) {      /* Open input */
        printf("Cannot reopen %s. Abort\n", argv[1]);
        exit(EXIT_FAILURE);
    }
    fseek(fpout, ØL, SEEK_SET);
}


/*****
                          write_doubles()

    This function generates a sequence of random doubles
    and writes them to a file.

    Argument list:      void

    Return value:       void
*****/
void write_doubles(void)
{
    int i;
    double vals[MAXVALS];

    for (i = Ø; i < MAXVALS; i++) {
        vals[i] = (double) rand();
    }

    for (i = Ø; i < MAXVALS; i++) {
        fwrite((void *) &vals[i], (size_t) sizeof(double),
               (size_t) 1, fpout);
    }
    fclose(fpout);
}
```

```
/*****
                        open_files()

    Function that attempts to open both the input and
    output disk data files. If either fopen() call fails,
    the program aborts.
*****/
void open_files(int argc, char *argv[])
{
    if (argc != 2) {
        printf("Usage: program outputfile:");
        exit(EXIT_FAILURE);
    }

    if ((fpout = fopen(argv[1], "wb")) == NULL) {    /* Open output */
        printf("Cannot open %s. Abort\n", argv[1]);
        exit(EXIT_FAILURE);
    }
}
```

The program is similar to listing 10.4, except it uses only one command line argument. First, the program calls open_files() to check for the proper number of command line arguments. If two arguments are not present, an error message is issued and the program aborts; otherwise, the program attempts to open the file.

The file name to be used by fopen() is held in argv[1]. Notice that fopen() has been changed to work with a binary data file by using the "wb" mode flag. If all goes well, fpout will contain a valid FILE pointer after fopen() is called.

File Positioning

As you probably know, the hardware required to read a disk involves moving a disk read-write head over the media. Although disk I/O must concern itself with tracks, blocks, sectors, and a lot more, you can simplify things considerably if you think of a disk as though you took the blocks, sectors, and tracks and laid them end-to-end to form a tape. Figure 10.3 shows how you might imagine the tape.

As shown in figure 10.3, when a file is opened, the disk drive's read-write head may be at the start of the file (for example, when using the "w" mode for fopen( )), or it might be at the end of file (for example, "a" mode).

Fig. 10.3. A data file viewed as a tape.

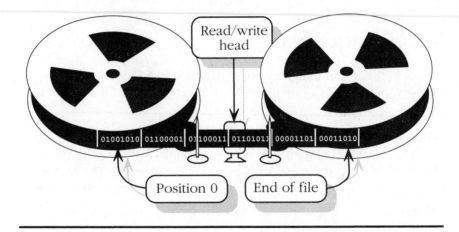

Sequential and Random Disk Files

If you read the file depicted in figure 10.3 as a smooth left-to-right movement of the disk read-write head, you are using sequential access to read the file. If, for example, the disk head moved from the beginning of file to position (1), you might read all of the financial data for the shipping department of a company. The same movement on a cassette player might be thought of as playing one song.

Suppose, however, that the marketing department's financial data is at position (4), and you want to read that data before you read the shipping department's data. You could solve this by performing a sequential read from the beginning of the file to position (4) and simply ignoring the information in-between; but that isn't very efficient.

A better way involves retracting the disk read-write head, placing it over position (4), lowering the disk head, and reading the data. When you have read the end-of-file mark, you can lift the head, move to the beginning of the file, and then read the shipping department's data. Reading a file in such a manner relies on *random access* file techniques. Random access file operations allows us to skip around on a disk reading and writing only on those disk positions that interest us.

Because the high-level disk functions like fread() and fputs() are essentially sequential read-write functions, you need additional functions that allow you to move the disk head from the current position to some new position. The fseek() and ftell() functions provide that capability.

fseek() and *ftell()*

The call to fseek() in the open_file() function in listing 10.5 may not be necessary, but it has been used anyway. The general form for fseek() is

```
fseek(FILE *fp, long int offset, int where)
```

where offset is a byte displacement from a position specified by where. Using the analogy from figure 10.3, fseek() allows you to move the disk head from its present position to offset bytes from where. The argument where represents three positions as indicated by the following three values:

SEEK_SET   Displacement relative to the beginning of the file (usually 0)

SEEK_CUR   Displacement relative to the current position in the file (usually 1)

SEEK_END   Displacement relative to the end of the file (usually 2)

The call in the program uses ØL for offset and SEEK_SET for where. (The capital letter L indicates that the constant is a long data type. The symbolic constants are defined by the ANSI standard and are found in the stdio.h header file.) This means that we want to offset 0 bytes relative to the beginning of the file. In other words, we are at the beginning of the file. For example, if the call were

```
fseek(fpout, -8L, SEEK_END)
```

the position would be 8 bytes from the end of the file. The fseek() function provides an easy way to move within the file in a random fashion.

The ftell() function has the form

```
ftell(FILE *fp)
```

and tells you where you are in a binary file relative to the beginning of the file. The return value is a `long` and represents the number of bytes from the beginning of the file to the present position.

`ftell()` may not return an exact count of the bytes for an ASCII file due to conversions that may take place. For example, the newline character represents a carriage-return linefeed combination but often is stored in the file as a single character. Therefore, `ftell()` can give an accurate count for a binary file, but may not do so for a text file.

Programming Tip

Remember That the File Offset Is a *long int*

One of the most common mistakes made when using `fseek()` is not defining the second argument to be a `long` data type. If you leave the L off the second argument, the compiler is going to think the constant is an `int`. For many compilers, this means only two bytes are sent to `fseek()` when four bytes are expected. This usually will not work too well.

When using an integer constant for the second argument to `fseek()`, always follow it with a capital L. Using the capital L also makes it easier to distinguish the L from the digit 1. That is,

```
fseek(fpout, 1L, Ø)
```

is easier to decipher than is

```
fseek(fpout, 11, Ø)
```

which could look like an eleven byte displacement.

The `write_doubles()` function simply generates 100 (`MAXVALS`) random numbers, each of which is a `double` data type. The standard library function rand() returns integer values, so we use a cast to force the return value to be a double.

The fwrite() function has the form

```
fwrite(void *buff, size_t size,   size_t num, FILE *fpout);
```

The void pointer as the first argument is used to indicate that a pointer to any data type can be used as the buffer for the output data. Both size and num have type specifiers of size_t, which is an implementation-defined typedef for the integer-type of data returned from the sizeof() operator. (Quite often size_t is a typedef for an unsigned data type.) Variable size is the size of one data item that we want to write to the file. Variable num tells fwrite() how many of those items are stored in buff and are to be written to the file. Therefore, fwrite() writes size * num bytes pointed to by buff to the file pointed to by fpout.

Could we have used

```
fwrite(&val[Ø], sizeof(double), (size_t) MAXVALS, fpout);
```

and done away with the loop to write the data to the file? No problem. This would write out all 100 doubles with a single call to fwrite() and avoid the overhead associated with the loop.

Finally, the call fclose() closes the data file. If we are going to read it in the next function call, why close it? The reason is twofold. First, if the file is opened in write mode, you cannot read the file. Second, the data is actually being written not to the disk file itself, but to the FILE buffer associated with fpout. If something happened between writing and reading the data (such as some form of hardware failure), you would probably lose some of the data because it is sitting in the FILE buffer and has not actually been written to disk. The call to fclose() "flushes" the buffer to the disk, and the data then is stored on disk.

The call to open_file() reopens the file by reusing the same FILE pointer. Notice that the modulus operator is used to determine whether a newline needs to be printed or not. Whenever i modulo 10 is zero (that is, i is 0, 10, 20, etc.), a newline is printed and columns of ten numbers result.

The fread() function

```
fread( (void *) &temp, sizeof(double),  (size_t) 1, fpout);
```

reads the data file one double at a time. Notice the first argument used in the function call to fread(). The ANSI standard defines the first argument as a pointer to void, although many compiler vendors follow the UNIX System V definition of a pointer to char. (We have shown the ANSI version.) The important thing to notice is that the first argument must be a pointer, which means fread( ) expects an lvalue. By using the address-of operator (&) in front of temp, we are sending the lvalue of temp to the function. Because of the next two arguments to fread( ), one double will be written into the lvalue supplied as the first argument. In other words, we fill in temp with the double stored on the disk. The call to printf( ) then prints the value out in a field of five character digits with no decimal places.

After all 100 doubles are displayed, fclose( ) closes the file and the program ends. Reading and writing binary data files is not much different than ASCII files. Just make sure that you fopen( ) the file for binary reading or writing.

Using *fscanf()* with *fprintf()*

Before leaving high-level file I/O, you should know about fscanf( ) and how it can be used with the fprintf( ) function. The general form is

```
fscanf(char *fp, char * control_string,...)
```

The fscanf( ) function allows you to read a file that contains formatted data, such as might be written with fprintf( ). Listing 10.6 shows an example of how these two functions may be used together.

Listing 10.6. Formatted Output with fprintf( ) *and* fscanf( )

```
#include  <stdio.h>
#include  <stdlib.h>

#define FIELDW  "%4d"

FILE *fpout;
void open_files(int argc, char *argv[], char *mode);

void main(int argc, char *argv[])
{
    int i, num;

    open_f(argc, argv, "w");

    for (i = Ø; i < 1Ø; i++)
        fprintf(fpout, FIELDW, i);

    fclose(fpout);
```

```
    open_f(argc, argv, "r");
    for (i = Ø; i < 1Ø; i++) {
        fscanf(fpout, FIELDW, &num);
        printf("%d", num);
    }
    fclose(fpout);

}
/*****

                            open_f()

    Function opens a data file in the mode passed into the function.

    Argument list:      int argc        argument counter from command line
                        char *argv[]     argument vector
                        char *mode      the method used for opening file

    Return value:       void
*****/

void open_f(int argc, char *argv[], char *mode)
{
    if (argc != 2) {
        printf("Usage: program outputfile:");
        exit(EXIT_FAILURE);
    }

    if ((fpout = fopen(argv[1], mode)) == NULL) {    /* Open output */
        printf("Cannot open %s. Abort\n", argv[1]);
        exit(EXIT_FAILURE);
    }
}
```

The program is invoked from the command line with a second argument, which is the name of the output file. The open_f() call receives the command line information and the mode in which the file will be used. This way the function can do the "double-duty" of opening the file for reading or writing, depending upon what is passed to the function in mode.

After the file is opened, a for loop is used to write 10 integers to the file using fprintf(). We used a "%4d" control string (FIELDW) for fprintf(), which means the integers are written as four characters to the file. Because only one digit is actually used for the values of i, the field is filled in with three blank spaces. Think about the problem this creates: Each digit requires four bytes in the file even though integers (are assumed to) require only two bytes. The problem is how to read the data back into the program with all of those extra blank spaces.

The `fscanf()` function provides an easy solution. If we use the same control string in `fscanf()` to retrieve the data, everything should stay in sync. The `fscanf()` reads the data from the file four bytes at a time and then forms an integer value from the four bytes. It knows to use four bytes when reading the data because the format string (`FIELDW`) is the same as that used to write the data.

Once the integer is formed by `fscanf()`, it is written into the `lvalue` associated with the conversion character in the control string. That is, the `"%4d"` tells `fscanf()` that the argument to be read is an integer and that an `lvalue` for that integer follows after the control string. Because `fscanf()` must know where in memory to place the data just read from the file, the arguments to `fscanf()` must resolve to `lvalues`. This is why `num` has the address-of operator in front of it; it provides `fscanf()` with a memory address (`lvalue`) of where the data is to be stored after the conversion.

Once `fscanf()` has read the data, converted it, and then written it into `num`, the blank spaces have been removed, and `num` has the appropriate integer value as stored in the data file.

> If you use `fprintf()` to write data to a file, chances are that `fscanf()` is going to provide the easiest means of reading that data back from the file.

At this time, you may want to browse through your standard library documentation and examine the high-level file functions provided with your compiler. Others are available to you and may prove useful in certain situations.

Low-Level File I/O

The remainder of this chapter discusses low-level file I/O, even though the ANSI standard does not support low-level file I/O functions in its description of the standard C library. However, because there is such a large body of pre-ANSI C source code that uses low-level file I/O, I thought it necessary to include the information in this chapter.

I encourage you to write all of your future C code with high-level file I/O to enhance your programs' portability. However, you also should know how low-level file I/O works so that you can understand and use the work of others who precede you.

Low-level file I/O puts us one step closer to the underlying disk operating system. In fact, low-level file I/O under UNIX is done through direct calls to the operating system. Other operating systems may not provide the same calls. Therefore, the designer of the compiler must "build" these call from the disk primitives (for example, BDOS calls in CP/M and MS-DOS) that do exist for the operating system. In either case, low-level file I/O is done in a way that is "convenient" for the host operating system.

open()

Before you can use a low-level disk file, you must open it by using the open() function call. The general form is

```
open(char *filename, int oflag, int mode)
```

where filename is a pointer to the name of the file to be opened and oflag sets the way in which the file will be used. The three basic modes of operation are

O_RDONLY	Open for reading (usually 0)
O_WRONLY	Open for writing (usually 1)
O_RDWR	Open for reading and writing (usually 2)

The values for the symbolic constants are defined in the fcntl.h header file. (This header file is defined in the UNIX System V definition. The symbolic constants are listed in table 10.2.) If the file is opened for writing and the file does not yet exist, it is created. If the file does exist, open( ) truncates it to zero length, effectively erasing its previous contents.

The mode variable assumes a value that defines the type of file that is created. *Caution*: The specific value is operating system dependent. (We will examine this variable when the creat( ) function is discussed later in this chapter.)

Programming Tip

Symbolic Constants for Low-Level File I/O

Many compilers supply a header file (UNIX uses fcntl.h) that contains a number of #defines for use with the open( ) function. The symbolic constants can be used individually or they may be bitwise OR'ed together for even more flexible operation. The most common symbolic constants are presented in table 10.2.

Table 10.2. Symbolic Constants for open( )

O_RDONLY	Open for reading only.
O_WRONLY	Open for writing only.
O_RDWR	Open for reading and writing.
O_APPEND	Open and move the file pointer to the end of the file for writing.
O_CREAT	Create a file. If the file exists, this flag has no effect. Otherwise, mode is set to 0.
O_TRUNC	If the file exists, truncate it to 0 length.
O_EXCL	If this and O_CREAT are set, the open will fail if the file already exists.

Notice that the last constant can provide you with a means for some defensive coding. For example,

```
open("test.c", O_WRONLY | O_CREAT, PMODE);
```

will create the file if it does not already exist and, if it does exist, it will open the file for writing. Because O_TRUNC is not OR'ed into oflag, this use of open() prevents you from opening a file for writing and losing its contents. PMODE (for example, permission mode) is a symbolic constant that assumes a value that is dependent upon the operating system being used. Because open() is not defined in the ANSI standard library, you must read your compiler's documentation for these and other open() options.

Our program examples will use the simpler oflag values rather than the OR'ed flags shown in table 10.2.

File Descriptors

Unlike high-level file I/O that uses FILE pointers for communication between disk files and your program, low-level file I/O uses file descriptors. A *file descriptor* is an integer value returned from the operating system for communication between your program and the disk data file. The file descriptor is returned by the operating system as a result of the call to open(). Once the file is opened, the file descriptor is used for all subsequent file I/O.

Actually, you already have used file descriptors in your programs. If you examine the file structure discussed in listing 10.6, you will see that the first member of the structure is the file descriptor. Because we were using FILE pointers, however, we never actually manipulated this member of the structure.

The following code fragment shows a typical example of how a file is opened using low-level file I/O:

```
if ((fd1 = open(argv[1], O_RDONLY)) == -1) {
    printf("Cannot open %s", argv[1]);
    exit(EXIT_FAILURE);
}
```

Using open() is similar to fopen(), except for three things. First, the second argument is an integer (0 through 2) instead of a character pointer ("r", "w", "a", etc.). Second, an integer file descriptor rather than a FILE pointer is returned from the call to open(). Third, because a file descriptor is the return value from open(), the check for a successful open() call is against an integer value rather than a NULL pointer. Most C implementations return -1 if the file could not be opened, but this may vary among compilers.

Now that you understand the similarity between high-level and low-level file functions and you understand what a file descriptor is, we can illustrate the rest of the low-level file functions by using a program example. Consider listing 10.7.

Listing 10.7. Low-Level File Example

```
#include <stdio.h>
#include <fcntl.h>
#include <stdlib.h>

#define ERR    -1
#define PMODE  Ø              /* WARNING: MS-DOS specific value */

int get_fd(int argc, char *argv[], int mode);
struct person get_data(void);
void show_friend(int fd);

struct person {
   char name[3Ø];
   int age, sex;
   double income;
   };

void main(int argc, char *argv[])
{
   int fd;
   struct person friend;

   fd = get_fd(argc, argv, O_WRONLY | O_TRUNC);
   friend = get_data();
   write(fd, (char *) &friend, (int) sizeof(friend));
   close(fd);

   fd = get_fd(argc, argv, O_RDONLY);
   show_friend(fd);
   close(fd);

}
```

```
/*****
                              show_friend()

    Function that gets the data about an individual from
    a disk file.

    Argument list:    int fd            file descriptor

    Return value:     void
*****/
void show_friend(int fd)
{
    struct person temp;

    read(fd, (char *) &temp, (int) sizeof(temp));
    printf("\n\nname: %s", temp.name);
    printf("\nage: %d   sex: ", temp.age);
    if (temp.sex)
        printf("female");
    else
        printf("male");
    printf("\nIncome: $%-10.2f", temp.income);

}
/*****
                              get_data()

    Function that gets the data about an individual from the user.

    Argument list:    void

    Return value:     struct person      structure with user's data
*****/
struct person get_data(void)
{
    char buff[20];
    struct person temp;

    printf("Enter the name: ");
    gets(temp.name);
    printf("Enter the age: ");
    temp.age = atoi(gets(buff));
```

```
    printf("Enter the sex (Ø = male, 1 = female): ");
    temp.sex = atoi(gets(buff));
    printf("Enter person's income: ");
    temp.income = atof(gets(buff));
    return temp;
}
/*****
                                get _fd()

        Function that gets a file descriptor for the output file.

    Argument list:      int argc        argument counter
                        char *argv[]     argument vector
                        int mode        mode of use

    Return value:       int fd          file descriptor
*****/

int get _fd(int argc, char *argv[], int mode)
{
    int fd;

    if (argc != 2) {
        printf("Usage: program outputfile:");
        exit(EXIT_FAILURE);
    }

    if ((fd = open(argv[1], mode)) == ERR) {    /* Open output */
        if ((fd = creat(argv[1], PMODE)) == ERR) {
            printf("Cannot open %s. Abort\n", argv[1]);
            exit(EXIT_FAILURE);
        }
    }
    return fd;
}
```

The program begins with #include directives for the standard header files plus fcntl.h, which contains the prototypes for the low-level file functions. Next a structure is declared that will be used for the input data for the program. One such structure named friend then is defined in main() for use in the program.

open() and creat()

Within main(), we first attempt to open the output file (as supplied from the command line) by the call to get _fd(). We have shown an alternative form for opening a file here. If you look at the get _fd() function in listing 10.7, you will see that we first attempt to open the file for writing and, if that fails, we then try to create the file. The code shown here will try to create the file if the open() call for writing should fail.

The second argument for creat() determines what type of access privilege is allowed when the file is created. Some operating systems support hidden and system files in addition to "normal" files. The symbolic constant PMODE typically is used to create a normal data file. Be sure to consult your documentation for the details about creat() and the possible values that PMODE can assume.

After the file is opened, a file descriptor (fd) is returned from the get _fd() call. The call to get _data() simply has the user supply the information requested about some friend. Notice that get _data() places all of the information in a structure of type person named temp. Because we have defined get _data() to return a struct person data type, we can return the structure back to main() after it has been filled in by the user. The concept of returning a structure from a function was not allowed in K&R C. The ANSI standard, however, allows us to return a structure from a function call. The temp structure returned from get _data() is then assigned into friend in main().

write()

Now all we have to do is write the data to the file. Reading from left to write, the call

```
write(fd, (char *) &friend, (int) sizeof(friend));
```

says "Write to the file associated with file descriptor fd the contents of friend (&friend) which consists of sizeof(friend) bytes of data." The casts are used so that the data passed to write() agrees with the prototype for write() as stored in fcntl.h. Therefore, the second argument of write() must always be an lvalue (that is, use the ampersand whenever the data item is not a pointer or an array). The third argument simply tells write() how many bytes to use from the item pointed to by the second argument.

close()

Finally, close() is called with fd as its argument. This call takes care of any cleanup that needs to be done on the file before the file is closed and the fd is freed.

The call to get _fd() again is called, but with a different mode value (O _RDONLY). Upon return, fd will once again be tied to the proper data file.

read()

The show _friend() defines a structure of type person into which the disk file information is to be read. The read() function then reads sizeof(temp) bytes from the disk into the lvalue associated with temp. In other words, the data from the file is read into the address where temp is stored in memory.

The rest of the program simply displays the data which was just read into temp from disk. After that has been done, control returns to main(), the file is closed, and the program ends.

lseek() and tell()

Listing 10.7 does a simple sequential write and read, using low-level file techniques. More sophisticated programs need the capability to do random reads and writes as well. The functions lseek() and tell() are the low-level equivalents for fseek() and ftell() discussed earlier.

For lseek(), the general form is

```
lseek(int fd, long offset, int where)
```

and is almost the same as fseek(), except the first argument is a file descriptor rather than a FILE pointer. The interpretation of offset and where is the same as for fseek(). The function

```
tell(int fd)
```

is the same as ftell(), except that a file descriptor is used instead of a FILE pointer. However, because these functions are not included in the standard library, you will need to consult your documentation for the specifics of their use.

When Files Aren't Files

If you have taken the time to look at the contents of the stdio.h header file, you probably saw several symbolic constants similar to those in the following list:

```
#define    stdin      &_iob[0]
#define    stdout     &_iob[1]
#define    stderr     &_iob[2]
```

As you saw earlier in this chapter, the _iob[] array is an array of FILE structures that holds the overhead information needed to use disk files. Stated simply, these are standard I/O definitions that can be used in C programs. (Some compilers will also implement stdlst for the list or printer device, but it is not defined by ANSI.) The defined symbolic constants stand for

stdin	Standard input device, usually the keyboard
stdout	Standard output device, usually the screen
stderr	Standard error device, usually the screen

Because each of these standard devices is a symbolic constant for the address (lvalue) of the FILE structure array, each may be treated as a FILE pointer. Therefore, if we wanted to let the user select whether output is to be sent to the screen, the standard error device, or a disk file, we might use code similar to that presented in listing 10.8.

Listing 10.8 uses an infinite while loop to force the user to select an option between 1 and 3. If the user does not enter a choice within the proper range, we continue to ask for the proper option. When the choice is within the proper range, the if test becomes True, and we break out of the while loop with c set to the choice.

A switch statement on c then sets the fpout FILE pointer to the appropriate output device. We will assume that open_file_device() gets all of the required information to open a file and returns a FILE pointer if option 3 is selected.

Listing (Fragment) 10.8. *User Selected Output Medium*

```
#define TRUE    1

FILE *fpout;
int c;
.
.
while (TRUE) {
    printf("Output to the: 1) screen 2) error device 3) file");
    printf("\n\n          Enter choice: ");
    c = getchar() - '0';
    if (c > 0 && c < 4)
        break;
}
switch (c) {
    case 1:              /* Screen  */
        fpout = stdout;
        break;
    case 2:              /* Standard error */
        fpout = stderr;
        break;
    case 3:              /* File     */
        fpout = open_file_device();
        break;
}
```

Converting a Character to an Integer

The statement

```
c = getchar() - '0';
```

is a quick-and-dirty way of converting a character to an integer. For example, if the user enters a character digit '1', it has an ASCII value of 49 (see Appendix A). Subtracting the ASCII value for a '0' digit character (48) gives a numeric (binary) value of 1. This is exactly what we want.

Output to the Screen and Smaller Code Size

C is used widely to program everything from large database projects to small programs that run microwave ovens. When you are working in pico-acres in a PROM (Programmable Read-Only Memory), code size is a critical factor. If you can shrink a program to the point where it saves one PROM chip, it can save a company millions of dollars.

One way of saving code space in a program is to avoid using huge functions that offer features not needed in your program. Perhaps the two worst offenders are printf() and scanf(). I have already played down the use of scanf(), but printf() is also very large. Part of the reason is because printf() must be able to cope with virtually every type of data available in C. If you are programming toasters, printf() is probably overkill. For example, consider listing 10.9.

Listing 10.9. *Short* printf( ) *Program*

```
#include <stdio.h>
#include <stdlib.h>

void main(void)
{
    printf("Hello world");
}
```

Listing 10.9 is the standard example of someone's first C program. With the compiler I use, the code size for the executable program was 9208 bytes. Now, consider listing 10.10.

Listing 10.10. *Short Program without* printf( )

```
#include <stdio.h>
#include <stdlib.h>

void main(void)
{
    write(fileno(stdout), "Hello world", 11);
}
```

Listing 10.10 is functionally equivalent to listing 10.9, but the executable program size was only 2160 bytes; less than one-fourth the size of program 10.9. The reason for the reduced code size is that write() is a simple function that isn't required to perform the variety of tasks expected of printf().

So how does it work? As you know, write() is a low-level output routine that expects a file descriptor as its first argument. Although stdout is associated with high-level file I/O, we also know that some file descriptor is associated with the stdout FILE structure. The library function fileno() is designed to retrieve a file descriptor from its associated FILE pointer. (Most compilers that provide low-level file I/O will supply this function in one form or another.) The rest of the write() arguments are simple: (1) the string constant we wish to print and (2) the number of characters in the string constant.

Obviously, you can also use variables if you wish. Suppose, for example, that buff[] is a character array with a message you want to display on the screen (or printer if you use stdlst). The write() call would be written

```
write(fileno(stdout), buff, strlen(buff));
```

The additional call to strlen() adds very little to the size of the program and allows you to use string variables rather than just constants.

Keep in mind that alternatives to printf() such as putchar() and puts() do exist in the standard library, and many of them will produce smaller and slightly faster programs. Also, there may be special functions supplied with your compiler that provide other alternatives, too. It may be worth your time to study your standard library documentation to see what little gems may be hidden away in there.

▼ Review Questions and Exercises

1. What is a FILE pointer and why is it important?

2. If you list your stdio.h file, you will probably see something like

    ```
    #define OPEN_MAX 1Ø
    ```

    and a comment stating that this is the number of files that are available. If that is the case, how many files can your program have open at one time?

3. Suppose that you need to know how large a binary file is at run time. How might you determine this information?

4. Why is a call to fclose() necessary when you are finished with a disk file?

5. Would you prefer to use high or low-level file I/O in a program? Why?

6. Write a program that will accept an input file name and one or more words on the command line. The program then opens the input file and searches the file for the sequence of words entered on the command line. Have the program print out the line number and the line where the match occurred, if any.

Answers

1. A FILE pointer is a typedef for a pointer to a structure that contains overhead information about a disk file. Such pointers are important because they serve as the communications link between your program and the system software that allows you to work with disk data files.

2. Although the answer to this question may vary among operating systems, the answer would typically be seven, because three of those 10 files are reserved for stdin, stdout, and stderr.

3. One way would be to do an fseek() to the end of the file, such as

```
fseek(fp, ØL, SEEK_END);
```

which places you at end-of-file. If you then perform an ftell(), the return value from ftell() is the number of bytes from the beginning of the file to its present position, which is EOF. This would be the size of the data file. Because of potential differences between character sets and internal character translations that might be made, this method is not guaranteed to work on text files.

4. Because high-level file I/O stores its input and output in a buffer, there may be information left in the buffer when you are finished using the file. One of the jobs of fclose() is to flush this buffer so that all the data from the program is written to disk.

5. Given the direction of the ANSI committee, future C programs should probably use high-level file I/O. It seems certain that all vendors of C compilers will provide as many of the standard library routines as are

possible to implement in the host environment. (Some have no meaning across operating systems, such as multiuser functions in a single-user operating system.) Therefore, the ease with which you can move a program from one environment to another should be easier if you use high-level I/O.

6. This program can be a useful utility, especially when you are working with multiple files and can't remember which one contains which sections of code. One solution might be as follows:

```
/* Disk File String Search */

#include <stdio.h>
#include <stdlib.h>
#include <string.h>

#define MAXSTR 256

FILE *fpin;

void search(char buff[]),
    make_string(int argc, char *argv[], char buff[]),
    open_file(int argc, char *argv[]);

void main(int argc, char *argv[])
{
    char buff[MAXSTR];

    open_file(argc, argv);
    make_string(argc, argv, buff);
    search(buff);
    fclose(fpin);
}
/*****
                              search()
```

Function that reads the input file one line at a time and searches for the pattern string. If a match is found, the line number and line with the match are displayed.

Argument list: char buff[]   buffer with pattern to find

Return value: void

```
*****/

void search(char buff[])
{
    char temp[MAXSTR], *ptr;
    int len, count;

    count = 1;
    len = strlen(buff);
    while (fgets(temp, MAXSTR, fpin) != NULL) {
        if ((ptr = memchr(temp, buff[Ø], strlen(temp))) == NULL) {
            count + +;
            continue;
        }
        if (memcmp(ptr, buff, len) == Ø) {
            printf("%5d %s\n", count, temp);
        }
        count + +;
    }

}

/*****
                            make_string()
```

Function converts the command line arguments argv[2] through argv[n] into a null-terminated string. Blank spaces are allowed from the command line.

Argument list:	int argc	argument counter from command line
	char *argv[]	argument vector
	char buff[]	buffer to hold string search pattern
Return value:	void	

```
*****/

void make_string(int argc, char *argv[], char buff[])
{
    int i;

    buff[Ø] = '\Ø';
    for (i = 2; i < argc; i + +) {      /* Build the string        */
        strcat(buff, argv[i]);
        strcat(buff, " ");
```

```
      }
      i = strlen(buff);
      buff[i - 1] = '\0';                  /* Get rid of trailing blank space  */
}
/*****
                              open_file()
```

Function checks for at least three command line arguments and then attempts to open the file.

Argument list: int argc   argument counter from command line
                         char *argv[]   argument vector   "

Return value: void

```
*****/
void open_file(int argc, char *argv[])
{
    if (argc < 3) {
        printf("Usage:program input_file search_string");
        exit(EXIT_FAILURE);
    }
    if ((fpin = fopen(argv[1], "r")) == NULL) {
        printf("Could not open %s", argv[1]);
        exit(EXIT_FAILURE);
    }
}
```

I think you owe it to yourself to figure out what the program does. It uses only ANSI standard function calls, or those provided in the program. The code that searches for the string is crude, but it can still search a 30-page document in less than 10 seconds on a PC-type computer. (For some alternative pattern matching ideas, see my article "Pattern Matching Alternatives: Theory vs. Practice," *Computer Language*, Nov., 1987, pp. 34-44.)

11

The C Preprocessor

Concepts in This Chapter

- ❏ The various preprocessor directives
- ❏ Parameterized macros
- ❏ ANSI header files

The C preprocessor is a program that examines a C source file and performs certain modifications on the file based upon instructions, or directives, to the preprocessor. The ANSI standard has expanded these directives substantially, and we will examine each of these directives in this chapter.

Macro Substitution Using the *#define* Directive

In a number of program examples in this book, the #define preprocessor directive has been used to create a symbolic constant for use in a program. The general form is

357

```
#define macro_name  substitution_text
```

where macro_name is replaced with substitution_text throughout the program. A typical example might be

```
#define MAXSIZE      128
...
char buff[MAXSIZE];
```

This book has also pointed out that the C preprocessor replaces the symbolic constant MAXSIZE with the *text* 128 at every point in the program (except within quoted strings). Because there is a textual substitution of 128 for each occurrence of MAXSIZE throughout the program, a #define preprocessor directive is often referred to as a "macro substitution" or, more simply, just a "macro."

Using *#undef*

In some circumstances, it is desirable to "undefine" a macro after it has been used. For example, if you are writing a series of screen functions, you might use

```
#define COLUMNS  80
#define ROWS     24

/* Perhaps several screen functions that use COLUMNS and ROWS */

#undef COLUMNS
#undef ROWS

#define COLUMNS  40
#define ROWS     16

/* New screen functions with different COLUMNS and ROWS */

#undef COLUMNS
#undef ROWS
```

The #undef cancels the existing replacement text for the COLUMNS and ROWS symbolic constants. If need be, you could then redefine these two constants. By redefining the constants, you could have a number of functions, using different values for COLUMNS and ROWS. If the #undef were not used, however, any new #defines for COLUMNS or ROWS would produce a "multiply defined" error message.

Using Parameterized Macros

What this book has not shown to this point is that macros may also have arguments. If a macro has an argument, it is called a *parameterized macro*. The classic example is a parameterized macro that squares a number, such as

```
#define  square(x)   (x) * (x)

...
...
val = 5;
y = square(val);
```

This will produce a value of y that is equal to 25. Again, because there is textual substitution, the preprocessor pass produces code for the compiler that looks like

```
val = 5;
y = (val) * (val);
```

Indeed, some compilers have a compile-time option that lets you examine the source code after the preprocessor pass is completed. This would allow you to see the actual substitutions that took place during the preprocessor pass.

Parentheses and Parameterized Macros

Are the parentheses necessary in the square() macro? Let's see what would happen if they were not used.

```
#define  square(x)   x * x

...
...
val = 5;
y = square(val + 1);
```

Notice hat the macro has been used in the form val + 1. In the absence of parentheses, the expansion by the preprocessor becomes

```
y = val + 1 * val + 1;
```

However, because of the precedence of operators, the expansion becomes

```
y = 5 + 1 * 5 + 1;
y = 5 + 5 + 1;
y = 11;
```

which is not correct. By using parentheses, you ensure that expressions are evaluated in the proper order, such as

```
y = (5 + 1) * (5 + 1);
y = 6 * 6;
y = 36;
```

Side Effects of Parameterized Macros

Another problem you should know about is the danger of performing certain operations with parameterized macros. These side effects can occur even when parentheses are used. Consider the square() macro using the following increment operation

```
y = square(val ++);
```

This use of the macro expands to

```
y = (val ++) * (val ++);
```

If val equals 5 prior to invoking the macro, the first use of val would be 5, the second use of val would be 6, and val would end up with the value of 7 because there are two post-increments of val. The result would be

```
y = 5 * 6;
y = 30;
```

although the expected result was probably 36 (that is, 6×6) when it was called with square(val ++).

As a general rule, you should perform all operations on a macro parameter prior to using the macro.

You could solve the square problem by performing the increment before using the square() macro, as in

```
val + +;
y = square(val);
```

which would yield the correct result.

Advantages and Disadvantages of Macros

Many standard library functions are actually implemented as macros. For example, the "is" functions (for example, islower(), isupper(), isdigit(), etc.) used to perform certain tests on characters are often implemented as macros. (To see these macros, examine the ctype.h header file.) Clearly, these functions could also be implemented as "real" standard library functions rather than macros. What is the difference between a library function and a macro?

First, because a macro is a textual substitution in a program, the code for that macro appears at each point in the program where you use it. This has the advantage that you avoid the overhead associated with a function call (for example, pushing arguments on the stack) and your program will execute slightly faster. The disadvantage is that code size increases because the code for the macro is duplicated each time the macro is used in the program. If a standard library function is used instead of a macro, the code only appears once in the program—code size is smaller. The price, however, is slightly slower code because of the overhead associated with a function call.

Another advantage of macros is that they are not data-specific. Using our square() macro,

```
val = 5;
y = square(val);
```

val can be any data type and the macro will produce the correct result. That is, val could be an int, long, or a double and the macro would produce the correct result. On the other hand, a square() function requires that the data type be specified when the function is defined. For example,

```
double square(double x)
{
    return x * x;
}
```

The type specifier and the prototype require that the function be defined for a given data type (a double in this example). Whereas one macro could handle all of your "squaring" needs, you would need to write a new square() function for each data type if a function is used. (Perhaps the best function approach would be to write a square() function for a double data type and then cast the value returned from the function to the desired data type.) A macro can be an efficient solution when different data types can be used by the same macro.

ANSI and Macros Versus Functions

The ANSI committee recognized that some programmers need the smallest code possible and would be willing to sacrifice some speed for smaller code size. The committee also knew that others would prefer macros because of their speed and could care less about code size. Because programming requirements differ, ANSI suggested that wherever possible, every macro also have an equivalent function in the standard library. Therefore, if the ctype.h header file has an islower() macro, there should also be an islower() function in the standard library. This gives you the right to choose the macro or function according to your own needs.

Keep in mind that, if square() is not a macro that has been #defined in the source code file, it then becomes the linker's responsibility to find the function in a library file. If the linker cannot find square() and it is still unresolved, an "unresolved external" error will be issued by the linker. This error message simply means the linker could not find the function in the libraries you told it to search. (Quite often this error message is caused by misspelling a function name.)

File Inclusion Using *#include*

Every program in this book has used an #include for the stdio.h header file. The general form has been

```
#include <file_name>
```

Forcing the Compiler To Use a Function

Suppose that you want to use the `islower()` function rather than its corresponding macro. How can you force the compiler to avoid the macro and use the function? Actually, there are a number of ways. The most obvious is to not #include the `ctype.h` header file. Not including that header file in the program will cause the linker to link in the `islower()` function from the standard library.

Not including the `ctype.h` header file is not a very elegant solution to the problem, however. First, there may be other information in the header file that you need to use in the program. Second, you lose the type-checking advantages of prototyping if you omit the related header file.

Is there any approach that allows us to have our cake and eat it too? Still another solution is to "undefine" the macro. Although this approach would allow you to #include the necessary header file in the program, you would still lose the benefits of prototyping.

Is there a way to include the header file and retain the type checking protection of prototyping? Yes, there is.

One of the rules of parameterized macros is that there can be nothing between the macro name and the opening parenthesis. That is, a blank space between `islower` and `()` is not allowed in a macro. So `islower(x)` is a valid macro name, but `islower (x)` is not. This seems to offer the simple solution of inserting a space between the function name and its opening parenthesis. Because the compiler knows that there can be no space between the macro name and the parenthesis, it would know not to use the macro, but cause the function to be linked in.

Unfortunately, some compilers may not allow a space after a function name. However, all compilers should accept

```
flag = (islower)(c);
```

as a valid function call, but not a valid macro invocation. Because the function name is enclosed in parentheses, the compiler knows that `islower()` cannot be a macro and must be a function.

In the strict interpretation, the left (<) and right (>) angle brackets mean that the search for `file_name` is done in some implementation-defined manner. In actual practice, this usually means that the current working directory is the last place searched (and it may not be searched at all).

On the other hand, in

```
#include "file_name"
```

where the angle brackets are replaced with double quotation marks, the search for `file_name` begins in the directory where the source file is located. This is usually the current working directory, but the details are implementation-defined.

The `file_name` should constitute a valid file name for the host operating system, but should not contain a newline character, quotes, angle brackets, or the comment characters /* or */.

You should consult your compiler's documentation for specifics on how the quotes versus angle brackets are processed by your compiler as well as details on what is a valid file name for your host operating system.

Conditional Compilation with *#if*

The preprocessor recognizes a variety of conditional compilation directives. The conditional preprocessor directives include those shown in table 11.1.

Table 11.1. Conditional Preprocessor Directives

Directive	Interpretation
#if	conditional if
#elif	else - if
#else	else
#endif	end of if or elif
#ifdef	if defined
#ifndef	if not defined

The general form for the #if directive is

```
#if exp
```

where exp is a constant expression. For example,

```
#if MOOD == 1
     #define FEELING     "Good"
#else
     #define FEELING     "Bad"
#endif
```

In this example if MOOD is equal to 1, the symbolic constant FEELING is given the replacement text "Good". If MOOD equals anything other than 1, FEELING is defined as "Bad". Notice the parallel between the if...else and the #if...#else. The purpose of the #endif is to tell the preprocessor where the end of #if is.

The #elif directive is new with the ANSI standard and extends the #if conditional. It is similar to an else-if syntax. For example,

```
#if PERSON == 1
     #define STATUS   "Single"
#elif PERSON == 2
     #define STATUS   "Married"
#elif PERSON == 3
     #define STATUS   "Divorced"
#elif PERSON == 4
     #define STATUS   "Widowed"
#else
     #define STATUS   "Unknown"
#endif
```

As you can see, the addition of the #elif provides a much simpler way to perform multiple tests than did the pre-ANSI preprocessor directives. If the #elif were not used, you would have to use a long series of #if-#endif directives. #elif is consistent with common coding practices and accomplishes a given task in fewer words.

The directives #ifdef and #ifndef provide a means of testing whether an identifier is yet defined in the program. For example, some compilers provide a symbolic constant named TRUE (usually with the value of 1), while others do not. If you are using different compilers, this can be a problem. Therefore, you might see something like

```
#ifndef TRUE
     #define TRUE 1
#endif
```

which says "If the symbolic constant TRUE is not defined, #define TRUE to be equal to 1." Another variation might be

```
#ifdef SYSV
     #include  <unix.h>
#selse
     #include  <msdos.h>
#endif
```

Notice that the #ifdef simply tests for a previous definition of the symbolic constant SYSV—the test is for an identifier, not a constant expression.

ANSI also allows a different way of writing the #ifdef and #ifndef, using the new preprocessor operator called defined. With this new operator, the above example could be written

```
#if ! defined TRUE
     #define TRUE 1
#endif
```

and

```
#if defined SYSV
     #include  <unix.h>
#else
     #include  <msdos.h>
#endif
```

Either form will produce the same results.

Compiling Multiple Files with Global Data

As you write larger and more complex programs, you will find it beneficial to break the program down into several modules, or source files. When you do this, keeping track of where the global variables are defined and where they are simply declared can get a bit messy. The preprocessor, however, provides a simple way of keeping things straight.

Let's suppose you have a number of global variables used in a program and that all global variables are contained in a header file called globals.h. To keep things simple, we will assume that there are only two modules for the program. Module 1 contains main(), and Module 2 contains support code for the program. Now let's see how we might write the globals.h header file:

```
/*  globals.h */
#ifdef EXT
      extern
#endif
      double x, y, z;
```

For things to work properly, variables x, y, and z can be defined in only one module, but must be declared (with the extern keyword) in the other module. Now suppose that the two modules begin with the following two lines:

```
/*  Module 1 */

#include "globals.h"

     .

     .

/*  Module 2 */

#define EXT 1
#include "globals.h"
```

When Module 1 is compiled, globals.h is read into the program. However, because EXT is not defined in Module 1, the #ifdef causes the extern keyword to be omitted. Therefore, after the preprocessor pass, globals.h ends up in Module 1 as though it were written

```
double x, y, z;
```

In other words, we have *defined* variables x, y, and z in Module 1.

Now look at what happens when Module 2 is compiled. Because EXT is defined *before* globals.h is read, the #ifdef causes the replacement in Module 2 to become

```
extern double x, y, z;
```

which means that we are *declaring* variables x, y, and z in Module 2. Because we can declare a variable as often as we wish, but can only define a variable once, the technique described here does exactly what we need to do for our globals to work correctly in the program. If you need more than two modules, just #define EXT prior to reading globals.h in each of the additional modules and everything will work as before.

Other Preprocessor Directives: #line, #error, #pragma

The #line preprocessor directive has the general form

    #line number "filename"

but can also be written

    #line number

where number is the line number of the next line in the source file named filename. If the filename is omitted, it is assumed to be the last name used for filename. The #line directive is used for diagnostics in debugging. For example, the line

    #line 1 "module1.c"

causes the compiler to refer to the source file as module1.c and the line number at the point of the #line directive is line 1. The new file name and line number now become the reference points for compiler diagnostics and error messages.

The #error preprocessor directive has the general form

    #error message

where message is normally a string containing some form of error message. The compiler vendor can prepend their own string to message.

The #pragma directive has the form

    #pragma implementation_defined_action

The action caused by a #pragma is determined by the compiler vendor. You will have to check your compiler's documentation to see whether any #pragmas are supported for your compiler and what they might do.

Predefined Preprocessor Identifiers

ANSI has reserved several identifiers for use by the preprocessor. These names are fixed and cannot be #undefed. The list of identifiers are presented in table 11.2.

Table 11.2. *Predefined Preprocessor Identifiers*

__LINE__	The present line number in the source file
__FILE__	The name of the file being compiled as a string
__DATE__	The date of the compile as a string
__TIME__	The time of the compile as a string
__STDC__	Evaluates to the constant 1 if the compiler is an ANSI standard conforming compiler

---

Listing 11.1 presents a simple example of how these identifiers may be used.

Listing 11.1. *Using Predefined Identifiers*

```
#include <stdio.h>

int main()
{
    printf("line = %d\n", __LINE__);
    printf("file = %s\n", __FILE__);
    printf("date = %s\n", __DATE__);
    printf("time = %s\n", __TIME__);
    printf("stdc = %d\n", __STDC__);
}
```

The output of the program (called prepro.c) was

```
line = 6
file = prepro.c
date = Jul 31 1988
time = 22:13:1Ø
```

(The __STDC__ was actually removed from the source program shown in listing 11.1 because the compiler was not yet a conforming ANSI compiler.)

This completes the discussion of the preprocessor directives. It is worth repeating that the preprocessor is just that—a pass on the source code that takes place prior to compilation. The preprocessor has several features that make some tasks easier than they would be otherwise. You should take the time to digest what has been presented above.

ANSI Standard Header Files

All vendors supply header files with their C compilers. However, prior to the work by the ANSI committee, the header files that were in use were not standardized in terms of either name of content. Only a few shared common names (such as stdio.h) and fewer still shared common content.

The ANSI committee recognized the need to standardize both the name and content of header files. For the most part, the header file names and contents have been standardized along functional lines. The string.h header file, for example, deals with string functions. ctype.h is concerned with character functions, and so forth. The new standards for both name and content of header files should enhance program portability.

What follows is a list of each of these standard header files and a brief description of what is contained in the header file. For a complete description, see the *C Standard Library* (Purdum and Leslie, Que Corporation).

assert.h

The assert.h header file contains the assert() macro which can be used to test an expression in a program at run time. For example, consider listing 11.2.

Listing 11.2. Using the `assert()` *Macro*

```
#include <stdio.h>
#include <assert.h>

int main()
{
    int i, j;
    i = rand();
    j = 5;
    assert(i);
    printf("%d", j / i);
}
```

When the expression that is the argument for the `assert()` macro returns a value that is logical False, the program will display

```
Assertion failed: (expression), file (filename), line  (nnn)
```

If `rand()` would return a value of zero for `i` and the file is named `test.c`, the display would be

```
Assertion failed: i, file test.c, line 11
```

showing that `i` had a value of 0. Note that the expression that is the argument for `assert()` can be more complex than a single variable. For example,

```
assert( (a + b) == 1Ø);
```

would also be permissible. The advantage of the `assert()` macro for debugging is that you can, in effect, remove the `assert()` macro by simply placing a `#define NDEBUG` prior to the `#include <assert.h>`. Some compilers provide a compiler switch (which is often `-DNDEBUG`) that also removes the `assert()` code from the program. The `assert()` macro in conjunction with the `NDEBUG` macro provides an easy way to toggle debug code in or out of a program without editing the source file. Check your compiler's documentation to see whether the `assert()` macro (and the `-D` compile switch) is available.

ctype.h

The ctype.h header file contains a number of character-testing macros of the is* family (for example, isdigit(), isupper(), etc.) plus the tolower() and toupper() macros.

errno.h

The errno.h file contains symbolic constants that can be used in error processing. This file assumes that a variable named errno has been defined by the vendor of the compiler. (ANSI assumes errno is defined as a volatile int.) This variable may be used in certain standard library functions (for example, perror()). See your compiler's documentation for details on errno and supporting functions.

float.h

The float.h file contains information about how floating point numbers are represented by the compiler. Primarily, it contains symbolic constants that explain such things as floating point precision, minimum and maximum floating point values, epsilon values, and the like.

limits.h

The limits.h header file has information about the minimum and maximum values that various data types can assume for the compiler. For example, the file will contain a number of symbolic constants that tell the minimum and maximum values for a char, int, long, and other data types.

locale.h

Inclusion of the locale.h header file in the ANSI standard is a formal recognition that C may exist in environments where ASCII is not the host character set. For example, while we use the decimal point for separating dollars and cents, it may be a comma or raised dot in other character sets. The purpose of this header file is to collect these "locale-specific" differences in one place.

math.h

The math.h header file contains various function prototypes and macros used by various math functions. Most of the functions in this header file return a double data type.

setjmp.h

The setjmp.h header file contains the function prototypes for the setjmp() and longjmp() functions plus a typedef for jmp_buf. As you may recall, the goto statement is limited to transferring program control to a point within the current function block. That is, a goto cannot send program control to a label that is outside of the function block in which the goto is used. Because there may be times when you need to send control outside of the current function block (perhaps because of an error condition), the setjmp() and longjmp() functions are made available. Listing 11.3 provides a simple program to demonstrate how setjmp() and longjmp() are used.

Listing 11.3 includes the setjmp.h header file so that the function prototypes and the typedef for jmp_buf are available. Two variables of type jmp_buf (env1 and env2) are defined. The purpose of these two "environment" variables is to hold the status of the program at the time they are set when a setjmp() call is made. (You can think of these variables as being able to hold a copy of the CPU registers, stack pointer, etc.) *The only value that can be returned by* setjmp() *is 0.*

The first call to setjmp() uses env1 as its argument which is filled in with the program environment that exists when setjmp() is called. Because setjmp() can only return 0, we skip the call to func1() and the else part of the first if statement is executed. The program now falls into the second if statement.

Once again, the program calls setjmp() but with env2 as its argument. This means that env2() is filled in with the status of the program as it presently exists. As before, setjmp() returns a 0 so that func2() is not called; then the program calls func3().

In func3(), a message is displayed and the longjmp() call is executed using env2 as its first argument. This has the effect of returning program control to the status that existed when env2 was set. However, because the second argument to longjmp() is a 1, the second if statement becomes logical True, and func2() is executed.

Listing 11.3. setjmp() *and* longjmp()

```
#include <stdio.h>
#include <setjmp.h>

jmp_buf env1, env2;
void func1(void), func2(void), func3(void);

int main()
{
   if (setjmp(env1))
      func1();
   else {
      if (setjmp(env2))
         func2();
      else
         func3();
   }
}

void func1(void)
{
   printf("Now we're in func1\n");
}

void func2(void)
{
   printf("Now we're in func2\n");
   longjmp(env1, 1);
}

void func3(void)
{
   printf("Now we're in func3\n");
   longjmp(env2, 1);
}
```

The code in func2() is virtually the same as func3(), except that env1 is used as the first argument of the longjmp() call. This means program control resumes at the status that existed when env1 was sent. Because longjmp() returns a value of 1, the first if statement is now viewed as logical True, and the call to func1() is executed. The output of the program, therefore, is

```
Now we're in func3
Now we're in func2
Now we're in func1
```

Notice that we have been able to jump to different points in the program from outside the main( ) function block. The setjmp( ) and longjmp( ) functions are quite powerful and are well worth studying.

signal.h

The purpose of the signal.h header file is to provide a means for coping with special conditions that might arise during program execution. Often these exceptional conditions are for processing interrupts and error conditions that might exist. The details will be influenced by both the compiler and operating system being used.

stdarg.h

The stdarg.h header file is concerned with functions and macros that are used to process functions that use a variable number of arguments. Most of the information presented is used by the vprintf( ) function.

stddef.h

The stddef.h file will list variable names and macros that are reserved for use by the compiler. It will also contain several typedefs used by a number of functions or operators. For example, this file contains the size_t typedef for the data type returned by the sizeof operator.

stdio.h

The stdio.h file is used whenever any type of I/O is done in a program —which means virtually all programs. It contains numerous prototypes, macros, and other information necessary to perform program I/O.

stdlib.h

The stdlib.h file contains the function prototypes and macros used by the utility functions provided as part of the C standard library. It appears that these utility functions are found in this file because they do not fit nicely into any of the other header files.

string.h

As the name might suggest, the string.h file contains the function prototypes and macros necessary to perform string processing in a program. Chances are, you will use string.h a lot.

time.h

The time.h file contains the function prototypes, macros, and typedefs for those functions that are concerned with either time or dates. This file also contains a structure definition that is used to hold time information.

As a general rule, you should include a header file in your program any time you use a function that is prototyped in that header file. It would be worth your time to list the contents of each header file shipped with your compiler to see what is contained therein. The list here is not exhaustive and special header files are often shipped with each compiler (such as dos.h). Keep the listings of these header files for future reference.

▼ Review Questions and Exercises

1. What is the difference between a macro and a parameterized macro?

2. What are the advantages and disadvantages of macros versus functions?

3. Write a macro that determines whether a number is odd or even. The macro should return 1 if the number is odd and 0 if it is even.

4. How can conditional compilation be used effectively when writing programs for more than one type of machine?

5. Why should you #include a header file in a program even when the program works without it?

6. Examine the list of header files in this chapter and categorize the header files along functional lines. What does your list look like?

▼ Answers

1. A simple macro is usually just a symbolic constant involving a text replacement in the program. A parameterized macro also involves text replacement, but the macro has one or more arguments associated with it.

2. A macro results in inline code whereas a function is like a subroutine call. Because the macro avoids the overhead associated with a function call, macros tend to execute somewhat faster. Also, macros are not data-specific. The disadvantage is that, because a macro does produce inline code, each use of the macro duplicates the code for that macro. As a result, macros tend to increase code size if the macro is used more than once in a program.

3. One way might be as follows:

```
#include  <stdio.h>
#include  <stdlib.h>

#define  oddeven(x) (x % 2)

int main()
{
   char buff[2Ø];
   int i, j;

   printf("Enter a number: ");
   i = atoi(gets(buff));

   j = oddeven(i);
   printf("number = %d odd-even flag = %d\n", i, j);
}
```

The oddeven() macro simply performs a modulus operation on the argument. If this approach is used, the macro can only be used with integer numbers (including longs) because the modulus operator cannot be used with floating point numbers.

4. C is known to be a fairly portable programming language. However, portability problems most often appear in the I/O sections of a program. If you could isolate certain variables, macros, and symbolic constants that vary among machines and place them in their own header file, conditional compilation might make things a bit simpler. For example, if you are writing a program for an IBM PC, a UNIX system, and a Macintosh, you might use

```
#if COMPUTER == PC
    #include "pc.h"
#elif COMPUTER == UNIX
        #include "unix.h"
#else
        #include "mac.h"
#endif
```

The approach described here also illustrates the importance of isolating system-dependent variables and constants into one place so that they can be located easily.

5. Many programs will work without including the header file. However, if you do not #include the header file, you lose the benefits of prototyping (type checking on function arguments). In addition, if some of the functions return values other than (the default data type of) int, it may take you some debugging time to find the problems in your program. Also, there may be symbolic constants or typedefs (such as FILE) that are critical to the proper use of certain functions.

6. Your list will be different than mine, but it might be similar to

assert.h, errno.h	Debugging and error processing
ctype.h	Character processing
float.h, limits.h	Defines sizes of certain data types and how some data types are processed
locale.h	Geographic differences affecting the compiler
math.h	Mathematical processing
setjmp.h	Non-local goto processing
signal.h	Interrupt (and error) processing
stdarg.h	Variable argument processing

stddef.h	Compiler specific variables and typedefs
stdio.h	Input/Output processing
stdlib.h	Utility functions (catch-all)
string.h	String processing
time.h	Time and date processing

ASCII Codes and the Extended Character Set

This appendix had two parts: a table showing ASCII codes, and a table showing the Extended Character Set available on IBM PCs and compatible computers. Codes for the characters are given in decimal, hexadecimal, octal, and binary notation. (For an introduction to binary, hexadecimal, and octal notation, see Appendix D.)

ASCII Codes

Control characters (codes 0 through 31) are identified by their names and by their control-key equivalents.

Decimal	Hex	Octal	Binary	ASCII	
0	00	000	00000000	^@	NUL
1	01	001	00000001	^A	SOH
2	02	002	00000010	^B	STX
3	03	003	00000011	^C	ETX
4	04	004	00000100	^D	EOT
5	05	005	00000101	^E	ENQ
6	06	006	00000110	^F	ACK
7	07	007	00000111	^G	BEL
8	08	010	00001000	^H	BS
9	09	011	00001001	^I	HT
10	0A	012	00001010	^J	LF
11	0B	013	00001011	^K	VT
12	0C	014	00001100	^L	FF
13	0D	015	00001101	^M	CR
14	0E	016	00001110	^N	SO
15	0F	017	00001111	^O	SI
16	10	020	00010000	^P	DLE
17	11	021	00010001	^Q	DC1
18	12	022	00010010	^R	DC2
19	13	023	00010011	^S	DC3
20	14	024	00010100	^T	DC4
21	15	025	00010101	^U	NAK
22	16	026	00010110	^V	SYN
23	17	027	00010111	^W	ETB
24	18	030	00011000	^X	CAN
25	19	031	00011001	^Y	EM
26	1A	032	00011010	^Z	SUB
27	1B	033	00011011	^[	ESC
28	1C	034	00011100	^\	FS
29	1D	035	00011101	^]	GS
30	1E	036	00011110	^^	RS
31	1F	037	00011111	^_	US
32	20	040	00100000	(space)	
33	21	041	00100001	!	
34	22	042	00100010	"	
35	23	043	00100011	#	

Decimal	Hex	Octal	Binary	ASCII
36	24	044	00100100	$
37	25	045	00100101	%
38	26	046	00100110	&
39	27	047	00100111	'
40	28	050	00101000	(
41	29	051	00101001	)
42	2A	052	00101010	*
43	2B	053	00101011	+
44	2C	054	00101100	,
45	2D	055	00101101	−
46	2E	056	00101110	.
47	2F	057	00101111	/
48	30	060	00110000	0
49	31	061	00110001	1
50	32	062	00110010	2
51	33	063	00110011	3
52	34	064	00110100	4
53	35	065	00110101	5
54	36	066	00110110	6
55	37	067	00110111	7
56	38	070	00111000	8
57	39	071	00111001	9
58	3A	072	00111010	:
59	3B	073	00111011	;
60	3C	074	00111100	<
61	3D	075	00111101	=
62	3E	076	00111110	>
63	3F	077	00111111	?
64	40	100	01000000	@
65	41	101	01000001	A
66	42	102	01000010	B
67	43	103	01000011	C
68	44	104	01000100	D
69	45	105	01000101	E
70	46	106	01000110	F
71	47	107	01000111	G
72	48	110	01001000	H
73	49	111	01001001	I
74	4A	112	01001010	J
75	4B	113	01001011	K
76	4C	114	01001100	L

Decimal	Hex	Octal	Binary	ASCII
77	4D	115	01001101	M
78	4E	116	01001110	N
79	4F	117	01001111	O
80	50	120	01010000	P
81	51	121	01010001	Q
82	52	122	01010010	R
83	53	123	01010011	S
84	54	124	01010100	T
85	55	125	01010101	U
86	56	126	01010110	V
87	57	127	01010111	W
88	58	130	01011000	X
89	59	131	01011001	Y
90	5A	132	01011010	Z
91	5B	133	01011011	[
92	5C	134	01011100	\
93	5D	135	01011101	]
94	5E	136	01011110	^
95	5F	137	01011111	_
96	60	140	01100000	`
97	61	141	01100001	a
98	62	142	01100010	b
99	63	143	01100011	c
100	64	144	01100100	d
101	65	145	01100101	e
102	66	146	01100110	f
103	67	147	01100111	g
104	68	150	01101000	h
105	69	151	01101001	i
106	6A	152	01101010	j
107	6B	153	01101011	k
108	6C	154	01101100	l
109	6D	155	01101101	m
110	6E	156	01101110	n
111	6F	157	01101111	o
112	70	160	01110000	p
113	71	161	01110001	q
114	72	162	01110010	r
115	73	163	01110011	s
116	74	164	01110100	t
117	75	165	01110101	u
118	76	166	01110110	v

Decimal	Hex	Octal	Binary	ASCII
119	77	167	01110111	w
120	78	170	01111000	x
121	79	171	01111001	y
122	7A	172	01111010	z
123	7B	173	01111011	{
124	7C	174	01111100	|
125	7D	175	01111101	}
126	7E	176	01111110	~
127	7F	177	01111111	DEL

Extended Character Set

These characters are available only on IBM PCs and compatible computers.

Decimal	Hex	Octal	Binary	ASCII
128	80	200	10000000	ç
129	81	201	10000001	ü
130	82	202	10000010	é
131	83	203	10000011	â
132	84	204	10000100	ä
133	85	205	10000101	à
134	86	206	10000110	å
135	87	207	10000111	ç
136	88	210	10001000	ê
137	89	211	10001001	ë
138	8A	212	10001010	è
139	8B	213	10001011	ï
140	8C	214	10001100	î
141	8D	215	10001101	ì
142	8E	216	10001110	Ä
143	8F	217	10001111	Å
144	90	220	10010000	É
145	91	221	10010001	æ
146	92	222	10010010	Æ
147	93	223	10010011	ô
148	94	224	10010100	ö
149	95	225	10010101	ò
150	96	226	10010110	û
151	97	227	10010111	ù
152	98	230	10011000	ÿ
153	99	231	10011001	ö
154	9A	232	10011010	Ü
155	9B	233	10011011	¢
156	9C	234	10011100	£
157	9D	235	10011101	¥
158	9E	236	10011110	₧
159	9F	237	10011111	ƒ
160	A0	240	10100000	á
161	A1	241	10100001	í
162	A2	242	10100010	ó
163	A3	243	10100011	ú
164	A4	244	10100100	ñ

Decimal	*Hex*	*Octal*	*Binary*	*ASCII*
165	A5	245	10100101	Ñ
166	A6	246	10100110	a
167	A7	247	10100111	o
168	A8	250	10101000	¿
169	A9	251	10101001	⌐
170	AA	252	10101010	¬
171	AB	253	10101011	½
172	AC	254	10101100	¼
173	AD	255	10101101	¡
174	AE	256	10101110	«
175	AF	257	10101111	»
176	B0	260	10110000	░
177	B1	261	10110001	▒
178	B2	262	10110010	▓
179	B3	263	10110011	│
180	B4	264	10110100	┤
181	B5	265	10110101	╡
182	B6	266	10110110	╢
183	B7	267	10110111	╖
184	B8	270	10111000	╕
185	B9	271	10111001	╣
186	BA	272	10111010	║
187	BB	273	10111011	╗
188	BC	274	10111100	╝
189	BD	275	10111101	╜
190	BE	276	10111110	╛
191	BF	277	10111111	┐
192	C0	300	11000000	└
193	C1	301	11000001	┴
194	C2	302	11000010	┬
195	C3	303	11000011	├
196	C4	304	11000100	─
197	C5	305	11000101	┼
198	C6	306	11000110	╞
199	C7	307	11000111	╟
200	C8	310	11001000	╚
201	C9	311	11001001	╔
202	CA	312	11001010	╩
203	CB	313	11001011	╦
204	CC	314	11001100	╠
205	CD	315	11001101	═

Decimal	Hex	Octal	Binary	ASCII
206	CE	316	11001110	╬
207	CF	317	11001111	╧
208	D0	320	11010000	╨
209	D1	321	11010001	╤
210	D2	322	11010010	╥
211	D3	323	11010011	╙
212	D4	324	11010100	╘
213	D5	325	11010101	╒
214	D6	326	11010110	╓
215	D7	327	11010111	╫
216	D8	330	11011000	╪
217	D9	331	11011001	┘
218	DA	332	11011010	┌
219	DB	333	11011011	█
220	DC	334	11011100	▄
221	DD	335	11011101	▌
222	DE	336	11011110	▐
223	DF	337	11011111	▀
224	E0	340	11100000	α
225	E1	341	11100001	β
226	E2	342	11100010	Γ
227	E3	343	11100011	π
228	E4	344	11100100	Σ
229	E5	345	11100101	σ
230	E6	346	11100110	μ
231	E7	347	11100111	τ
232	E8	350	11101000	Φ
233	E9	351	11101001	θ
234	EA	352	11101010	Ω
235	EB	353	11101011	δ
236	EC	354	11101100	∞
237	ED	355	11101101	ϕ
238	EE	356	11101110	$\in$
239	EF	357	11101111	$\cap$
240	F0	360	11110000	$\equiv$
241	F1	361	11110001	$\pm$
242	F2	362	11110010	$\geq$
243	F3	363	11110011	$\leq$
244	F4	364	11110100	$\lceil$
245	F5	365	11110101	$\rfloor$
246	F6	366	11110110	$\div$
247	F7	367	11110111	$\approx$

Decimal	Hex	Octal	Binary	ASCII
248	F8	370	11111000	°
249	F9	371	11111001	•
250	FA	372	11111010	·
251	FB	373	11111011	$\sqrt{}$
252	FC	374	11111100	n
253	FD	375	11111101	^{2}
254	FE	376	11111110	■
255	FF	377	11111111	

B

IBM-Specific
Programming Examples

This appendix discusses some programming examples that are specific to the IBM® PC, XT, AT, PS/2™, and compatible machines using MS-DOS. The topics covered include

- ❑ Character sets graphics
- ❑ Using MS-DOS interrupts
- ❑ Simple CGA graphics
- ❑ Programming the speaker port

The purpose of this appendix is to introduce you to some of the special things you can do on an IBM personal computer (or compatible). We decided not to make this appendix a complete chapter for two reasons. First, all of the chapters in the book should work with little or no change on almost any computer system. Clearly, the material covered in this appendix will not run on machines other than IBM PC or compatible machines (although the algorithms and concepts can be extended to other machines). Second, the entire field of computer graphics is much too robust to think of giving it complete coverage in a single chapter. The purpose of graphics in this appendix is simply to give you an idea of the resources available to you and provide enough guidance that you can experiment on your own.

Character Graphics

The easiest type of graphics to use on the IBM Personal Computer (PC from now on) is character graphics. As you know (and can see in Appendix A), the ASCII character set is defined for the binary values 0 through 127. However, given that a character occupies eight bits on the PC, there are 256 (that is, 2^8) possible bit patterns available for a single character. This leaves binary values 128 through 255 free for special (non-ASCII) characters. The special characters are often referred to a *special graphic characters*, or the *extended character set*.

Listing B.1 simply displays the special graphic characters available on the PC.

Listing B.1. Special Character Graphics

```
#include <stdio.h>

#define START   128
#define END     256

void main(void)
{
    int i, j;
    for (j = Ø, i = START; i < END; i++, j++) {
        if (j % 1Ø == Ø) {
            printf("\n");
        }
        printf("%3d %c  ", i, i);
    }
}
```

The program is little more than a `for` loop that displays the special graphic character set. The output of the program is shown below in figure B.1

As you can see, the graphic character set includes math symbols, Greek letters, boxes, lines, and other special characters. As listing B.1 shows, you can output any of these graphic characters by using `printf()` and the `%c` conversion character.

Fig. B.1. *Output of listing B.1.*

128	Ç	129	ü	130	é	131	â	132	ä	133	à	134	å	135	ç	136	ê	137	ë
138	è	139	ï	140	î	141	ì	142	Ä	143	Å	144	É	145	æ	146	Æ	147	ô
148	ö	149	ò	150	û	151	ù	152	ÿ	153	Ö	154	Ü	155	¢	156	£	157	¥
158	₧	159	ƒ	160	á	161	í	162	ó	163	ú	164	ñ	165	Ñ	166	ª	167	º
168	¿	169	⌐	170	¬	171	½	172	¼	173	¡	174	«	175	»	176	░	177	▓
178	▓	179	│	180	┤	181	╡	182	╢	183	╖	184	╕	185	╣	186	║	187	╗
188	╝	189	╜	190	╛	191	┐	192	└	193	┴	194	┬	195	├	196	─	197	┼
198	╞	199	╟	200	╚	201	╔	202	╩	203	╦	204	╠	205	═	206	╬	207	╧
208	╨	209	╤	210	╥	211	╙	212	╘	213	╒	214	╓	215	╫	216	╪	217	┘
218	┌	219	█	220	▄	221	▌	222	▐	223	▀	224	α	225	ß	226	Γ	227	π
228	Σ	229	σ	230	µ	231	τ	232	Φ	233	Θ	234	Ω	235	δ	236	∞	237	ø
238	ε	239	∩	240	≡	241	±	242	≥	243	≤	244	⌠	245	⌡	246	÷	247	≈
248	°	249	·	250	·	251	√	252	ⁿ	253	²	254	■	255			

By studying the output presented in figure B.1, you can see that the character corresponding to number 218 looks like the upper left corner of a box. Number 201 also looks like the upper left corner of a box, but with a double line. The task is obvious: You need to write a function that draws a box on the screen by using character graphics.

Designing a Box Function with Character Graphics

Before you write a box( ) function, you should probably give some thought as to how it might be used in a program. Perhaps the box will surround a message to highlight the importance of the message. Error messages could make use of a box. Perhaps the box will be moved to different parts of a screen to draw the user's attention to that part of the screen. This technique is often used when the screen looks like a form that must be filled in by the user.

The box drawn by this function should be "placeable" at any point on the screen. It also seems important that you should be able to draw boxes of different sizes. Because the extended character set includes characters for both single and double lines, you should make these two alternatives available to the user. In other words, the box( ) function should be able to

- ❑ Place a box at any point on the screen
- ❑ Draw any sized box (within screen limits)
- ❑ Draw single or double line boxes

These design goals seem straightforward enough, but certain problems must be addressed before you write the box( ) function.

Any programmer who goes to the trouble of drawing a box will want to start with a "clean" screen first. Therefore, you need to write a clear( ) function. Second, because you want to be able to place the box at any point on the screen, you need a way of moving the cursor to a given position on the screen before drawing the box. Therefore, you will also need a curpos( ) function. Because these two functions probably will either be called before (or as part of) the box( ) function, let's tackle these two functions first.

Using the ROM BIOS

Every PC has a section of read-only memory (ROM) that contains the Basic Input-Output System (BIOS) software. Within this software are a number of text and graphics drivers that can be called by using interrupt 16 (or 0x10 hex). Most of the services available in the ROM BIOS assume that the CPU registers contain certain value prior to calling interrupt 0x10. Therefore, the first thing you must do as a C programmer is provide a means of initializing the CPU registers and calling an interrupt. (The reader who expects to do much programming using BIOS or related routines should investigate Terry Dettman's *DOS Programmer's Reference,* Que Corporation, 1988.)

Fortunately, virtually all C compilers for the PC provide a header file called dos.h that contains the necessary definitions to allow for initialization of the registers as well as one or more functions to execute the interrupt. The function that you will use is called int86( ) and has the general form

```
int int86(int num, union REGS *ireg, union REGS *oreg)
```

where num is the number of the interrupt (0x10 in our case), and two unions of type REGS. The typedef for REGS is usually defined as

```
struct XREG{
    unsigned ax,bx,cx,dx,si,di;
};

struct HREG{
    char al,ah,bl,bh,cl,ch,dl,dh;
};
```

```
union REGS {
    struct XREG x;
    struct HREG h;
};
```

As you can see, the union is capable of holding either the HREG or XREG type of structure. Given the way a union works, only one of the structures can occupy the REGS union at one time. Notice that the XREG structure members are unsigned integers while the HREG structure are chars.

Clearing the Screen

Function 0x07 of interrupt 0x10 initializes a specified window to blanks by scrolling the window down. Specifically, the required initialization of the registers is presented in table B.1

Table B.1. *Register Settings To Scroll a Window*

Register	Meaning
AH	Function number (0x07)
AL	number of lines to scroll (the entire window is cleared if 0)
BH	Attribute for blanked area (usually 0)
CH	Upper left y coordinate
CL	Upper left x coordinate
DH	Lower right y coordinate
DL	Lower right x coordinate

Function 0x07 returns nothing useful from the function call, so you need not worry about what is returned from the interrupt call. (Although function 0x07 scrolls the window down, you could call function 0x06 to scroll the window up. All of the other register values remain unchanged.)

Given the information in table B.1, you can now write the function to clear the screen. The code appears in listing B.2.

Listing B.2 (Fragment). *Clear Screen Function*

```
/*****
                              clrscr()

        Function that clears the screen and places the
    cursor at the upper left corner (location Ø,Ø or the "home"
    position) through a call to function ØxØ7 of interrupt Øx1Ø.

    Argument list:        void

    Return value:         void

*****/

#include  <dos.h>

void clrscr(void)
{
    union REGS ireg;

    ireg.h.ah = ØxØ7;
    ireg.h.al = Ø;
    ireg.h.ch = Ø;
    ireg.h.cl = Ø;
    ireg.h.dh = 24;         /* There are 25 lines - Ø thru 24   */
    ireg.h.dl = 79;         /* There are 8Ø columns - Ø thru 79 */
    ireg.h.bh = Ø;          /* Assume a black background         */

    int86(Øx1Ø, &ireg, &ireg);
}
```

As you might guess, the int86() function simply moves the values of the structure members to the appropriate registers and executes an interrupt 0x10. The end result is a clear screen. Because the function does not return a useful value, we have "reused" the input register as the second argument to the call. If an interrupt returns a value, you may have to define a second REGS union so that you can preserve the input and return register values.

Listing B.3 (Fragment). *A Window* scroll() *Function*

```
/*****
                              scroll()

        Function scrolls a window that is wide by deep units
    starting at the upper left corner of the window as defined
    by row-col.
```

Argument list: int row the upper left row position

int col the upper left column pos

int wide the width of the window

int deep the depth of the window

int num the number of lines to
scroll

Return value: void

*****/

```c
#include  <dos.h>

void scroll(int row, int col, int wide, int deep, int num)
{
   union REGS ireg;

   ireg.h.ah = 0x07;
   ireg.h.al = num;
   ireg.h.ch = row;
   ireg.h.cl = col;
   ireg.h.dh = row  + deep;
   ireg.h.dl = col  + wide;
   ireg.h.bh = 0;          /* Assume a black background       */

   int86(0x10, &ireg, &ireg);
}
```

Programming Tip

Writing "Smarter" Code

You can make better use of the clrscr() function than shown in
listing B.2. Because function 0x07 is really a window-scrolling
function, you could write a scroll() function and make clrscr()
a special case. Consider listing B.3.

With the scroll() function defined as in listing B.3, you could write the
clrscr() function as a special case macro by using scroll(), as in

```c
#define clrscr()   scroll(0,0,79,24,0)
```

which would accomplish the same task as before, but you now have the scroll() function available for use, too.

If you are interested, you could set the ah member of ireg to 0x06 and scroll the window in the opposite direction. As an experiment, try printing something in a window and call the scroll() function with 0x06 and 0x07 in the ah structure member. If you have a color monitor, you could also experiment with color values for the bh member. It is also interesting to print some text on the screen and scroll one or two lines up and then down, using full and partial screen sizes for the window.

Cursor Positioning

Positioning the cursor also uses interrupt 0x10, but uses a different function number. Table B.2 shows the proper values for initializing the structure members.

Table B.2. *Register Settings for Cursor Positioning*

Register	Meaning
AH	Function number (0x02)
BH	Page number (0 in graphics mode)
DH	y coordinate
DL	x coordinate

Function 0x02 does not return a meaningful value. The code for the function is presented in listing B.4.

Listing B.4 (Fragment). *Cursor-Positioning Function*

```
/*****
                              cursor()

          Function places the cursor at the position defined
     by row-col.

     Argument list:      int row      the row position
                         int col      the column position
```

```
    Return value:        void
*****/

#include <dos.h>

void cursor(int row, int col)
{
    union REGS ireg;

    ireg.h.ah = 2;
    ireg.h.bh = Ø;
    ireg.h.dh = row;
    ireg.h.dl = col;
    int86(Øx1Ø, &ireg, &ireg);
}
```

Once again, the int86() function call performs most of the work and we reuse the input REGS union as the second argument.

With the clrscr() and cursor() functions taken care of, you can finally write the box() function.

The *box()* Function

Listing B.5 shows the source code for the box() function.

Listing B.5. *The* box() *Function*

```
/*****
                        box()

    Function scrolls a window that is wide by deep units
    starting at the upper left corner of the window as defined
    by row and col.

    Argument list:      int row       the upper left row
                        int col       the upper left column
                        int wide      the width of the box
                        int deep      the depth of the box
                        int bars      1 = single bar, 2 = double
                                      bar for drawing box
```

```
        Return value:        void
*****/
#include <stdio.h>
#include <string.h>            /* Use memory.h for UNIX System V  */
#include <fcntl.h>             /* For the write() function        */

#define ifbars(x,y)    (c=(bars==1)?(x):(y))

#define UL  218                /* These are for single-line boxes */
#define UR  191
#define LL  192
#define LR  217
#define VB  179
#define HB  196

#define DUL 201                /* These are for double-line boxes */
#define DUR 187
#define DLL 200
#define DLR 188
#define DVB 186
#define DHB 205

#define MAXWIDE   80           /* Maximum screen width for text */

void box(int row, int col, int wide, int deep, int bars)
{
    char c, buff[MAXWIDE];
    int fd, i;

    fd = fileno(stdout);
                /* Get the file descriptor */

    ifbars(HB, DHB);

    memset(buff, c, wide);              /* Fast memory set */

    cursor(row, col);
    ifbars(UL, DUL);
    write(fd, &c, sizeof(char));
    ifbars(HB, DHB);
    write(fd, buff, wide);
    ifbars(UR, DUR);
    write(fd, &c, sizeof(char));
    ifbars(VB, DVB);
```

```
for (i = 1; i <= deep + 1; i++) {
   cursor(row + i, col);
   write(fd, &c, sizeof(char));
   cursor(row + i, col + wide + 1);
   write(fd, &c, sizeof(char));
}
cursor(row + deep + 1, col);
ifbars(LL, DLL);
write(fd, &c, sizeof(char));
ifbars(HB, DHB);
write(fd, buff, wide);
ifbars(LR, DLR);
write(fd, &c, sizeof(char));
}
```

One of the implicit goals of all programming is to make the code as fast and small as possible. For these reasons, you probably should avoid printf() —it is a very large function and is slower than some available alternatives.

First, let's examine the arguments to the box() function.

```
box(int row, int col, int wide, int deep, int bars)
```

Although a box can be defined by giving the coordinates for opposite corners, we chose to provide the upper left row-column coordinates along with the width and depth of the box(). The last argument (bars) determines whether the box is drawn with one or two lines.

Prior to the box() function, there is a fairly long list of #defines for the various graphics characters used to draw the box. The meaning of the symbolic constants will be clear if you have run the program in listing B.1.

Inside the box() function, several working variables are defined and then the fileno() function is used to determine the file descriptor for the screen (that is, stdout). This is done so that you can use the faster write() function instead of printf().

The statement

```
ifbars(UL, DUL);
```

is a macro that is defined prior to the start of the box() function. The macro expands into a ternary that assigns a single or double-bar character into c. The argument bars determines which of the two arguments to ifbars() is selected. The macro is called each time the character c needs to be changed.

The next statement

```
memset(buff, c, wide);
```

is a call to a standard library function that quickly initializes buff[] with wide counts of character c. The memset() function will be faster than using a loop to initialize buff[]. This enables you to avoid using a loop to draw the top and bottom parts of the box.

The call to write()

```
write(fd, &c, sizeof(char));
```

simply causes the character in c to be written to the screen. The write() function will be faster and smaller that the printf("%c", c) alternative. (Try using putchar() and see whether it is smaller and faster.) Recall that ANSI does not support the low-level I/O functions. However, most compilers do supply the write() function and the fcntl.h header file.

The rest of the code is more or less a repeat of the ideas presented earlier. Character c is reset each time we encounter a corner of the box() and the for loop is used to print the vertical sides of the box.

You should be able to write your own test program to experiment with the box() function. While you are experimenting, you might consider what to do if one of the arguments to box() is out of bounds (for example, row = 30, or column = 90, etc.).

Graphics (Non-text) Drawing

Drawing with the special graphics character set suffers from two major limitations. First, you are restricted to the predefined special character set. Second, the resolution of the drawing is very limited (typically 80 ×25). Most PC display devices are capable of higher resolution in a non-text mode.

Function 0x00 of interrupt 0x10 allows you to select the video mode that you wish to use (provided you have the necessary hardware). Table B.3 presents the different modes that are possible.

Table B.3. Video Modes

Video Mode	Description
0x00	40x25 BW
0x01	40x25 color
0x02	80x25 BW
0x03	80x25 color
0x04	320x200 4 color graphics
0x05	320x200 4 color graphics (no color burst)
0x06	640x200 2 color graphics
0x07	Monochrome adapter text
0x0d	320x200 16 color (EGA)
0x0e	640x200 16 color (EGA)
0x0f	640x350 monochrome graphics (EGA)
0x10	640x350 4 to 16 color (EGA)
0x12	640x480 16 color (VGA)

When function 0x00 of interrupt 0x10 is invoked, the ah member of the REGS structure is initialized to the function number (0x00) and the al member of the structure is initialized to the mode desired from table B.3. Obviously, you cannot do EGA graphics unless you have the required EGA hardware. Most PCs, however, should allow you to experiment with the first six mode selections in table B.3.

Turning on a Pixel

Up to this point, we have only been concerned with placing characters on the screen. What you will do in this section is find a way to use the screen in a non-text mode.

If you think of your screen as a matrix of dots, text characters are form by turning specific dots on or off. Each of the dots is called a *pixel*. In the graphics mode, you are not constrained by the dot patterns that form ASCII or special graphics characters. Each pixel can be treated as an individual element in the matrix that forms the screen.

Obviously, using the graphics mode assumes you know how to turn on a single pixel. To turn a pixel on, you must first change the screen mode from its normal text status to the graphics status. This is done by function 0x00 of interrupt 0x10. Function set_mode() in listing B.6 shows how you can set the screen mode to one of the modes presented in table B.3.

The do_dot() is designed to turn on a single pixel at a given screen location. This is done by using function 12 (0x0c) of interrupt 0x10. Given that the upper left pixel is location 0,0, you can pass a pair of coordinates to do_dot() and turn that pixel on. Listing B.6 demonstrates how these two functions might be used.

Listing B.6. *Turn a Pixel On*

```
#include  <stdio.h>
#include  <stdlib.h>
#include  <dos.h>

void set_mode(int mode), do_dot(int x, int y);

int main()
{
   char buff[2Ø];
   int i, x, y;

   clrscr();
   printf("Enter x value: ");            /* Get x-y values    */
   x = atoi(gets(buff));
   printf("Enter y value: ");
   y = atoi(gets(buff));

   set_mode(4);                          /* Set graphics mode */

   printf("Write a dot at %d:%d", x, y);
   do_dot(x, y);
   getchar();                            /* Wait for Enter    */


   set_mode(3);                          /* Back to text mode */
}

/*****

                        set_mode()

        Function sets the screen mode using a mode value from
   Table B.3.
```

```
        Argument list:      int mode      the screen mode value

        Return value:       void

*****/

void set _mode(int mode)
{
    union REGS ireg;

    ireg.h.ah = Ø;
    ireg.h.al = mode;
    int86(Øx1Ø, &ireg, &ireg);
}


/*****
                                do _dot()

        Function writes a pixel on the screen mode by using the
    coordinates passed into the function.

        Argument list:      int x         the x coordinate
                            int y         the y coordinate

        Return value:       void

*****/

void do _dot(int x, int y)
{
    union REGS ireg;

    ireg.h.ah = Øx0c;
    ireg.h.al = 1;
    ireg.x.dx = x;
    ireg.x.cx = y;
    int86(Øx1Ø, &ireg, &ireg);
}
```

The program should look fairly familiar to you, given the other functions
and programs in this appendix. Note that the screen is reset to text mode
by a second call to set _mode( ) before the program ends. If you fail to reset
the screen to text mode, the text you see on the screen after the program
has ended might look a bit strange. (You could use the MS-DOS MODE
command to reset the screen if you forget. Use *MODE CO80* for color
monitors or *MODE BW80* otherwise.)

There are a number of graphics books available that present algorithms for drawing lines, circles, and many other types of graphics. You could use the do_dot() function to replace the point(), dot(), or pixel() routines used in those algorithms to build your own graphics function library.

Using the Speaker Port

You can program the speaker port on the PC to produce a variety of sounds. The 8255 Programmable Peripheral Interface (PPI) chip is responsible for most input-output operations on the PC. The PPI has two input (using ports 0x60 and 0x62) and one output (port 0x61) registers. The BIOS contains a routine (that is, BEEP) to sound the speaker during power-on by using the 8253 Timer chip. (Details on how to use the various ports and registers can be found in the *IBM Technical Reference Manual*.) By communicating with the PPI and the Timer chip, you can produce various tones on the PC's speaker.

Listing B.7 uses the PC's speaker to play a brief "song." (Because my only musical talent is limited to playing the chalkboard, the digital song values have been determined by someone else with a better sense of rhythm.)

Listing B.7. Play a Tune

```
#include <stdio.h>
#include <stdlib.h>
#include <dos.h>

#define BEEPPORT    97
#define ON          79
#define TIMER       182
#define FREQPORT    66
#define T_MODEPORT  67

#define REST        99
#define SPEED       15     /* Given for 7.2 MHz AT; Try 5 for a PC */
#define FAST        1230L  /* Another trial-error value        */
#define END         0

static int notes[] = {
        131, 147, 165, 174, 196, 220, 250,
        262, 294, 330, 350, 392, 440, 494
        };
```

```c
static int song[] = {    /* Each group = 1 measure */
      9,     10, 11,     11, 10,  9, 8,
      7, 7,  8,  9,       9,  8,  8,

      9,     10, 11,     11, 10,  9, 8,
      7, 7,  8,  9,       8,  7,  7,

      8,     9,  7,       8,  9, 10, 9, 7,
      8, 9, 10,  9, 8,    7,  8,  4, REST,

      9,     10, 11,     11, 10,  9, 8,
      7, 7,  8,  9,       8,  7,  7, END
      };

static int length[] = {    /* Each group = 1 measure */
      4, 2, 2,           2, 2, 2, 2,
      2, 2, 2, 2,        3, 1, 4,

      4, 2, 2,           2, 2, 2, 2,
      2, 2, 2, 2,        3, 1, 4,

      4, 2, 2,           2, 1, 1, 2, 2,
      2, 1, 1, 2, 2,     2, 2, 2, 2,

      4,     2, 2,       2, 2, 2, 2,
      2, 2, 2, 2,        3, 1, 2, 2
      };

void tone(int freq, int time), rest(int time);

void main()
{
  int i;

  for (i = 0; song[i] != END; i++) {
   if (song[i] == REST) {
     rest(length[i] * SPEED);
     continue;
   }
   tone(notes[song[i]], length[i] * SPEED);
  }
}

void tone(int freq, int time)
{
    int hibyt, lobyt, port;
    long i, count, divisor;
```

```
        divisor = 1190000L / freq;
        lobyt = (int) divisor % 256;
        hibyt = (int) divisor / 256;
        outportb(T_MODEPORT, TIMER);
        outportb(FREQPORT, lobyt);
        outportb(FREQPORT, hibyt);
        port = inportb(BEEPPORT);
        outportb(BEEPPORT, ON);

        count = FAST * time;
        for (i = 0; i < count; i++)
            ;
        outportb(BEEPPORT, port);

        count /= 8;
        for (i = 0; i < count; i++)
            ;

}

void rest(int time)
{

    long j, count;

    count = FAST * time;
    for (j = 0; j < count; j++)
        ;
    count /= 8;
    for (j = 0; j < count ; j++)
        ;
}
```

The program begins with a number of #defines, most of which are hardware dependent. Note that SPEED and FAST may vary with the type of PC you are using. Some experimentation will be necessary to get things to sound right. The numbers shown here are good starting values.

The notes[] array contains the frequency for the notes that can be played in the program (the value 262 is the approximate frequency for middle C). The song[] array is the song to be played, and the length[] array tells how long each note is held. In main(), a loop is used to play the song by calls to tone().

The tone() function is passed the frequency of the note to be played and the duration of the note. The frequency passed to tone() is used to provide the correct values to the timer port, and time determines how long the note is played. The outportb() function sends a byte value (for example, TIMER) to the port specified (T_MODEPORT) to initialize the timer mode register. The second and third calls to outportb() set the frequency.

> *Note*: outportb() is not a portable function and is designed to send a byte value, not a word (for example, two bytes), to the port. Some compilers for the PC provide an outport() function that does output a word to the specified port. Be sure not to confuse the two functions.

The call to inport() gets the status of the speaker port and saves it in port. We now call outportb() again to turn the speaker on. The count value determines how long the speaker remains turned on. The final call to outputb() turns the speaker off and control returns to main() for the next note in the song.

It's up to you to figure out what the song is.

As you might notice, there are a lot of "magic numbers" in the program, most of which may have to be changed somewhat to get the song to sound like a song. If things sound a bit strange on your system, begin experimenting with different values for SPEED and FAST. If you wish, you could also rewrite the program to play different songs stored in data files. Try using command line arguments to select the file.

C Products

In this appendix, I present short descriptions about various C products that might prove useful to you. The purpose of this section is not to review a product or give it an endorsement. Rather, the descriptions are meant to give you some idea of what the product is and what you might expect from it before you buy.

I have tried to group the products into general categories. However, just because your interest might be database programming, don't assume that other sections offer nothing useful for you. Miscellaneous Tools and Utilities, for example, should have something for everybody regardless of specific interests.

Unless stated otherwise, products are for the IBM PC and compatibles. We do urge you to contact the companies listed for current pricing, supported compilers, and other product information before purchasing any product.

C Compilers and Interpreters

Aztec C86, Ver. 4.1B
Manx Software Systems
P.O. Box 55
Shrewsbury, NJ   07701
(201) 542-2121

The C86 compiler reviewed here is the Commercial version and includes the compiler, macro assembler, librarian, linker, editor, *two* debuggers (sdb and db), plus several useful utilities (such as a MAKE and profiler). The manual covers everything but is a little difficult to use. Unlike most vendors that arrange library functions in alphabetical order, Manx splits the library into two (system) groups. (This is similar to the UNIX System V organization.) However, you may have trouble finding things if you don't know to which group a particular function belongs.

The code produced by the compiler is often much smaller than that produced by other compilers, although execution times are pretty much near the average. Unlike many of the other compilers reviewed, C86 is capable of generating ROMable code and does permit inline assembler code. The standard library is fairly complete, but many MS-DOS functions found in other compilers are missing. (This might be because Manx does support other environments and wants its library portable across those environments.) The editor and debuggers are very functional, but lack the menuing approach common to other MS-DOS compilers.

Manx markets several varieties of this compiler. The Commercial compiler ($499.00) is the one described previously. The Developer System ($299.00) is much the same, but excludes library source code. The Standard System ($199.00) excludes the source, UNIX utilities, and the editor. Because Manx offers compilers and cross compilers for several systems, this compiler could be a very good choice for those moving between those systems.

Turbo C Ver. 1.5
Borland International
4585 Scotts Valley Drive
Scotts Valley, CA   95066
(800) 543-7543

Borland is well known for producing a quality product at a reasonable price, and Turbo C is no exception. The compiler supports five memory models including data aggregates larger than 64K. The package includes the compiler, editor, and linker. The library now includes a number of graphics (with fonts) and windowing functions (and fonts) that appear to be fairly fast. The documentation includes three manuals: a user's guide, a reference, and an additions and enhancements manual (added with version 1.5).

You can compile, edit, and link a program from within the editor or you can compile programs from the command line. Compile times are fast, with much of the time gain due to the very fast linker used by Turbo C. (Most competitors use Microsoft's linker.) The generated code is fast in most benchmarks and code size is smaller than most competitors. The library is complete and most of the ANSI language is implemented. The function descriptions are complete, but they do not contain much in the way of examples. The integrated environment is easy to learn through the menuing system common to many Borland products. Version 2.0 has recently been announced and includes a source code debugger. At $149.95, Turbo C is a good choice.

MacC and MacC Toolkit
Consulair Corp.
140 Campo Drive
Portola Valley, CA   94025
(415) 851-3272

The MacC compiler is a full K&R C compiler with many (but not all) ANSI extensions. The compiler does support structure passing and assignment, void, and enum data types. Prototyping is not supported but inline assembler using #asm and #endasm is. There are other features that will seem strange to MS-DOS programmers but make perfect sense on the Macintosh (for example, \p at the beginning of a string generates a Pascal string. Useful, since the Mac's operating system was written in Pascal). The compiler has a host of compile-time switches to do things like outputting assembler source files, turning off floating point support routines, and others. The documentation is easy to read, but the library descriptions are pretty terse.

The package also has a number of tools that will prove useful. A program editor is supplied, and you can compile a program without leaving the editor. The package also includes an assembler, linker and librarian, Mac run-time interface, path manager, Macsbug debugger, and a Resource manager. Source code is provided for many of the tools. In some cases, the tools are function shells that make it easier to use the standard library routines. Because of the way the operating system works on the Mac, these tools can be a big help. The manual also presents a list of the operating system calls that can be accessed by MacC.

The MacC compiler is a complete package and benchmarks show it to be a good performer. Price is $425.00. The same compiler without most of the support products is available for $80.00.

DeSmet DC88
C Ware
P.O. Box 428
Paso Robles, CA   93447
(805) 239-4620

The DC88 compiler package has several additional features. In addition to the compiler, you get a source code debugger, the SEE program text editor, an assembler, and its own proprietary linker and librarian. The compiler also has a number of useful utility programs, including a program profiler. The compiler produces code for the small memory model (64K code, 64K data) only, but an option allows overlays to be generated for larger programs using these constraints. The compiler recognizes special preprocessor directives (#asm) for including assembler source directly in the C source file. The manual is fairly easy to use, although no index is provided.

The compiler is very fast, usually compiling faster than any other compiler reviewed. Another factor contributing to the speed is the nonstandard linker (called Bind) provided with the package. (The Microsoft linker used by most other companies often takes more time than does the compiler.) There is an optional program, however, that can convert the Bind format to produce standard OBJ files. Execution speed is a little slower than most. Still, with a price of $99.95, you get a lot for the money.

Eco-C88
Ecosoft Inc.
6413 N. College Ave.
Indianapolis, IN   46220
(800) 952-0472

Note: It should be stated at the outset that this compiler is produced by the author's company and the opinions expressed might be biased.

Eco-C88 supports four memory models and most ANSI extensions. (All programs in this book were written with Eco-C88.) The package includes a full-screen, multi-window program editor with on-line help for the editor and standard library functions. Programs can be edited, compiled, and linked from within the editor or from the command line. The editor marks program errors in the source file with a red cursor and an error message appears near the bottom of the editor screen.

The standard library has over 225 functions, each explained in prototype form and with a short program rather than code fragment. The compiler allows the user to select the level of lint-like error checking desired and there is no cascading of false error messages. The package also includes a multi-window, source code debugger. Code size, compile time, and execution speed are good. Price is $99.95, and source code to the standard library is available for $25.00. Windowing and graphics packages are available for less than $40.00 each.

C-terp
Gimpel Software
3207 Hogarth Lane
Collegeville, PA   19426
(215) 584-4261

C-terp is a full-featured C interpreter rather than a compiler. Unlike a compiler that passes over the entire source code and (ultimately) produces an executable program, an interpreter acts on the source code a line at a time and takes the action specified but under the control of the interpreter. The advantage is that you can halt program execution and examine variables during program execution. The disadvantage is that interpreters tend to be slower in program execution than are compilers. When you consider the time spent *compiling* and running a program, C-terp is not at much of a disadvantage. C statements are tokenized in one pass and then C-terp interprets these tokens. Programs execute quite fast under the interpreter.

The manual is written clearly (even witty in places) and instructions are easy to follow. The major sections discuss the C-terp menu, the editor, language reference, debugging, standard library, and how to link into external libraries.

Gimpel Software offers versions of C-terp that "mate" with other vendor's C compilers. That is, code written under C-terp during the development process can be compiled with a C compiler provided by another vendor. This gives you the development advantages of an interpreter and the speed advantages of a compiler. Price is $298.00. (Check with vendor for special pricing on some compilers.)

C++
Guidelines Software, Inc.
P.O. Box 749
Orinda, CA   94563
(415) 254-9183

C++ is an object-oriented language developed by Bjarne Stroustrup and
AT&T Bell Labs. C++ is an extension of C and is designed to reduce some
of the "problem areas" in C, especially in terms of complex types and
structures. As you probably know by now, C gives you a great deal of
freedom, which means you may occasionally shoot yourself in the foot.
C++ is more structured, but also safer because of that structure.

In a real sense, C++ is a preprocessor for a standard C compiler. That is,
C++ code in the input source file becomes compilable C source code as
the output file. It follows that knowing C before learning C++ will make
the transition easier. The package includes AT&T's version 1.2 C++ translator, runtime libraries, a copy of Stroustrup's book on C++, sample programs, and a user's manual. The output from Guidelines' C++ is designed
for compilation with Microsoft's C compiler. The price is $295.00.

Lattice C, C-Sprite, LMK
22 W600 Butterfield Road
Glen Ellyn, IL   60137
(312) 858-7950

The Lattice C compiler is one of the more mature compilers in the MS-DOS
C market. The compiler provides for five memory models including aggregates that exceed 64K. No editor or debugger are supplied as part of the
compiler. The documentation consists of two manuals, the first serves as a
language reference and explains how to use the compiler, and the second
describes the standard library. The discussion of the standard library includes numerous examples and is very good, although the functions are in
K&R style rather than prototype form. Compile time, code size, and execution times are average.

C-Sprite is the debugger designed for use with the Lattice compiler but
doesn't use the windowing environment common to many other MS-DOS
debuggers. However, C-Sprite does give better hooks into the code at the
assembler level than some debuggers. This allows you to view the code at
both the source or assembler level (with generated labels). It also has
support for overlaying linkers—a feature uncommon to most debuggers.

LMK is a MAKE utility that simplifies the compile process by keeping track of how all of a program's source modules interrelate. Most software projects are built up from several C source files. Typically, all modules save one tend to stabilize quickly—it's that one module that gets recompiled over and over. The MAKE utility keeps track of what has and has not been changed since the last compile and only compiles those modules that need to be recompiled. This can save a lot of time. The documentation is well written and also explains how to use the macro language included with LMK.

The price for the Lattice C compiler has been dropped to $450.00 and is available for MS-DOS, Amiga, and other cross-compilers. Lattice is one of the few companies to offer a full compiler for the Amiga and has a pending release for OS/2. The C-Sprite debugger sells for $175.00 and can be used with other compilers. The LMK Make utility sells for $195.00 and can also be used with other compilers. The company also markets a number of other (non-C) products of use to end users and programmers.

High C
MetaWare
903 Pacific Ave., Suite 201
Santa Cruz, CA   95060
(408) 429-6382

From the first time you open it, High C looks like a professional product. The reference manual is over two inches thick and contains major sections on using the compiler, a discussion of the standard library (using ANSI conventions), and a section that presents an introduction to C. I might add that this is one of the few packages that consistently uses the proper distinction between "declare" and "define" in its introductory material. The compiler generates code for the Intel 80xxx family and NEC's V-20 chip. They also market an 80386 version (not reviewed here).

Installation is simple, but takes a lot of disk space for the compiler; a little over 1 meg. No editor or debugger is included, but there is a section on debugging that should prove useful to most programmers. Most of the library functions have a complete program to illustrate the use of the function. Five memory models are supported, including aggregates that can exceed 64K. The compiler has numerous compile switches and #pragmas that give the user a wide variety of options. Price is $595.00.

Watcom C, Version 6.0
Watcom Systems, Inc.
415 Phillip St.
Waterloo, Ont.   N2L 3X2
CANADA
(519) 886-3700

Although Watcom is a recent entry into the microcomputer marketplace, they have been in the mainframe market for years. This is a nice package. First, you get five small, albeit complete, manuals: for the compiler and its tools (overlaying linker, librarian, MAKE, and others), the editor, the library reference, the user's guide, and the language reference. Next, you get four multi-fold reference cards for the debugger, editor, library, and C language reference. All of the printed material is professionally done with a clean, easy-to-read layout. Everything fits neatly into a bookshelf box for convenient use.

The editor is a full-screen editor capable of editing multiple files with the features you'd expect from a programming editor. The editor features on-line help for the editor and library functions. The debugger is also complete and has a macro language that lets you configure the command language to suit your own needs. The compiler supports five memory models, including aggregates exceeding 64K. The compiler is large (using over 2 meg of disk space for everything) and all of its optimization techniques make its compile times a bit slower than some of the alternatives. Still, it produces fast code and is one of the best professional-quality compilers available. Price is $295.00.

Although not included for review, Watcom also produces Express C which does include the compiler, editor, and debugger for $75.00.

Function Libraries

C Tools Plus
Blaise Computing Inc.
2560 Ninth St., Suite 316
Berkeley, CA   94710
(415) 540-5441

C Tools Plus is a set of over 130 functions for string handling, screen and keyboard handling, windows, menus, file, memory, printer, utility, and interrupt processing. The documentation begins with an explanation of the organization of the functions and related introductory material. Each function is explained and includes a short code fragment showing how the function might be used. (The menu and window functions look very useful.) Source code for all functions is included in the purchase price of $129.00. Although not supplied for inclusion in this text, the company also markets several other packages, including an asynchronous communications package for $175.00.

Vitamin C, VCScreen
Creative Programming
Box 112079
Carrollton, TX   75011
(214) 416-6447

Vitamin C is a set of 150 library functions covering the areas of data entry, keyboard handling, menuing, windowing, plus utility routines. Each function is described fully and includes a short code fragment showing how the function might be used. The documentation is well organized, easy to read, and most popular compilers are supported. (UNIX and XENIX versions should be ready by the time this text goes to press.)

Although all of the functions should prove useful to any C programmer, the windowing functions are quite complete and can be used to write some very nice data entry and "pop-up" type screens and windows. Another plus is that the source code is included in the package price—a good way to learn more advanced C techniques. Vitamin C sells for $225.00.

The company also produces VCScreen which allows you to draw data input forms on the screen and then generate the C code for those screens. An editor allows you to define the data screen, the attributes used, input prompts, type of cursor, and so forth. The manual is a bit terse for my liking, but things work as stated. The package assumes that you have the Vitamin C library, as those functions are used in generating the C source code for the screens. VCScreen is $100.00.

C Utility, Essential Graphics, Essential Communications, Resident C
Essential Software
P.O. Box 1003
Maplewood, NJ   07040
(914) 762-6605

C Utility, Essential Graphics, Essential Communications are each a set of library functions designed for different tasks. The C Utility library contains over 300 functions for data input and validation, DOS services, date and time, sort-compare, string, keyboard, and file functions plus many more. The functions include some that you probably wouldn't have thought of on your own . . . I know I didn't. (Price: $185.00)

Essential Graphics includes over 150 functions for the CGA, EGA, Hercules, VDC, DEB, and Tecmar graphics devices. All of the graphics primitives (line, circle, arc, etc.) that you would expect are included, plus bars, hatching, even light pen and mouse functions. Eight different fonts are also provided with the package. (Price: $250.00)

Essential Communications is a library of functions designed to simplify working with asynchronous data devices. Numerous devices are supported including IMODEM, XMODEM, XON/XOFF, plus others. A monitor/debugger named Breakout is also available. The manual contains an introductory chapter on communications protocols, RS-232 standard, modem operations, UART specifications, and other information needed to use the library effectively. (Price: $185.00, or $250.00 with Breakout)

Resident C provides functions that allow you to write TSR (Terminate and Stay Resident) and ISR (Interrupt Service Routine) programs. Some of the example programs use functions from the Utility library. The manual has a good introductory discussion about TSR and ISR programs. (Price: $99.00)

All of Essential's products have good manuals with examples plus sample code fragments for each function. Each package also includes the source code.

Greenleaf Library Series
Greenleaf Software
1411 LeMay Drive, Suite 101
Carrollton, TX   75007
(214) 446-8641

The Greenleaf Comm library is a set of about 140 library functions designed for various asynchronous communications. Numerous devices are supported including XMODEM, XON/XOFF, RTS/CTS, Hayes, plus others. The manual is well organized and includes discussions on using async communications devices. Each function is documented fully with a sample code fragment using the function. Source code is included with the package price of $185.00.

The Greenleaf Functions consist of about 280 functions covering the following topics: video and graphics, string, keyboard, serial I/O, DOS, time and date, and utility functions. The manual begins with an introductory discussion of the general areas of coverage. Following the introduction, each function is discussed thoroughly, and, unlike some other libraries, most have a complete program example (rather than a code fragment). A reference card with a list of the functions is also provided. Source code is included in the $185.00 price.

The Greenleaf Sample library consists of 112 library functions in the general areas of async communications, windows, menus, graphics, date-time, and keyboard functions. The manual is well written with each function clearly explained and a program or code fragment showing how the function is used. The price is $95.00.

db_VISTA
Raima Corp.
3055 112th Ave. NE
Bellevue, WA   98004
(206) 828-4636

db_VISTA is more than a set of library functions; it is a professional database development system. Three manuals come with the package. The first two are a user's guide and a reference manual for db_VISTA. The database can support multiple users, file and record locking, LAN support, transaction logging and timestamping, and virtual memory disk caching, making it fast even with very large databases. (The relationship between access time and database size is virtually linear with db_VISTA rather than exponential as with other relational database management systems.)

The second manual details the use of db_QUERY; the structured query language used for the database. The Database Definition Language (DDL) is patterned after C and is used to define the content and structure of the database. Query procedures can be "on the fly" or through predefined query procedures. The manuals are well written and with sufficient examples that most programmers should be able to write their own databases even without prior experience.

db_VISTA is available for MS-DOS, UNIX, XENIX, VMS, and OS/2 at prices from $595.00 to $3,960.00 which includes 60 days of free technical support.

Miscellaneous Tools and Utilities

Tree Diagrammer, Source Print
Aldebaran Laboratories, Inc
3339 Vincent Road
Pleasant Hill, CA   94523

Tree Diagrammer is designed to read a C source file and generate an organizational chart showing the functions that are called in the program and their order of use. Tree Diagrammer may be run through a menu system or directly from the DOS command line. Unlike some similar programs, #includes are processed automatically.

Source Print is a print utility that also can produce a structure outline of the program, emphasize printing on keywords, create titles, beautify the program, exclude parts of a program from the output, and perform a number of formatting tasks.

It should be noted that both programs not only work for C, but also with BASIC, Pascal, Modula-2, FORTRAN, and dBASE programs. The price for Tree Diagrammer is $77.00 and Source Print is $97.00.

Peabody
Copia International Ltd.
1964 Richton Dr.
Wheaton, IL   60187
(312) 665-9830

Peabody is a memory-resident reference manual that can be called upon at any time to provide information on C keywords, syntax rules, and standard library functions. Although Peabody can be used by itself, it is most useful when you are writing a C program with your program editor. If, for example, you cannot remember the proper order for a standard library function, just move your editor's cursor on the function name, press two keys, and up comes a description of the function. The same method can be used for keywords, too. You can also order a table of ASCII characters, extended keyboard codes, and compiler options for the Peabody version—all of this in a very fast and smooth operation. Although the version sent was not written for my favorite compiler, Peabody worked perfectly with it. This could save you *A LOT* of reference manual time, especially if you are just getting started with C. The price is $100.00.

ScreenStar
Essential Software
P.O. Box 1003
Maplewood, NJ   07040
(914) 762-6605

ScreenStar is a screen development tool that comes with a screen editor (SSED) to generate a screen. Through a series of commands, you can use SSED to layout a form, generate attributes for fields within the form (such as foreground and background colors), use lines and boxes, and just about anything else you might need to design a screen. The screen definition can then be saved to disk (in a compressed format). The highlight of the system is that SSED can then generate C source code for the screen just defined, enabling you to compile and link the source code for the screen into an application program. Also provided are almost 100 support functions for the package. Although SSED is most useful for generating data screens (that is, screens that are used to prompt the user for data input), almost any screen can be defined with it. The compiled output of SSED seems very fast. A project or two should more than compensate for the $99.00 price tag; source is another $99.00.

PC-lint
Gimpel Software
3207 Hogarth Lane
Collegeville, PA   19426
(215) 584-4261

Lint is a UNIX utility that examines C source code for syntactical and semantic errors. A syntax error is simply a violation of the rules of the language. A semantic error is more subtle. For example, the sentence "The dog meowed." obeys all the rules for an English sentence, but the context is wrong. The purpose of lint is to catch those errors that are valid C syntax, but may prove troublesome during program debugging. Therefore, lint is designed to pick off the "fluff" of a program that could cause problems later.

Error messages from PC-lint are divided into two groups: those with numbers between 1 and 199 are syntax errors, and those with numbers between 500-599 are most likely semantic errors (that is, the have bug potential). Each error message is discussed in the manual.

PC-lint's power comes from a host of runtime switches that give the user control over what PC-lint does. The manual is easy to read and discusses many of the ANSI enhancements to C and how these are processed by PC-lint. Twelve different compilers are supported. Using PC-lint on a daily basis could give you a pretty good measure of how your coding is progressing by counting the number of errors produced by PC-lint. Price is $139.00.

---

risC
International Microcomputer Software, Inc.
1299 Fourth St.
San Rafael, CA   94901
(415) 454-7101

The risC compiler is described as a blend of three concepts: (1) Reduced Instruction Set Computers (RISC), (2) the C language, and (3) High-level Assembler Languages (HAL's). The risC compiler is an efficient, object oriented high-level assembler language tool that has C-like constructs but is more closely related to assembler than C. To check the claim of tight and fast executing code, I compiled the classic Sieve benchmark. Most C compilers execute sieve on an IBM AT in about 5 seconds with a code size of 9K (some as much as 20K). The risC compiler produce an EXE file of less than 1100 bytes and executed in less than 2 seconds. If you like assembler and C, this is worth checking out. Price is $80.

VIP
Mainstay
5311-B Derry Ave.
Agoura Hills, CA   91301
(800) 628-2828

This program is kinda' neat. VIP is a visual programming tool for the Apple Macintosh. VIP provides basic classes for objects (`char`, `int`, etc.), logic forms (`if...then...else`, `switch`, etc), and procedures (draw a line, call up system routine, etc.). By selecting combinations of objects, logic forms, and procedures (almost 200 of them are available) with a mouse, you combine these basic program types to form a complete program. Because VIP is an interpreter, you can run and test programs immediately. VIP programs are created and run within the VIP editor (which also has a built-in debugger). The manual is easy to read and understand and has a nice layout. Even a beginner should have simple programs running in less than an hour.

After the program is written, you can use an optional VIP translator that will translate the program in VIP form to C or Pascal. At the time of this writing, the Lightspeed and MPW C compilers are supported. Mainstay claims that the compiled programs run between two and six times faster than the native VIP programs (even though the programs are reasonably fast anyway). VIP is priced at $125.00 and a VIP translator is $90.00. Other support modules for ISAM's, speech processing, building databases are also available at nominal cost.

MetaWindow
Metagraphics
4575 Scotts Valley Dr.
Scotts Valley, CA   95066
(408) 438-1550

MetaWindow is not just a windowing system but a graphics package complete with line drawing, circle, ovals, arcs, icons, rubberbanding, dragging, mouse support, menus, windows, multiple coordinate systems, proportionally spaced fonts, and many other features. All graphics functions seem very fast, especially fill operations. (The MetaWindow graphics driver is installed prior to running a program. There is no royalty for using the driver, however.) The manual is good, and the chapter that explains how various graphics devices and coordinate systems work is particularly well written. Function documentation uses the K&R style, and there are lots of examples and very good explanations for all topics. Over 70 graphics devices are supported including PS/2, VGA, and MCGA. C, Pascal, and FORTRAN versions are available. Price is $195.00.

C Programmer's Toolbox, Volumes I and II
MMC AD Systems
Box 360845
Milpitas, CA   95035
(408) 263-0781

The C Programmer's Toolbox is a collection of programming utilities for IBM PC and compatibles. Volume I consists of 12 programs, of which the most interesting are CFlow and PMon. CFlow traces the function hierarchy of a program during runtime, including the runtime library calls and which functions are called by whom. PMon presents a variety of statistics concerning where a program spends its time during execution. A nice touch in PMon is that DOS system calls are identified along with a short description (it saves you the trouble of looking them up). PMon alone is worth the $79.95 price.

Volume II contains 11 programs of which CXref and CritPath are the highlights. CXref is a cross referencing program that generates a number of reports about variable usage in a program. CritPath derives a program's critical path (that is, the sequence of functions that consumes the most execution time) plus a number of other reports—it looks most useful. Volume II is priced at $79.95, or you can get both volumes for $130.00.

C-scape
Oakland Group
675 Massachusetts Ave.
Cambridge, MA   02139
(800) 233-3733

C-scape is an "interface management system" that can create text and prompts for data entry, context-sensitive help screens, pop-up windows, a variety of menus (Lotus, pull-down, "slug", and others), data validation, and other screen managment tasks. The manual is thorough, well organized, easy to read, and each function is fully described. The code generated by C-scape is also clean and easy to read. Although the libraries are specific for each compiler, source code is provided. The price is $299.00.

The company also markets a screen editor called Look and Feel Screen Designer with fewer features for $50.00. The company offers other products (and training) for MS-DOS, UNIX, and XENIX operating systems.

Panel, Panel Plus
Roundhill Computer Systems
P.O. Box 8107
Englewood, NJ   07631
(201) 569-2265

Panel is a screen design and management system for creating data entry and output screens. Panel Plus has the same basic goal, but contains many advanced features and programs for design and testing a screen. Both products use an editor to create a screen. Input fields can be built and the data entered can be validated as part of the screen-generating process. Once the screen is designed the way you want it, the screen is saved and ready for compilation. Screens can be compiled and linked into the program or saved as disk files for reading at runtime. Although the version received was for a different compiler (most popular compilers are supported), everything compiled without a hitch. Both products include a user's manual and descriptions of how various features and functions are used. (The Panel Plus documentation uses a larger typeface and is easier to read for us old folks.) The price for Panel is $129.00 and Panel Plus varies from a low of $495.00 for MS-DOS to $9,950 for 8800 VMS.

ISAM and BTree (v2.5)
Softfocus
1343 Standbury Dr.
Oakville, Ont.   L6L 2J5
(416) 825-0903

A B-Tree is a short form for Binary Tree and is a common technique used to organize data. The problem with a B-Tree is that it can become unbalanced if a large number of similar items are added to a list (e.g., a lot of people with a name starting with 'A'). BTree v.2.5 is a variant of a binary tree except effort is made to keep the tree balanced (a balanced tree minimizes search times). A discussion of how BTree works is included in the manual. All functions needed to use their BTree are included in source and are described in the user's manual. The documentation states that they have ported the code for BTree to several different machines and it never took over an hour. Because I found this hard to believe, I tried to compile the source code for their library. It compiled on the first try without change! Price is $75.00.

ISAM is an abbreviation for Indexed Sequential Access Method for reading and writing data to a file. ISAM v.2.5 is a library of routines designed to make writing an application program using indexed records as simple and painless as possible. Each function is described in the manual and a short code fragment shows how each function might be used. The function descriptions use the K&R style, but using the libraries should not be a problem. Examples provided in the manual will also help you to use and understand how ISAM works if it is new to you. Price is $40.00 but you need BTRee, too. Contact Softfocus for combined price.

Screen Maker
SoftScience Corporation
P.O. Box 42905
Tucson, AZ   85733
(602) 326-4679

Screen Maker is a productivity tool for creating data entry and output screens. When Screen Maker is invoked you are placed in an editor that allows you to draw boxes using character graphics of your choice, define input fields, change colors or other screen attributes (for example, blink), plus a host of other options. Once the screen has been defined, you can generate the source code for the screen. Not only can Screen Maker generate C source, it can also produce BASIC, Pascal, and dBASE code. The source code is then compiled with your favorite C compiler. Although my compiler of choice is not on the list, the code did compile after two minor changes in the program. The manual is short, but things are pretty intuitive from within the editor. The price is $75.00.

Slate Printer Management System
The Symmetry Group
P.O. Box 26195
Columbus, OH   43226
(614) 431-2667

Slate consists of three major components: S_Print, Slate, and Slatelib. The S_Print program is a full-featured text processor capable of producing high-quality documents, forms, manuals, etc. Slate and Slatelib work together to form a printer management system for communicating with over 350 different types of printers. C is used to interface with Slate through a large variety of commands that can be used to format the text. Commands include underlining, boldface, sub- and supercript, italics, changing fonts and font sizes, line spacing, select margins, plus a host of other commands.

The Slate commands are used in conjunction with numerous C functions to provide total control of the output going to the printer. This would be especially useful for anyone involved with custom programming. At the time of this writing, the number of compilers was somewhat limited. However, they are adding new compilers to the list all the time. Check with the vendor before ordering. Slate is $299.00 and S_Print is $150.00, or both for $349.00.

EMACS, CMACS
UniPress SOftware, Inc.
2025 Lincoln Hwy.
Edison, NJ   08817
(800) 222-0550

EMACS is full-screen text editor born on the UNIX operating system. It features multiple windows, commands that can do anything you could want an editor to do (and some you probably never thought of), and even has its own programming language "MLisp" for extending or modifying the command structure. Windows can be opened to the shell, allowing operating system communications or even running programs from within the editor. EMACS is available for MS-DOS, UNIX, XENIX, and VMS, and a Macintosh version should be available by the time you read this. Prices vary from $250.00 (Macintosh) to $7,000.00 (mainframe) in binary form. Source is available for $7,000.00.

CMACS is a derivative of EMACS, but designed for the C programmer. If you type a C keyword, the editor supplies necessary parentheses and braces automatically and positions the cursor in the proper spot for syntax filling. On-line help is available for the standard library and the language itself. CMACS can match an error message file with a C source file for easier program correction, expand preprocessor directives, undo commands, cut-paste between windows, plus a host of other facilities. Another plus from using the EMACS family is that the editor is found on a wide range of systems—once you learn EMACS, there's a good chance you won't have to learn another editor. CMACS prices range from $645.00 for a single user to $9,950.00 for mainframes.

The C Workshop
Wordcraft
3827 Penniman Ave.
Oakland, CA   94619
(800) 227-2400, ex. 955

I'm not sure where this product should be placed because it's more than just one product. It is a screen-based tutorial on C, but it also includes a book and built-in compiler as part of the tutorial. Pressing special function keys while running the tutorial enters the program editor where programs can be written, compiled, and run. When you have finished, another stroke of a function key, and you pick up where you left the tutorial. This would allow you to experiment as you read the tutorial. The tutorial and compiler are geared to K&R C, but this is still a useful product at a bargain price of $70.00.

C Source Code and Journals

Note: Although more and more vendors are supplying C source code with their packages, you can never have enough "sources for C source." Listed here are companies and publications that are good places to find complete listings of C source code.

Austin Code Works
11100 Leafwood Lane
Austin, TX   78750
(512) 253-0785

This company sells a number of the commercial packages presented in this appendix plus public domain (or shareware) products. You can buy just about everything from the complete source code to a (subset) C compiler or interpreter for $20.00 to a multitasking operating system for $100.00. Almost any of their products provide an excellent source for learning new coding techniques plus are good values, too. Call or write for a current list of products.

The C Users Journal
2120 W. 25th Street, Suite B
Lawrence, KS   66046
(913) 841-1631

This publication specializes in C articles and columns. Rarely is there an issue that doesn't contain something useful for C programmers at all levels of programming experience. It is also a good read for keeping up with current C products available in the market.

Computer Language
500 Howard Street
San Francisco, CA   94105
(415) 397-1881

Computer Language does not specialize in any one language, but covers most popular languages. Articles cover a wide spectrum of topics, and will be of interest to novice and experienced programmer alike. (Historically, the February issue is the annual C issue.)

Dr. Dobb's Journal of Software Tools for the Professional Programmer
501 Galveston Drive
Redwood City, CA 94063
(415) 366-3600

This magazine has been around for over 10 years, and I've always found it to be an excellent source of code in C and other languages. *Dr. Dobb's* continues to publish complete listings, while other magazines have stopped that practice. Just about every issue has a C listing or two that you can learn from.

Binary, Octal, and Hexadecimal Numbering Systems

Despite all the things a computer can do, it only understands two things: on and off (or 1 and 0). In other words, a computer only understands data presented in base 2, or binary. Although this format is convenient for the computer, binary doesn't work well for people who are used to decimal (base 10) arithmetic.

Base 8 (octal) and base 16 (hexadecimal) numbering systems are often used in C programming. This appendix is an introduction to those numbering systems. Before we discuss the octal and hexadecimal numbering systems, however, we must first consider binary numbers.

Binary Numbering System

Only two states are possible when working in binary: on and off. That is, each *bi*nary digi*t*, or bit, can be only on or off at any given moment. The *on* state, represented by a 1, is usually some positive reference voltage in the computer (for example, +5 volts). The following discussion uses the ASCII character set as a point of reference, because ASCII characters are used frequently in C.

The ASCII (American Standard Code for Information Interchange) character set uses 7 data bits. With bit 0 defined as the least significant bit (LSB), ASCII characters use only bits 0 through 6, for a total of 7 bits. For example, some microcomputers use an 8-bit data bus to communicate data throughout the system. However, when the data consists of ASCII characters, the most significant bit (MSB), which is bit 7, is usually ignored or stripped away. Therefore, when we talk about ASCII characters, we are actually concerned with bits 0 through 6; the MSB is not used.

Because a bit can be in one of two states (on or off, 0 or 1), an 8-bit data word can have 256 (or 2^8) distinct patterns. Each bit can be thought of as 2 raised to a power, as shown in figure D.1. The numeric value of a bit is 2 raised to a power equal to its bit position (numbering starts with 0 and reads from right to left). The decimal values are listed in figure D.1 to make the relationships clearer.

Fig. D.1. *Values of bits in a data word.*

Power of 2:	2^7	2^6	2^5	2^4	2^3	2^2	2^1	2^0
Decimal value:	128	64	32	16	8	4	2	1
	0	1	0	0	0	0	0	1
Bit position:	7	6	5	4	3	2	1	0

The MSB is not used, so the largest number we can represent in the ASCII character set is 127. Because 0 is also included in the range, 128 different bit patterns are available for the ASCII character set.

In figure D.1, the bits are "on" in positions 0 and 6, which have decimal values equal to 1 (or 2^0) and 64 (or 2^6), respectively; thus, the value of the data word is 65. If you consult the ASCII table in Appendix A, you will find that decimal 65 is the ASCII code for the letter A. The binary representation for A is 01000001. (Notice that the MSB is "off," or zero.)

Because people don't think in terms of binary numbers, other numbering systems are often used: octal (base 8) and hexadecimal (base 16).

Octal Numbering System

The octal numbering system divides binary digits into fields of 3 bits each, starting with the LSB. Table D.1 shows that 3 bits can represent 8 numbers (0 through 7).

Table D.1. *Binary and Octal Representation for Numbers 0 through 7*

Binary	Octal
000	0
001	1
010	2
011	3
100	4
101	5
110	6
111	7

If we want a number larger than 7, we must "roll over" into the next field of 3 bits. The binary representations for 8, 9, and 63 are shown in table D.2.

Table D.2. *Range of Values in Two 3-bit Fields*

Field 2 (3 bits)	Field 1 (3 bits) 6 bits total
001	000 = 8
001	001 = 9
111	111 = 63

To represent a number greater than 63, we must go to a third field. But the width of our data word is only 8 bits, so only 2 bits remain for the third field. Therefore, the largest possible octal number for the third field is 3. Sample values for the binary, octal, and decimal representations of the 3 fields are shown in table D.3. As you can see, binary 01000001 is 101 in octal and 65 in decimal. Again, these values are the ASCII code for the letter A.

Table D.3. *Binary, Octal, and Decimal Values in Three Fields.*

Maximum value (255 decimal):

	Field 3 (2 bits)	Field 2 (3 bits)	Field 1 (3 bits)	Total 8 bits (1 byte)
Binary	11	111	111	11111111
Octal	3	7	7	377
Decimal	128 +64	32 +16 +8	4 +2 +1	255

Sample value (65 decimal):

	Field 3 (2 bits)	Field 2 (3 bits)	Field 1 (3 bits)	Total 8 bits (1 byte)
Binary	01	000	001	01000001
Octal	1	0	1	101
Decimal	64	0	1	65

To use the character constant A in C, you may write

```
#define LETTER_A    '\Ø1Ø1'
```

Although you can define the letter A in this way, most C programmers prefer

```
#define LETTER_A    'A'
```

because you can more easily understand what is being defined.

Appendix A lists the ASCII codes in the binary, octal, and decimal numbering systems. A significant advantage of octal over binary is that the same information can be conveyed in 3 octal digits rather than 8 binary digits.

Hexadecimal Numbering System

Hexadecimal (or *hex*) is a base-16 numbering system in which each digit represents 4 binary digits. Four bits can represent 2^4 (or 16) unique numbers. Because 0 is a valid number, the 4 binary digits can represent a number from 0 through 15.

We must be able to count from 0 through 15, but we encounter a problem when we try to represent the numbers 10 through 15 with single characters. For this reason, hexadecimal notation uses the letters A through F to represent the numbers 10 through 15, as shown in table D.4.

Table D.4. Hex Representation of Numbers 0 through 15

Decimal	Hex	Binary
0	0	0000
1	1	0001
2	2	0010
3	3	0011
4	4	0100
5	5	0101
6	6	0110
7	7	0111
8	8	1000
9	9	1001
10	A	1010
11	B	1011
12	C	1100
13	D	1101
14	E	1110
15	F	1111

To represent a number larger than 15, we must again "roll over" into the next 4-bit hex field. The binary and hex representations for 16 are shown in table D.5.

Table D.5. Hex Representation of Decimal 16

Field 2 (4 bits)	Field 1 (4 bits)	
0001	0000	
1	0	= 16 (decimal)

Therefore, 10 hex is 16 decimal. Note the base-2 power relationship between fields and values (refer to fig. D.1): $1 \times 2^4 = 16$.

Problems can arise, however. If you see the number 10 written somewhere in a program, how can you tell whether the number represents 10 decimal or 10 hex? Octal is less of a problem, especially when all 3 fields are represented. (For example, 012 is 10 decimal.) Because of this potential area of confusion, C compilers expect to find *0x* before a hex number. To use a hex constant equivalent to 16 decimal, we write 0x10.

If we want to define the same constant in octal, we must supply a leading 0. In octal, a decimal 16 is defined as 020. Therefore, an ASCII escape character is *27 decimal, 0x1b hex,* or *033 octal.* Representations of the letter A are shown in table D.6.

Table D.6. *Binary, Octal, and Hex Representations for the Character A*

Notation	Field Values	Character
Binary	01000001	= A (ASCII)
Octal	1 0 1	= A
Hex	4 1	= A
Decimal	64 + 1 = 65	= A

The hex number 0x41 is the ASCII representation of the letter A.

You should be able to verify that the largest 8-bit number in hex is FF, which corresponds to 255 decimal:

11111111 (binary) = 377 (octal) = FF (hex) = 255 (decimal)

One advantage of hexadecimal numbers is that 2 hex numbers can represent 8 binary digits; hex numbers are shorter. Because hex numbers use fields of 4 binary digits, numeric representations in hex are easier, especially if you're working with computers that use address and data fields whose sizes are even multiples of 4 bits.

Index

437

B

C

D

V

W

Y

More Computer Knowledge from Que

SELECT QUE BOOKS TO INCREASE
YOUR PERSONAL COMPUTER PRODUCTIVITY

Debugging C

by Robert Ward

If you've spent hours looking for bugs in your C programs, *Debugging C* is for you. Robert Ward's "theory of debugging" explains the difficulty in debugging C programs and shows how to treat debugging as a tiered scientific procedure. This book also presents specific techniques for identifying and correcting common C problems. Let *Debugging C* help you eliminate hours—maybe days—of time, toil, and raging frustration from your programming tasks!

Finding this book among the flotsam and jetsam of computer publishing is like finding a $100 bill in the street.

—Ray Duncan,
Dr. Dobb's Journal

Using Assembly Language

by Allen Wyatt

Using Assembly Language shows you how to make the most of your programs with assembly language subroutines. This book helps you understand assembly language instructions, commands, and functions— how they are used and what effects they produce. You will learn to develop and manage libraries of subroutines, successfully debug subroutines, access BIOS and DOS services, and interface assembly language with Pascal, C, and BASIC. Now you can harness assembly language's speed, versatility, flexibility, and code compaction—with Que's *Using Assembly Language*!

C Quick Reference

*Developed by
Que Corporation*

Put C functions at your fingertips with *C Quick Reference*. This compact guide provides immediate access to information often buried in traditional text. *C Quick Reference* makes it easy to find information on essential commands and keywords, important concepts, and proper programming protocol. Speed up *your* C programming with the quality information in Que's *C Quick Reference*.

DOS Programmer's Reference

by Terry Dettmann

Intermediate and advanced programmers will find a wealth of information in Que's *DOS Programmer's Reference*. Designed for serious applications programmers, this "nuts and bolts" guide contains sections on DOS functions and their use; IBM-specific programs; expanded and extended memory; and the use of DOS with various languages, such as C, BASIC, and assembly language. A combination of tutorial and reference, this text helps you gain a greater understanding of what your operating system has to offer. Choose *DOS Programmer's Reference*, the definitive guide to DOS applications programming.

ORDER FROM QUE TODAY

Item	Title	Price	Quantity	Extension
76	DOS Programmer's Reference	$24.95		
107	Using Assembly Language	24.95		
60	Debugging C	19.95		
868	C Quick Reference Guide	6.95		

Book Subtotal _____
Shipping & Handling ($2.50 per item) _____
Indiana Residents Add 5% Sales Tax _____
GRAND TOTAL _____

Method of Payment

☐ Check   ☐ VISA   ☐ MasterCard   ☐ American Express

Card Number _____ Exp. Date _____

Cardholder's Name _____

Ship to _____

Address _____

City _____ State _____ ZIP _____

If you can't wait, call **1-800-428-5331** and order TODAY.
All prices subject to change without notice.

FOLD HERE

_____

_____

_____

_____

Place
Stamp
Here

Que Corporation
P.O. Box 90
Carmel, IN 46032

REGISTRATION CARD

Register your copy of *C Programming Guide*, 3rd Edition, and receive information about Que's newest products. Complete this registration card and return it to Que Corporation, P.O. Box 90, Carmel, IN 46032.

Name _____ Phone _____

Company _____ Title _____

Address _____

City _____ State _____ ZIP _____

Please check the appropriate answers:

Where did you buy *C Programming Guide*, 3rd Edition?

- ☐ Bookstore (name: _____)
- ☐ Computer store (name: _____)
- ☐ Catalog (name: _____)
- ☐ Direct from Que _____
- ☐ Other: _____

How many computer books do you buy a year?

- ☐ 1 or less   ☐ 6–10
- ☐ 2–5   ☐ More than 10

How many Que books do you own?

- ☐ 1   ☐ 6–10
- ☐ 2–5   ☐ More than 10

How long have you been programming in C?

- ☐ Less than 6 months
- ☐ 6 months to 1 year
- ☐ 1–3 years
- ☐ More than 3 years

What influenced your purchase of *C Programming Guide*, 3rd Edition?

- ☐ Personal recommendation
- ☐ Advertisement   ☐ Que catalog
- ☐ In-store display ☐ Que mailing
- ☐ Price   ☐ Que's reputation
- ☐ Other: _____

How would you rate the overall content of *C Programming Guide*, 3rd Edition?

- ☐ Very good   ☐ Satisfactory
- ☐ Good   ☐ Poor

How would you rate the *Programming Tips*?

- ☐ Very good   ☐ Satisfactory
- ☐ Good   ☐ Poor

How would you rate the *review questions and exercises*?

- ☐ Very good   ☐ Satisfactory
- ☐ Good   ☐ Poor

How would you rate the *tear-out Quick Reference Card*?

- ☐ Very good   ☐ Satisfactory
- ☐ Good   ☐ Poor

What do you like *best* about *C Programming Guide*, 3rd Edition?

What do you like *least* about *C Programming Guide*, 3rd Edition?

How do you use *C Programming Guide*, 3rd Edition?

What other Que products do you own?

For what other programs would a Que book be helpful?

Please feel free to list any other comments you may have about *C Programming Guide*, 3rd Edition.

_____

_____

_____

_____

_____

_____

FOLD HERE

Que Corporation
P.O. Box 90
Carmel, IN 46032